**2019 3rd EDITION**

KB079952

## 이번 시험에 나온 문제로 다음 시험의 적중률을 보장할까요?

파고다 어학원 토익 전문 연구진 108인은
다음 시험 적중률로 말합니다!

...

## 이번 시험에 나온 문제를 풀기만 하면, 내 토익 목표 점수를 달성할 수 있을까요?

파고다 토익 시리즈는
파고다 어학원 1타 강사들과 수십 만 수강생이
함께 만든 토익 목표 점수 달성 전략서입니다!

파고다 어학원 1타 토익 강사들의
토익 목표 점수 달성 전략 완전 정리

# 최신 경향 실전 모의고사 10회분
# 900~990점 목표

**내 위치를
파악했다면
목표를 향해
나아갈 뿐!**

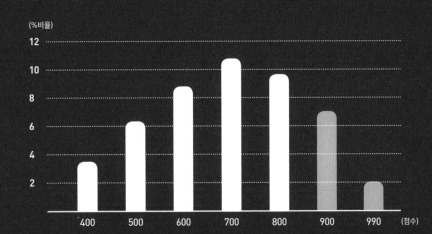

# 파고다 토익 프로그램

## 독학자를 위한 다양하고 품부한 학습 자료

세상 간편한 등업 신청으로 각종 학습
자료가 쏟아지는
**파고다 토익 공식 온라인 카페**
http://cafe.naver.com/pagodatoeicbooks

- 교재 Q&A
- **교재 학습 자료**
- 나의 학습 코칭
- 정기 토익 분석 자료
- 기출 분석 자료
- 예상 적중 특강
- 논란 종결 총평

온라인 모의고사 2회분
받아쓰기 훈련 자료
단어 암기장
단어 시험지
MP3 기본 버전
MP3 추가 버전(1.2배속 등)
추가 연습 문제 등 각종 추가 자료

## 매회 업데이트! 토익 학습 센터

시험 전 적중 문제, 특강 제공

시험 직후 실시간 정답, 총평 특강, 분석 자료집 제공

## 토익에 풀! 빠져 풀TV

파고다 대표 강사진과 전문 연구원들의
다양한 무료 강의를 들으실 수 있습니다.

---

# 600     700     800

| 기본 완성 RC | 실력 완성 RC | 고득점 완성 RC |
|---|---|---|
| **토익 문법·독해·어휘 입문서** | **토익 개념&실전 종합서** | **최상위권 토익 만점 전략서** |
| 토익 초보 학습자들이 단기간에 쉽게 접근할 수 있도록 토익의 필수 개념을 집약한 입문서 | 토익의 기본 개념을 확실히 다질 수 있는 풍부한 문제 유형과 실전형 연습문제를 담은 훈련서 | 기본기를 충분히 다진 토익 중고급자들의 고득점 완성을 위해 핵심 스킬만을 뽑아낸 토익 전략서 |

3rd Edition

실전 모의고사 10회분

Vol. 1

RC

뽀개기 적중실전

초　　판 1쇄 발행　2016년　4월　29일
개 정 판 1쇄 발행　2016년　12월　26일
개정2판 8쇄 발행　2022년　7월　12일

**지 은 이** | 파고다교육그룹 언어교육연구소
**펴 낸 이** | 박경실
**펴 낸 곳** | Wit&Wisdom 도서출판 위트앤위즈덤
**임프린트** | **PAGODA Books**
**출판등록** | 2005년 5월 27일 제 300-2005-90호
**주　　소** | 06614 서울특별시 서초구 강남대로 419, 19층(서초동, 파고다타워)
**전　　화** | (02) 6940-4070
**팩　　스** | (02) 536-0660
**홈페이지** | www.pagodabook.com

**저작권자** | ⓒ 2019 파고다아카데미

**ISBN　978-89-6281-825-3 (13740)**

도서출판 위트앤위즈덤　　www.pagodabook.com
파고다 어학원　　　　　　www.pagoda21.com
파고다 인강　　　　　　　www.pagodastar.com
테스트 클리닉　　　　　　www.testclinic.com

3rd Edition

벼락치기

실전 모의고사 10회분

적중
실전

RC

Vol. 1

# 목차

## >> TEST

**파고다토익** 적중 실전 **RC**

▶ 해설서 유료 다운로드 (3,000원)   http://www.pagodabook.com
http://www.pagodastar.com

# 이 책의 구성과 특징

>> **PART 5** GRAMMAR 토익 입문자들에게 꼭 필요한 기초 토익 문법과 핵심 기본 문제 유형을 학습한다.
문장의 구조와 틀을 이해하고 해석하는 능력을 길러 각 문제를 푸는 방법을 익힌다.
VOCA Part 5, 6, 필수 동사, 명사, 형용사, 부사 어휘를 핵심 어휘 문제로 풀어본다.

>> **PART 6** Part 5에서 학습한 어법 적용 문제, 어휘 문제, 글의 흐름상 빈칸에 알맞은 문장을 삽입하는 문제에도
충분히 대비한다.

>> **PART 7** 문제 유형별 해결 전략과 지문의 종류 및 주제별 해결 전략을 학습한다.

## 실전 모의고사 10회분 VOL.1

토익의 유형에 대한 철저한 분석을 통해 예상 적중 문제 10회분 모의고사를 구성하였다. 개정판은 가장 최근 기출문제 경향을 정확하게 반영하여 정기 시험 전에 실제 문제와 가장 유사한 문제로 충분히 훈련, 준비할 수 있다.

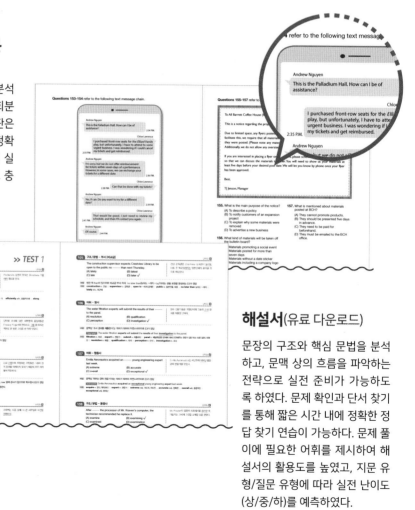

## 해설서(유료 다운로드)

문장의 구조와 핵심 문법을 분석하고, 문맥 상의 흐름을 파악하는 전략으로 실전 준비가 가능하도록 하였다. 문제 확인과 단서 찾기를 통해 짧은 시간 내에 정확한 정답 찾기 연습이 가능하다. 문제 풀이에 필요한 어휘를 제시하여 해설서의 활용도를 높였고, 지문 유형/질문 유형에 따라 실전 난이도 (상/중/하)를 예측하였다.

# 유료 해설서 온라인 구매방법

온라인 해설서
구매 바로 가기

| 구매방법 1 | 구매방법 2 |
|---|---|
| 1. www.pagodastar.com으로 접속 후, 회원가입 및 로그인을 한다. | 1. www.pagodabook.com으로 접속 후, 왼쪽 메뉴에서 "영어→토익"을 클릭한다. |
| 2. 홈페이지 상단 메뉴의 "과목선택" 탭에서 "교재/상품권"을 클릭한다. | 2. 파고다 토익 적중 실전 RC Vol. (3rd Edition)을 클릭한다. |
| 3. 파고다 토익 적중 실전 RC Vol. (3rd Edition) 해설서를 구매한다. (3,000원) | 3. 도서 정보 하단에 "해설서 구매하기"를 선택한다. |
| 4. 구매 후, "내 강의실" 탭에서 "온라인 교재 다운로드"를 클릭한다. | 4. 연동된 파고다 스타 홈페이지에서 회원가입 후 해설서를 구매한다. (3,000원) |
| | 5. 구매 후, 파고다 스타 홈페이지의 "내 강의실" 탭에서 "온라인 교재 다운로드"를 클릭한다. |

## PART 5

각 문제별로 문제유형을 표시하고 유형별로 전략을 제시하여 빠르게 정답을 찾아내는 방법을 수록하였다. Key word 부분에서 정답을 빨리 골라낼 수 있는 힌트들을 제시하였고 Key point 부분에서는 중요 문법사항을 정리하였다.

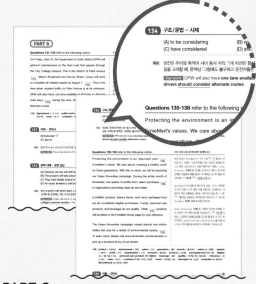

## PART 6

상세한 해설로 문맥을 파악해서 고르는 Part 6 문제에 완벽하게 대비할 수 있으며, 마찬가지로 Key word 부분에서 정답을 빨리 골라낼 수 있는 힌트들을 제시하였고 Key point 부분에서는 중요 문법사항을 정리하였다.

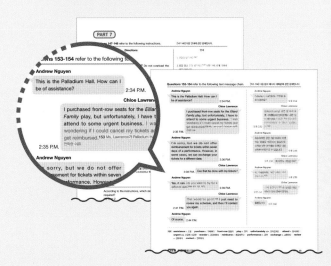

## PART 7

가장 최신 기출문제를 바탕으로 한 실제 시험과 가장 유사한 문제로만 구성되어 어떤 유형의 문제라도 완벽하게 대비할 수 있다. 힌트가 되는 부분을 빠르게 파악할 수 있는 전략을 제시했으며, Part 7의 핵심인 패러프레이징을 모든 문제에 정리해 두었다.

# 토익이란?

TOEIC(Test Of English for International Communication)은 영어가 모국어가 아닌 사람들을 대상으로 일상생활 또는 국제 업무 등에 필요한 실용 영어 능력을 평가하는 시험입니다.

상대방과 '의사 소통할 수 있는 능력(Communication ability)'을 평가하는 데 중점을 두고 있으므로 영어에 대한 '지식'이 아니라 영어의 실용적이고 기능적인 '사용법'을 묻는 문항들이 출제됩니다.

TOEIC은 1979년 미국 ETS(Educational Testing Service)에 의해 개발된 이래 전 세계 150개 국가 14,000여 개의 기관에서 승진 또는 해외 파견 인원 선발 등의 목적으로 널리 활용하고 있으며 우리나라에는 1982년 도입되었습니다. 해마다 전 세계적으로 약 700만 명 이상이 응시하고 있습니다.

## ❯❯ 토익 시험의 구성

| | 파트 | 시험 형태 | | 문항 수 | 시간 | 배점 |
|---|---|---|---|---|---|---|
| 듣기 (LC) | 1 | 사진 문제 | | 6 | 45분 | 495점 |
| | 2 | 질의응답 | | 25 | | |
| | 3 | 짧은 대화 | | 39 | | |
| | 4 | 짧은 담화 | | 30 | | |
| 읽기 (RC) | 5 | 단문 빈칸 채우기 | | 30 | 75분 | 495점 |
| | 6 | 장문 빈칸 채우기 | | 16 | | |
| | 7 | 독해 | 단일 지문 | 29 | | |
| | | | 이중 지문 | 10 | | |
| | | | 삼중 지문 | 15 | | |
| 계 | | | | 200 | 120분 | 990점 |

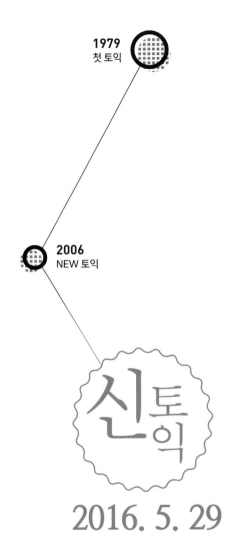

1979
첫 토익

2006
NEW 토익

신토익

2016. 5. 29

## 토익 시험 접수와 성적 확인

토익 시험은 TOEIC 위원회 웹사이트(www.toeic.co.kr)에서 접수할 수 있습니다. 본인이 원하는 날짜와 장소를 지정하고 필수 기재 항목을 기재한 후 본인 사진을 업로드하면 간단하게 끝납니다.

보통은 두 달 후에 있는 시험일까지 접수 가능합니다. 각 시험일의 정기 접수는 시험일로부터 2주 전까지 마감되지만, 시험일의 3일 전까지 추가 접수할 수 있는 특별 접수 기간이 있습니다. 그러나 특별 추가 접수 기간에는 응시료가 4,000원 더 비싸며, 희망하는 시험장을 선택할 수 없는 경우도 발생할 수 있습니다.

성적은 시험일로부터 16~18일 후에 인터넷이나 ARS(060-800-0515)를 통해 확인할 수 있습니다.

성적표는 우편이나 온라인으로 발급 받을 수 있습니다. 우편으로 발급 받을 경우는 성적 발표 후 대략 일주일이 소요되며, 온라인 발급을 선택하면 유효 기간 내에 홈페이지에서 본인이 직접 1회에 한해 무료 출력할 수 있습니다. 토익 성적은 시험일로부터 2년간 유효합니다.

## 시험 당일 준비물

시험 당일 준비물은 규정 신분증, 연필, 지우개입니다. 허용되는 규정 신분증은 토익 공식 웹사이트에서 확인하기 바랍니다. 필기구는 연필이나 샤프펜만 가능하고 볼펜이나 컴퓨터용 사인펜은 사용할 수 없습니다. 수험표는 출력해 가지 않아도 됩니다.

## 시험 진행 안내

시험 진행 일정은 시험 당일 고사장 사정에 따라 약간씩 다를 수 있지만 대부분 아래와 같이 진행됩니다.

### ≫ 시험 시간이 오전일 경우

| AM 9:30 ~ 9:45 | AM 9:45 ~ 9:50 | AM 9:50 ~ 10:05 | AM 10:05 ~ 10:10 | AM 10:10 ~ 10:55 | AM 10:55 ~ 12:10 |
|---|---|---|---|---|---|
| 15분 | 5분 | 15분 | 5분 | 45분 | 75분 |
| 답안지 작성에 관한 Orientation | 수험자 휴식 시간 | 신분증 확인 (감독교사) | 문제지 배부, 파본 확인 | 듣기 평가(LC) | 읽기 평가(RC) 2차 신분증 확인 |

* 주의: 오전 9시 50분 입실통제

### ≫ 시험 시간이 오후일 경우

| PM 2:30 ~ 2:45 | PM 2:45 ~ 2:50 | PM 2:50 ~ 3:05 | PM 3:05 ~ 3:10 | PM 3:10 ~ 3:55 | PM 3:55 ~ 5:10 |
|---|---|---|---|---|---|
| 15분 | 5분 | 15분 | 5분 | 45분 | 75분 |
| 답안지 작성에 관한 Orientation | 수험자 휴식 시간 | 신분증 확인 (감독교사) | 문제지 배부, 파본 확인 | 듣기 평가(LC) | 읽기 평가(RC) 2차 신분증 확인 |

* 주의: 오후 2시 50분 입실 통제

# 파트별 토익 소개

## PART 5 | INCOMPLETE SENTENCE
### 단문 빈칸 채우기

Part 5는 빈칸이 있는 문장이 하나 나오고, 4개의 선택지 중 빈칸에 가장 적합한 단어나 구를 고르는 문제로써 총 30문항이 출제된다.

| | |
|---|---|
| **문항 수** | 30문항 (101번 ~ 130번) |
| **문제 유형** | **[어형 문제]** 문제의 빈칸이 어떤 자리인지를 파악하여 네 개의 선택지 중에 들어갈 적절한 품사 및 형태를 묻는 문제이다. 보통 10문항 정도가 출제되는데 어형 문제는 품사에 관한 기초만 탄탄히 하면 쉽게 풀 수 있는 비교적 난이도가 낮은 문제이다. |
| | **[어휘 문제]** 어휘의 정확한 용례를 알고 있는지 묻는 문제로 같은 품사의 서로 다른 어휘가 선택지로 나온다. 어휘 문제는 다른 Part 5 문제들보다 어려운 편인 데다가 전체 30문항 중 절반가량이 어휘 문제일 정도로 출제 비중이 점점 높아지고 있다. |
| | **[문법 문제]** 문장의 구조 파악과 구와 절을 구분하여 전치사와 접속사 또는 부사 자리를 구분하고, 접속사가 답인 경우는 접속사 중에서도 명사절, 형용사절, 부사절을 구분하는 문제가 출제된다. 보통 6~7문항이 출제되는데 쉬운 문제부터 상당히 어려운 문제까지 난이도는 다양하다. |

**어형 문제** ≫

101. If our request for new computer equipment receives -------, we are going to purchase 10 extra monitors.

(A) approval                (B) approved
(C) approve                 (D) approves

**어휘 문제** ≫

102. After being employed at a Tokyo-based technology firm for two decades, Ms. Mayne ------- to Vancouver to start her own IT company.

(A) visited                  (B) returned
(C) happened                (D) compared

**문법 문제** ≫

103. ------- the demand for the PFS-2x smartphone, production will be tripled next quarter.

(A) Even if                  (B) Just as
(C) As a result of           (D) Moreover

정답 101. (A) 102. (B) 103. (C)

# PART 6

## TEXT COMPLETION
## 장문 빈칸 채우기

Part 6은 4문항의 문제가 있는 4개의 지문이 나와 총 16문항이 출제된다. 각각의 빈칸에 가장 적절한 단어나 구, 문장을 삽입하는 문제로 Part 5와 Part 7을 접목한 형태로 볼 수 있다.

| | |
|---|---|
| 문항 수 | 4개 지문, 16문항 (131번 ~ 146번) |
| 지문 유형 | 설명서, 편지, 이메일, 기사, 공지, 지시문, 광고, 회람, 발표문, 정보문 등 |
| 문제 유형 | **[어형 문제]** 빈칸의 자리를 파악하여 네 개의 선택지 중에 들어갈 적절한 품사 및 형태를 묻는 문제로 Part 5와 같은 유형의 문제들이다. 전체 16문항 중 3~4문항 정도가 출제된다. |
| | **[어휘 문제]** 네 개의 선택지 중 의미상 가장 적절한 어휘를 고르는 문제로, 전후 문맥을 파악하여 풀어야 하므로 Part 5의 어휘 문제들보다 어려운 편이다. 보통 5~6문항이 출제된다. |
| | **[문법 문제]** 구와 절, 즉 문장 구조를 파악하는 문제로 Part 6에서는 출제 빈도가 낮은 편이지만 Part 5보다 상당히 어려운 문제들로 출제된다. 전체 16문항 중 1~2문항 정도가 출제된다. |
| | **[문장 삽입 문제]** Part 7처럼 전반적인 지문의 흐름을 파악하여 4개의 선택지 중에 가장 적절한 한 문장을 선택하는 가장 난이도가 높은 문제이며, 지문마다 한 문제씩 총 4문항이 출제된다. |

---

**Questions 131-134** refer to the following e-mail.

To: sford@etnnet.com
From: customersupprt@interhostptimes.ca
Date: July 1
Re: Your Subscription

Congratulations on becoming a reader of *International Hospitality Times*. ----131.---- the plan you have subscribed to, you will not only have unlimited access to our online content, but you will also receive our hard copy edition each month. If you wish to ----132.---- your subscription preferences, contact our Customer Support Center at +28 07896 325422. Most ----133.---- may also make updates to their accounts on our Web site at www.interhosptimes.ca. Please note that due to compatibility issues, it may not be possible for customers in certain countries to access their accounts online. ----134.----. Your business is greatly appreciated.

*International Hospitality Times*

문법 문제 ≫

131. (A) Besides
(B) As if
(C) Under
(D) Prior to

어형 문제 ≫

133. (A) subscribe
(B) subscriptions
(C) subscribers
(D) subscribing

어휘 문제 ≫

132. (A) purchase
(B) modify
(C) collect
(D) inform

문장 삽입 문제 ≫

134. (A) We have branches in over 30 countries around the globe.
(B) We provide online content that includes Web extras and archives.
(C) We are working to make this service available to all readers soon.
(D) We would like to remind you that your contract expires this month.

정답 131. (C) 132. (B) 133. (C) 134. (C)

# PART 7

## READING COMPREHENSION
독해

Part 7은 지문을 읽고 그에 해당하는 각각의 질문(2~5개)에 알맞은 답을 고르는 문제이다. 지문의 종류가 다양하며 그 형태도 1개의 지문으로 된 것과 2개, 3개의 지문으로 된 것이 있다.

| | |
|---|---|
| 문항 수 | 54문항 (147번 ~ 200번) → 단일 지문: 10개 지문, 19문항<br>이중 지문: 2개 지문, 10문항<br>삼중 지문: 3개 지문, 15문항 |
| 지문 유형 | 편지, 이메일, 광고, 공지, 회람, 기사, 안내문, 웹페이지(회사나 제품소개, 행사 소개,<br>고객 사용 후기), 청구서 또는 영수증, 문자, 온라인 채팅 대화문 등 |
| 문제 유형 | - 주제·목적 문제<br>- 세부사항 문제<br>- 암시·추론 문제<br>- 사실확인 문제<br>- 동의어 문제<br>- 화자 의도 파악 문제<br>- 문장 삽입 문제 |

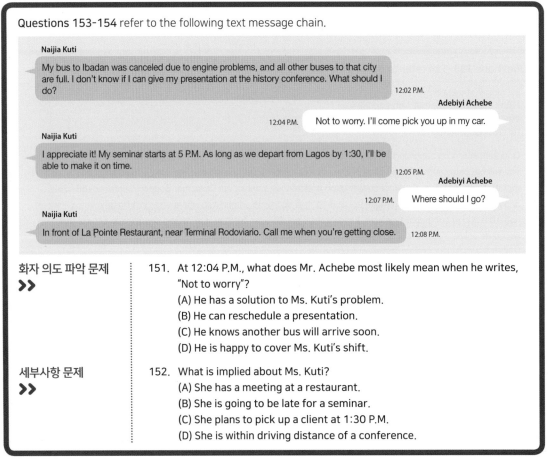

Questions 153-154 refer to the following text message chain.

**Naijia Kuti**
My bus to Ibadan was canceled due to engine problems, and all other buses to that city are full. I don't know if I can give my presentation at the history conference. What should I do?
12:02 P.M.

**Adebiyi Achebe**
12:04 P.M.   Not to worry. I'll come pick you up in my car.

**Naijia Kuti**
I appreciate it! My seminar starts at 5 P.M. As long as we depart from Lagos by 1:30, I'll be able to make it on time.
12:05 P.M.

**Adebiyi Achebe**
12:07 P.M.   Where should I go?

**Naijia Kuti**
In front of La Pointe Restaurant, near Terminal Rodoviario. Call me when you're getting close.   12:08 P.M.

화자 의도 파악 문제
▶▶

151. At 12:04 P.M., what does Mr. Achebe most likely mean when he writes, "Not to worry"?
(A) He has a solution to Ms. Kuti's problem.
(B) He can reschedule a presentation.
(C) He knows another bus will arrive soon.
(D) He is happy to cover Ms. Kuti's shift.

세부사항 문제
▶▶

152. What is implied about Ms. Kuti?
(A) She has a meeting at a restaurant.
(B) She is going to be late for a seminar.
(C) She plans to pick up a client at 1:30 P.M.
(D) She is within driving distance of a conference.

정답 151. (A) 152. (D)

Questions 158-160 refer to the following Web page.

http://www.sdayrealestate.com/listing18293

Looking for a new home for your family? This house, located on 18293 Winding Grove, was remodeled last month. It features 2,500 square feet of floor space, with 5,000 square feet devoted to a gorgeous backyard. Also included is a 625 square feet garage that can comfortably fit two mid-sized vehicles —[1]—. Located just a five-minute drive from the Fairweather Metro Station, this property allows for easy access to the downtown area, while providing plenty of room for you and your family. —[2]—. A serene lake is just 100–feet walk away from the house. —[3]—. A 15 percent down payment is required to secure the property. —[4]—. For more detailed information or to arrange a showing, please email Jerry@sdayrealestate.com.

세부사항 문제

**»**

158. How large is the parking space?
(A) 100 square feet
(B) 625 square feet
(C) 2,500 square feet
(D) 5,000 square feet

사실확인 문제

**»**

159. What is NOT stated as an advantage of the property?
(A) It has a spacious design.
(B) It has been recently renovated.
(C) It is in a quiet neighborhood.
(D) It is near public transportation.

문장 삽입 문제

**»**

160. In which of the positions marked [1], [2], [3], and [4] does the following sentence best belong?

"A smaller amount may be accepted, depending on the buyer's financial situation."

(A) [1]
(B) [2]
(C) [3]
(D) [4]

정답 158. (B) 159. (C) 160. (D)

# 학습 플랜

## 2주 플랜

| DAY 1 | DAY 2 | DAY 3 | DAY 4 | DAY 5 |
|---|---|---|---|---|
| TEST 01 | TEST 02 | TEST 03 | TEST 04 | TEST 05 |
| 시간 재고 풀기 | 시간 재고 풀기 | 시간 재고 풀기 | 시간 재고 풀기 | 시간 재고 풀기 |
| 채점하고 해설지로 복습 | 채점하고 해설지로 복습 | 채점하고 해설지로 복습 | 채점하고 해설지로 복습 | 채점하고 해설지로 복습 |
| RC 어휘집 외우기 (카페 다운로드) | RC 어휘집 외우기 (카페 다운로드) | RC 어휘집 외우기 (카페 다운로드) | RC 어휘집 외우기 (카페 다운로드) | RC 어휘집 외우기 (카페 다운로드) |

| DAY 6 | DAY 7 | DAY 8 | DAY 9 | DAY 10 |
|---|---|---|---|---|
| TEST 06 | TEST 07 | TEST 08 | TEST 09 | TEST 10 |
| 시간 재고 풀기 | 시간 재고 풀기 | 시간 재고 풀기 | 시간 재고 풀기 | 시간 재고 풀기 |
| 채점하고 해설지로 복습 | 채점하고 해설지로 복습 | 채점하고 해설지로 복습 | 채점하고 해설지로 복습 | 채점하고 해설지로 복습 |
| RC 어휘집 외우기 (카페 다운로드) | RC 어휘집 외우기 (카페 다운로드) | RC 어휘집 외우기 (카페 다운로드) | RC 어휘집 외우기 (카페 다운로드) | RC 어휘집 외우기 (카페 다운로드) |

## 4주 플랜

| DAY 1 | DAY 2 | DAY 3 | DAY 4 | DAY 5 |
|---|---|---|---|---|
| TEST 01<br><br>시간 재고 풀기<br><br>채점하고 해설지로 복습 | TEST 01 복습<br><br>RC 어휘집 외우기<br>(카페 다운로드) | TEST 02<br><br>시간 재고 풀기<br><br>채점하고 해설지로 복습 | TEST 02 복습<br><br>RC 어휘집 외우기<br>(카페 다운로드) | TEST 03<br><br>시간 재고 풀기<br><br>채점하고 해설지로 복습 |

| DAY 6 | DAY 7 | DAY 8 | DAY 9 | DAY 10 |
|---|---|---|---|---|
| TEST 03 복습<br><br>RC 어휘집 외우기<br>(카페 다운로드) | TEST 04<br><br>시간 재고 풀기<br><br>채점하고 해설지로 복습 | TEST 04 복습<br><br>RC 어휘집 외우기<br>(카페 다운로드) | TEST 05<br><br>시간 재고 풀기<br><br>채점하고 해설지로 복습 | TEST 05 복습<br><br>RC 어휘집 외우기<br>(카페 다운로드) |

| DAY 11 | DAY 12 | DAY 13 | DAY 14 | DAY 15 |
|---|---|---|---|---|
| TEST 06<br><br>시간 재고 풀기<br><br>채점하고 해설지로 복습 | TEST 06 복습<br><br>RC 어휘집 외우기<br>(카페 다운로드) | TEST 07<br><br>시간 재고 풀기<br><br>채점하고 해설지로 복습 | TEST 07 복습<br><br>RC 어휘집 외우기<br>(카페 다운로드) | TEST 08<br><br>시간 재고 풀기<br><br>채점하고 해설지로 복습 |

| DAY 16 | DAY 17 | DAY 18 | DAY 19 | DAY 20 |
|---|---|---|---|---|
| TEST 08 복습<br><br>RC 어휘집 외우기<br>(카페 다운로드) | TEST 09<br><br>시간 재고 풀기<br><br>채점하고 해설지로 복습 | TEST 09 복습<br><br>RC 어휘집 외우기<br>(카페 다운로드) | TEST 10<br><br>시간 재고 풀기<br><br>채점하고 해설지로 복습 | TEST 10 복습<br><br>RC 어휘집 외우기<br>(카페 다운로드) |

TES

# ST 1

# READING TEST

In the Reading test, you will read a variety of texts and answer several different types of reading comprehension questions. The entire Reading test will last 75 minutes. There are three parts, and directions are given for each part. You are encouraged to answer as many questions as possible within the time allowed.

You must mark your answers on the separate answer sheet. Do not write your answers in the test book.

## PART 5

**Directions:** A word or phrase is missing in each of the sentences below. Four answer choices are given below each sentence. Select the best answer to complete the sentence. Then mark the letter (A), (B), (C), or (D) on your answer sheet.

**101.** Thirty percent of Packerville businesses operate ------- Broadway Avenue.

(A) efficiently
(B) along
(C) sideways
(D) apart

**102.** Most responders to the internet survey are familiar with Freezey Yogurt, and 65 percent of ------- have purchased it at least once.

(A) them
(B) theirs
(C) themselves
(D) they

**103.** Companies expanding into new ------- frequently encounter difficulty because they do not understand the local culture.

(A) market
(B) markets
(C) marketed
(D) marketable

**104.** The Purchasing Department ------- to relocate to a larger office next month.

(A) predicts
(B) reports
(C) plans
(D) thinks

**105.** The construction supervisor expects Crestview Library to be open to the public no ------- than next Thursday.

(A) lately
(B) latest
(C) late
(D) later

**106.** The water filtration experts will submit the results of their ------- to the panel.

(A) resolution
(B) qualification
(C) perception
(D) investigation

**107.** Emilia Aeronautics acquired an ------- young engineering expert last week.

(A) extreme
(B) accurate
(C) overall
(D) exceptional

**108.** After ------- the processor of Mr. Kraven's computer, the technician recommended he replace it.

(A) examine
(B) examining
(C) examined
(D) examination

**109.** The number of personnel needed to prepare all the required items ------- on order size.

(A) depending
(B) to depend
(C) depends
(D) depend

**110.** The Ridgeline Park hike will be postponed if the weather is ------- hot on Sunday.

(A) uncomfortably
(B) essentially
(C) cautiously
(D) nearly

**111.** To work as a master electrician, Mr. Ranganathan is obligated to renew his professional certification ------- five years.

(A) still
(B) fewer
(C) every
(D) wherever

**112.** In response to student -------, Xavier College will host a series of professional development lectures.

(A) permit
(B) balance
(C) entry
(D) demand

**113.** After the seminar, the attendees were allowed a ------- amount of time to ask about the presentations.

(A) generous
(B) generousness
(C) generously
(D) generosity

**114.** The Bruder demonstration at the Kitchen Equipment Exhibition garnered much -------.

(A) interests
(B) interest
(C) interesting
(D) interested

**115.** The Vice President met French investors ------- a brunch yesterday in Nice.

(A) like
(B) when
(C) at
(D) had

**116.** The deadline for the monthly budget report was postponed to ------- comment from the board of directors.

(A) turn into
(B) use up
(C) allow for
(D) count on

**117.** Passengers must arrive at the airport ------- 1 hour prior to their flight's departure.

(A) by then
(B) so that
(C) as little
(D) at least

**118.** A team of chemical engineers is experimenting with panel coatings ------- can survive extreme conditions.

(A) then
(B) what
(C) into
(D) that

**119.** Argent Auto Parts Company manufactures higher-quality oil filters ------- its rivals do.

(A) such
(B) than
(C) where
(D) these

**120.** Buena Vista Outdoor is holding a big ------- sale since the store is moving to a new location.

(A) clearable
(B) clearance
(C) clearing
(D) cleared

*GO ON TO THE NEXT PAGE*

**121.** The Business Channel will broadcast a new program ------- to product development and innovative designs.

(A) introduced
(B) permitted
(C) arranged
(D) dedicated

**122.** Ms. Ming courteously ------- the position offered by Verrazano Imports Ltd.

(A) converted
(B) declined
(C) lessened
(D) restricted

**123.** ------- it is fairly difficult, the climbing wall at Masters Gym is very popular with members.

(A) Basically
(B) Although
(C) Overall
(D) Reasoning

**124.** Ms. Armor worked on the sales floor for three days before she was ------- introduced to the branch manager.

(A) presently
(B) formally
(C) considerably
(D) primarily

**125.** The bank's new policy allows you to refinance your mortgage according to a ------- 10-year plan.

(A) manages
(B) managing
(C) manageable
(D) manageably

**126.** Mr. Lee has requested a maintenance worker, ------- within two hours.

(A) preference
(B) preferable
(C) preferably
(D) prefer

**127.** Hexel Industries lowered operating costs, but even more significant for its future, it has strengthened its ------- advantage.

(A) diverse
(B) competitive
(C) sharp
(D) careful

**128.** Ms. Fitzpatrick regards dependability as a vital ------- for all her employees to possess.

(A) version
(B) trait
(C) instrument
(D) action

**129.** This shipment cannot ------- until we have obtained final approval.

(A) being processed
(B) to process
(C) has processed
(D) be processed

**130.** The cost of providing training instructors has been factored ------- the system installation fee.

(A) into
(B) from
(C) with
(D) onto

# PART 6

**Directions:** Read the texts that follow. A word, phrase, or sentence is missing in parts of each text. Four answer choices for each question are given below the text. Select the best answer to complete the text. Then mark the letter (A), (B), (C), or (D) on your answer sheet.

**Questions 131-134** refer to the following notice.

On Friday, June 22, the Department of Public Works (DPW) will perform maintenance on the main road that passes through the City College campus. This is the stretch of Palm Avenue ------- Maron Boulevard and Hoover Street. Crews will work to complete all
**131.**
needed repairs by August 1. -------. This is the time when student traffic on Palm
**132.**
Avenue is at its minimum. DPW will also have one lane available at all times so that the

road stays ------- during the work. Despite this, drivers ------- alternate routes.
**133.** **134.**

131. (A) between
    (B) from
    (C) above
    (D) among

132. (A) Subway service will still be available.
    (B) This project will take place during the college's summer vacation.
    (C) They had initially hoped to finish six months earlier.
    (D) An exact timeline is still being discussed.

133. (A) opens
    (B) opening
    (C) open
    (D) opener

134. (A) to be considering
    (B) will have considered
    (C) have considered
    (D) should consider

GO ON TO THE NEXT PAGE

**Questions 135-138** refer to the following notice.

Protecting the environment is an important part ------- ErnieMart's values. We care
                                                **135.**
about creating a healthy world for future generations. With this in mind, we will be

launching our Green November campaign. During the entire month of November, one

quarter of profits from select purchases ------- to organizations promoting clean air and
                                         **136.**
water.

ErnieMart produce, bakery items, and most packaged food are all considered eligible

purchases. Candy, personal care products, and beverages do not qualify.  Other -------
                                                                               **137.**
products will be listed on the ErnieMart home page for your reference.

The Green November campaign raised almost one million dollars last year for a variety

of environmental causes. -------. To learn more, please visit www.erniemart.com/
                         **138.**
erniecares or pick up a brochure at any of our stores.

**135.** (A) across
(B) as
(C) of
(D) through

**136.** (A) will contribute
(B) are contributing
(C) was contributed
(D) will be contributed

**137.** (A) unopened
(B) damaged
(C) excluded
(D) discontinued

**138.** (A) This time, we expect to triple that
amount.
(B) It has been a difficult time for our
association.
(C) Every participating company will be
charged for admission.
(D) This will be our last year of running
the campaign.

**Questions 139-142** refer to the following e-mail.

From: Londi Fumarolo
To: All Trek Fitness Center (TFC) members
Date: April 25
Subject: GymDirect

Dear TFC Members,

You ------- a message from our new billing agency, GymDirect. Included in it was a link
    **139.**
to our member Web site for all bill payment services. -------. Starting next month, all of
                **140.**
your billing will be processed through this Web site. You will not receive further

messages regarding your billing issues.

Furthermore, the message from GymDirect should contain a temporary login ID and

password. These should be used to access the site, and you should do ------- by the
                    **141.**
end of this week. -------, your temporary login information will expire.
      **142.**

Please give me a call at 1-800-555-1212 if you need assistance with this process.

Best regards,

Londi Fumarolo
TFC Member Services Manager

**139.** (A) might get
    (B) have been getting
    (C) should have gotten
    (D) will be getting

**140.** (A) Save this address for your convenience.
    (B) This page is not currently available.
    (C) We have several new facilities you can use.
    (D) Unfortunately, your account was billed incorrectly.

**141.** (A) other
    (B) so
    (C) again
    (D) both

**142.** (A) Meanwhile
    (B) However
    (C) At any time
    (D) After that

*GO ON TO THE NEXT PAGE*

**Questions 143-146** refer to the following letter.

March 15

Jarvis McMahon
1211 E. California Rd.
Fort Wayne, IN 46806

Dear Mr. McMahon,

This letter is in response to your ------- visit to our investor service center. At that time,
                                  **143.**
we discussed the possibility of moving your retirement savings to Kamberis Financial.

We would be very happy to assist you with this. ------- is a brochure explaining our
                                                **144.**
services and investment options, per your request. -------.
                                                   **145.**

Our investor service representatives are available at any time should you require
additional information or assistance. When you are ready, we will also handle the

process of moving your ------- from your present institution to Kamberis Financial.
                       **146.**

Once again, thank you for your interest in Kamberis Financial. We look forward to
working with you in the future.

Best regards,

James Cleary
Investor Services Associate

Kamberis Financial
219-555-1212

**143.** (A) further
(B) recent
(C) next
(D) delayed

**144.** (A) Enclose
(B) Enclosed
(C) Enclosing
(D) Enclosure

**145.** (A) We will waive your maintenance fee
for the first year.
(B) Your feedback will help us better
serve you in the future.
(C) Your investments have all been
selected and purchased.
(D) I think you will find that we have a
variety of excellent choices.

**146.** (A) suggestion
(B) edition
(C) account
(D) preference

# PART 7

**Directions:** In this part you will read a selection of texts, such as magazine and newspaper articles, e-mails, and instant messages. Each text or set of texts is followed by several questions. Select the best answer for each question and mark the letter (A), (B), (C) or (D) on your answer sheet.

**Questions 147-148** refer to the following instructions.

## Directions

**1.** Insert cash.

**2.** Open the door to insert garments. Do not overload the machine.

**3.** Insert soap and select appropriate temperature.

**4.** Close the door and press the start button to begin the wash.

**5.** In the event an alarm sounds, rearrange the contents of the machine so that they are balanced.

**6.** When finished, transfer items to the dryer within five minutes so that others can use the machine.

**147.** Where would the instructions most likely appear?

(A) At a car wash business
(B) At a laundry facility
(C) At a home appliance store
(D) At a clothing store

**148.** According to the instructions, which step is NOT always required?

(A) Step 2
(B) Step 4
(C) Step 5
(D) Step 6

*GO ON TO THE NEXT PAGE*

**Questions 149-150** refer to the following form.

## Arc IT Infrastructure

### Installation Request Form

**Client:** Rosewood Medical Clinic

**Contact:** linda.richards@rosewoodmc.com

**Address:** 35 Ash Ct., Fairfax VA 22030

**Date:** July 26

**Technician:** Roberta Coe

**Order #:** 8233

**Equipment:** 700m, Cat 5 cable

**Labor Estimate:** 4.5 hours

**Work Location:** East Wing

**Work Description:** Connect all computers and printers in all staff areas to network outlets, and test the connections. No access when surgeries are in progress. Finish during non-business hours (8:00 P.M. to 4:30 A.M.). Contact security at extension 457 in the lobby.

---

**149.** What is indicated about the job at Rosewood Medical Clinic?

(A) It will be done at night.
(B) It was paid for on July 26.
(C) It will need several workers.
(D) It is the first phase of a project.

**150.** What is implied about the Rosewood Medical Clinic?

(A) It is located near Arc IT Infrastructure's office.
(B) It has extended its operating hours.
(C) It is hiring new security staff.
(D) It has multiple building sections.

**Questions 151-152** refer to the following advertisement.

Jefferson Apartment Company (JAC):
# Our New Francis Street Apartments

JAC is opening a new apartment complex this fall. These great units are exclusively open to Madwell University students who don't want to live in dormitories but would still like to be a part of on-campus life. The complex is conveniently situated three blocks from Barrett Hall with great access to public transportation, all within a five-minute walk of the lovely nature trails in San Andreas Park. Enjoy our state-of-the-art fitness center, where you can engage in various recreational activities. All units include private kitchens and living room areas. The building also features a 24-hour laundry facility equipped with brand-new washers and dryers. Each tenant is provided with one parking spot in our large parking lot. Act quickly before all units fill up.

**151.** What does the advertisement promote?

(A) A university seminar series
(B) The opening of a new business
(C) Housing for a particular population
(D) Newly added hiking trails

**152.** What is NOT mentioned in the advertisement?

(A) Pricing
(B) Location
(C) Activities
(D) Parking

GO ON TO THE NEXT PAGE

**Questions 153-154** refer to the following text message chain.

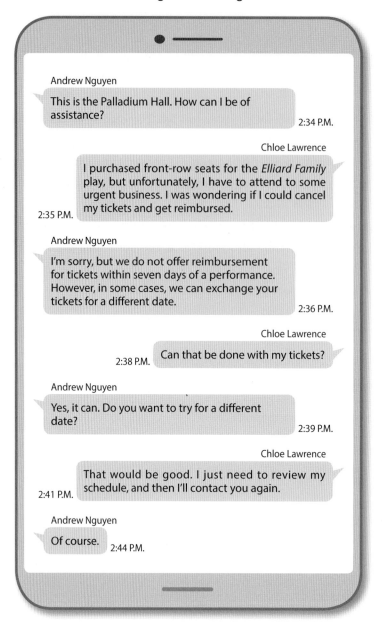

**Andrew Nguyen**

This is the Palladium Hall. How can I be of assistance?

2:34 P.M.

**Chloe Lawrence**

2:35 P.M.

I purchased front-row seats for the *Elliard Family* play, but unfortunately, I have to attend to some urgent business. I was wondering if I could cancel my tickets and get reimbursed.

**Andrew Nguyen**

I'm sorry, but we do not offer reimbursement for tickets within seven days of a performance. However, in some cases, we can exchange your tickets for a different date.

2:36 P.M.

**Chloe Lawrence**

2:38 P.M.

Can that be done with my tickets?

**Andrew Nguyen**

Yes, it can. Do you want to try for a different date?

2:39 P.M.

**Chloe Lawrence**

2:41 P.M.

That would be good. I just need to review my schedule, and then I'll contact you again.

**Andrew Nguyen**

Of course.

2:44 P.M.

**153.** Why does Ms. Lawrence contact the Palladium Hall?

(A) To offer some feedback
(B) To upgrade some seats
(C) To inquire about an artist
(D) To request a refund

**154.** At 2:41 P.M. what does Ms. Lawrence most likely mean when she writes, "That would be good"?

(A) She can buy new tickets immediately.
(B) She will do as Mr. Nguyen suggests.
(C) She can go to a show next week.
(D) She will watch a performance online.

**Questions 155-157** refer to the following notice.

To All Barrett Coffee House (BCH) Customers:

This is a notice regarding the proper use of our bulletin board.

Due to limited space, any flyers posted will remain on the board for a period of 14 days. To facilitate this, we require that all materials include a date sticker from BCH indicating when they were posted. (Please note: any materials that do not have this label will be removed.) Additionally, we do not allow any oversized flyers or multiple postings for the same event.

If you are interested in placing a flyer on our board, please schedule an appointment with us so that we can discuss the materials together. You will need to show us your materials at least five days before your desired post date. We will let you know by phone once your flyer has been approved.

Best,

TJ Jenson, Manager

**155.** What is the main purpose of the notice?

(A) To describe a policy
(B) To notify customers of an expansion project
(C) To explain why some materials were removed
(D) To advertise a new business

**156.** What kind of materials will be taken off the bulletin board?

(A) Materials promoting a social event
(B) Materials posted for more than seven days
(C) Materials without a date sticker
(D) Materials including a company logo

**157.** What is mentioned about materials posted at BCH?

(A) They cannot promote products.
(B) They should be presented five days in advance.
(C) They need to be paid for beforehand.
(D) They must be emailed to the BCH office.

GO ON TO THE NEXT PAGE

**Questions 158-160** refer to the following article.

---

## CityBeat.com/local

By Ekon Diallo
May 30

It has been 15 years since Tabatha Lin started out at Twain and Roth as a records clerk. Inspired by the firm's commitment to the local community, she enrolled in law school. These days, she is not only one of the prominent firm's partners, but also the leader of their effort to open a new law office dedicated to property law on Main Avenue.

Nowadays, Ms. Lin is often the first to arrive at the office and the last to leave. Even when she's out of the office, she's conducting research or meeting with new clients. However, she says she's happy to put in long hours. "We're building something special, and I'm honored to take part," she explains.

Ms. Lin says that her experience at every level of the firm informs the way she works today. She is approachable and thoughtful, taking time to listen to everyone, from the top litigators to the newest interns. "Everyone's perspective and experience are important," she says, "and no one can do their best work without help from others."

Ms. Lin believes that the firm has benefited from the opportunity to hire graduates from the top law schools in the country, but "teamwork and communication are always the biggest keys to success."

---

**158.** What is the main purpose of the article?

(A) To profile an attorney
(B) To publicize a vacant legal assistant position
(C) To discuss a recent trial
(D) To explain a law school's new policy

**159.** The word "informs" in paragraph 3, line 2, is closest in meaning to

(A) instructs
(B) invests
(C) influences
(D) interacts

**160.** What is mentioned about Twain and Roth?

(A) It recruits from prestigious universities.
(B) It recently relocated to a new office.
(C) It has won several big property cases.
(D) It has hired a number of new interns.

**Questions 161-163** refer to the following letter.

Kamala Williams
Ames Industries
32 Redwood Way
Salt Lake City, UT 84104

Dear Ms. Williams,

Two weeks ago, your final copy of *Micasa Magazine* was delivered, but we haven't received your renewal request. —[1]—. Over the past decade, *Micasa Magazine* has identified trends in flooring patterns, lighting, and effective management of indoor space. —[2]—. This informative resource for your business is worth much more than the $55 annual subscription fee. —[3]—. However, included with this notice is a renewal offer marked down 30 percent from the usual yearly subscription rate. Send it back before April 30 to take advantage of this special deal. —[4]—. Don't lose out on this valuable business resource. Act now!

Best regards,

Miles Stanford
Customer Services

ENCLOSURE

**161.** Who most likely is Ms. Williams?

(A) A broadcasting executive
(B) A magazine editor
(C) A corporate accountant
(D) An interior designer

**162.** What is offered to Ms. Williams?

(A) A discounted subscription
(B) Free advertising space
(C) An individual consultation
(D) Some product samples

**163.** In which of positions marked [1], [2], [3], and [4] does the following sentence best belong?

"This is a reminder in case you had not intended for this situation to occur."

(A) [1]
(B) [2]
(C) [3]
(D) [4]

GO ON TO THE NEXT PAGE

**Questions 164-167** refer to the following online chat discussion.

---

**Sharon West [1:02 P.M.]**

Hope everyone had a good lunch. The company is planning to hold an info session regarding our upcoming merger next Tuesday or Wednesday. I want to find out which day is best for each team. Participation is mandatory for all employees.

**Gloria Fukuzaki [1:04 P.M.]**

Well, Personnel will be unavailable all day on Tuesday because of job interviews. However, our schedule's pretty flexible on Wednesday. When will they be held?

**Sharon West [1:06 P.M.]**

We haven't set the exact times yet. All of the managers need to let us know their preferences first. Oliver, when would be good for you?

**Oliver Ferguson [1:08 P.M.]**

IT employees are usually busy during the afternoon, so Tuesday morning would be ideal.

**Sharon West [1:09 P.M.]**

We could probably hold two separate sessions if the event hall is open on those days. Gloria, do you mind seeing if the event hall is available?

**Gloria Fukuzaki [1:12 P.M.]**

According to the system, the event hall will be in use on Tuesday morning and Wednesday afternoon.

**Sharon West [1:14 P.M.]**

Would you please get in touch with the department that booked the event hall for Tuesday morning? Please check if they'd be willing to move their event. If they're OK with it, book the hall from 10:00 A.M. to 11:00 A.M. for both days.

**Gloria Fukuzaki [1:18 P.M.]**

Done. I just got off the phone with Ms. Cartman. We can use the event hall on both days now. I'll have my team attend on Wednesday morning.

**Oliver Ferguson [1:19 P.M.]**

We'll stick with Tuesday morning.

---

SEND

---

**164.** What is the main topic of the discussion?

(A) Meeting potential clients
(B) Updating a computer system
(C) Analyzing some survey results
(D) Scheduling an information session

**165.** What is indicated about Ms. Fukuzaki?

(A) She will not be available this week.
(B) She is a Personnel employee.
(C) She will postpone her appointment.
(D) She is Ms. Cartman's manager.

**166.** At 1:18 P.M., what does Ms. Fukuzaki imply when she writes, "Done"?

(A) She submitted an application form.
(B) She managed to reserve a venue.
(C) She completed a project early.
(D) She revised a document.

**167.** When will the IT team attend the session?

(A) On Tuesday morning
(B) On Tuesday afternoon
(C) On Wednesday morning
(D) On Wednesday afternoon

**Questions 168-171** refer to the following information.

---

### Midwest Interior Design Fair (MIDF), Dayton, Ohio

**Terms of Use**

**A. Contracts:** All approved exhibitors must complete and sign all related documents no later than two weeks before the event. Participants who fail to meet MIDF's strict guidelines for appropriate exhibit content will be denied booth space.

**B. Costs:** Booth spaces in the convention hall are made available to exhibitors from 9:00 A.M. to 7:00 P.M., which includes one hour before and after the hall is publicly accessible. Booths cost $435 per day or $800 for both days. There may be additional costs related to usage (refer to terms C and D).

**C. Booths:** Spaces provided to exhibitors in the convention hall are 14 feet by 14 feet. One floor outlet contains 4 sockets (120V). For furnishings, internet connectivity, or sign-printing services, please contact vendor_info@midf. org. Note that these services will incur additional fees. In addition, any booth that holds raffles, contests, or other events that might cause a crowd to gather must obtain MIDF's prior approval to ensure that the event does not create an excessive burden on fellow exhibitors. For all exhibitors offering refreshments, a $10 surcharge will be collected to cover the cost of waste removal.

**D. Distribution of Materials:** Exhibitors are permitted to give away informational materials, product samples, and promotional items. However, due to security restrictions, attendees are only permitted to carry bags issued by the convention hall. Therefore, we highly recommend that any distributed items be able to fit into a 5 inch by 15 inch opening.

---

**168.** According to the information, why might a booth request be rejected?

(A) An exhibitor's products are unsuitable for the event.
(B) A company did not make a payment on time.
(C) Company contact information was not provided.
(D) An exhibitor requires a larger booth size.

**169.** What is suggested about the Midwest Interior Design Fair?

(A) It lasts for two days.
(B) It offers attendees free internet access.
(C) It takes place annually in Dayton.
(D) It has a $10 entry fee.

**170.** According to the information, what is most likely an objective of MIDF employees?

(A) Drawing a large number of participants
(B) Ensuring that all exhibitors use available space fairly
(C) Making transportation arrangements for international attendees
(D) Grouping companies with similar products together

**171.** What is true about the MIDF exhibitors?

(A) They can have only a certain amount of employees.
(B) They must wear their ID badges at all times.
(C) Their booths will be inspected one hour before the fair begins.
(D) Their promotional items should not exceed a certain size.

*GO ON TO THE NEXT PAGE*

**Questions 172-175** refer to the following Web page.

LONDON (8 August) – ElliptiCorp, the creators of the popular mobile application, Insider, announced a new round of investments Tuesday night. The investments bring the company's valuation to $50 million. —[1]—. The investment was spurred by growing use of the app, which solicits dining recommendations from registered locals, rather than anonymous users.

"Our idea is pretty straightforward," said ElliptiCorp CEO Angela Moss. "We aim to guide people and their food preferences to the right place. The app allows users to read in-depth reviews about a restaurant's menu, location, and environment. Insider makes it easy to choose the best place to get a bite."—[2]—.

Although the site was designed with customers in mind, its popularity has certainly not been limited to its original target users. —[3]—. Daniel Miller, who runs one of London's oldest bistros, believes that Insider has helped improve declining sales. —[4]—. "We didn't know what was wrong at first since everyone said our food was great," said Miller. "However, after going through some reviews, we realized that we didn't have enough workers to provide timely service. We were able to remedy this situation within a month."

Insider is available for download in all major app stores or at ElliptiCorp.com/insider.

**172.** What is indicated about Insider?

(A) It appointed a new CEO.
(B) It was launched six months ago.
(C) Its posts come from area residents.
(D) Its users are unidentified.

**173.** According to the Web page, what is one function of the Insider application?

(A) Arranging food delivery
(B) Finding suitable eateries
(C) Reserving a table
(D) Purchasing kitchen supplies

**174.** What did Mr. Miller likely change?

(A) The prices of some products
(B) The number of employees
(C) The date of a training session
(D) The hours of a store

**175.** In which of the positions marked [1], [2], [3], and [4] does the following sentence best belong?

"Business owners are also making use of the application."

(A) [1]
(B) [2]
(C) [3]
(D) [4]

GO ON TO THE NEXT PAGE

**Questions 176-180** refer to the following article and e-mail.

---

## The Carverton Republic
## Business Spotlight

Beirut Café, owned and managed by Jean Christophe Ayoub, opened its doors a decade ago, and they remain open today thanks to his business knowledge. He had already worked in the food service industry for many years and understood that every restaurant takes time to build a reliable clientele and earn a profit. However, even Mr. Ayoub didn't expect the local economic downturn to last so long.

Mr. Ayoub spoke to the Carverton Chamber of Commerce last Tuesday, offering some advice to new restaurant owners. He emphasized that the long-term viability of a business depends on the surrounding community. "A lot of customers will go out to eat only a few times a month," he said. "So you need something unique to pull them to your restaurant."

"Carverton is a diverse community, and a lot of people are familiar with Lebanese cuisine," he explained, "that was a big help in the early years. There are also several specialty markets that provide excellent fresh ingredients."

Mr. Ayoub devoted much of his talk to the importance of being prepared for major expenses early on, especially for advertising. "Estimate how much you think effective ads will cost," he said, "and then triple it." That early investment in radio and newspaper promotions helped Beirut Café stay open and survive four hard years before the business became truly profitable.

Now that Mr. Ayoub's restaurant has a loyal following, his advice for retaining those customers is simple. "We try to keep our clientele eager to come back by creating weekly specials and offering discounts for regulars. Also, if there's a special request, my chefs will do their best to complete the order," he said. "After all, making customers happy is what it's all about."

---

| To | Mina Salazar <msalazar@dfu.edu> |
|---|---|
| From | Reza Kosch <rezak@carvertoncc.org> |
| Date | November 18 |
| Subject | News |

Dear Mina,

I was happy to hear that you graduated from culinary school. I'm sure that you've started looking for jobs, and so I'm writing to let you know of an opening in Carverton. The position is for a morning kitchen assistant who helps prepare ingredients, bake, and manage deliveries. The job posting can be found at www.beirutcafe.com/recruit. The owner was my classmate at Sullivan University. Don't forget to mention your experience cooking at the Mayer Summer Camp.

All the best,

Reza

**176.** In the article, the word "pull" in paragraph 2, line 4, is closest in meaning to

(A) stretch
(B) draw
(C) remove
(D) tear

**177.** How did Mr. Ayoub help his restaurant survive the economic downturn?

(A) He got a loan from the Carverton Chamber of Commerce.
(B) He only did business with local farms.
(C) He moved into a smaller building.
(D) He anticipated high initial costs.

**178.** What has contributed to Beirut Café's recent success?

(A) Its selection of organic ingredients.
(B) Its famous head chef.
(C) Its large selection of menu items.
(D) Its commitment to regular clientele.

**179.** Why did Mr. Kosch write the e-mail?

(A) To request that a Web site be changed
(B) To promote a new restaurant location
(C) To explain how to prepare a dish
(D) To announce an open position

**180.** What is suggested about Mr. Kosch?

(A) He went to school with Mr. Ayoub.
(B) He is hiring staff for his new restaurant.
(C) The Beirut Café sells a menu item designed by him.
(D) Ms. Salazar was his student at the culinary school.

GO ON TO THE NEXT PAGE →

**Eduline Lecture on Overseas Digital Marketing**

Have you been considering ways to boost international sales? Are you thinking of advertising on foreign Web sites? If you are, create an account on www.eduline.org to sign up for a series of interactive panels on Internet Marketing, which are provided to audiences abroad. Methods to attract business in markets across the world using simple computer tools will be discussed by a panel of marketing veterans. The lectures will be aired live on Thursday, October 17, from 3:20 P.M. to 6:30 P.M. (Hawaii Standard Time)

There will be a total of three presentations:
"Sell It with a Photo: Viral Image Sharing in China" - Mari Polk
"Taking Advantage of Automatic Translations" - Sora Han
"Utilizing Social Network Services in Vietnam" - Rene Torres

If you are having difficulty signing up online, contact Lars Orloff at 1-800-555-3627 anytime before October 15.

Busy at the time of the live event? Check out the Streams section on our Web site. Every event is available for viewing within 12 hours of the live broadcast.

---

www.eduline.org/feedback_survey/1017

Dear Josh Cortez,

Thank you for being a part of the Eduline Lectures on Overseas Digital Marketing. We invite you to provide some feedback in order to improve future sessions.

**Please rate the lectures (1 = not helpful to 5 = very helpful)**

| | |
|---|---|
| Usefulness of the lecture's subject | 5 |
| Presenter's information and clarity | 5 |
| Relevant examples to lecture topics | 5 |

**What did you like the most?**

Mr. Torres' presentation helped me get a much better idea of how I can market my products more effectively. It was delivered with real depth and passion. I appreciated that he allowed more time to answer all the participants' questions.

**What would you like to be improved in future lecture events?**

I currently live in London, and I had to wait until 1:20 A.M. to join the live broadcast. I'm sure many participants would appreciate it if there were more options for lecture times.

**181.** What is suggested about the lectures?

(A) They are only open to Hawaiian business owners.
(B) They will be offered throughout the month.
(C) They are intended for graduate students.
(D) They will be delivered online.

**182.** According to the advertisement, why should readers contact Mr. Orloff?

(A) To get access to the lectures
(B) To ask for a video file
(C) To propose new event topics
(D) To ask a speaker some questions

**183.** What is implied about the panelists?

(A) They are conference organizers.
(B) They are marketing professors.
(C) They have all been previously employed at Eduline.
(D) They have extensive experience in advertising abroad.

**184.** What is suggested about Mr. Cortez?

(A) He will move to London at the end of October.
(B) He plans to promote his merchandise in Vietnam.
(C) He often works extra hours.
(D) He participates in professional seminars often.

**185.** What aspect of the lectures does Mr. Cortez recommend changing?

(A) The venue
(B) The sign-up procedure
(C) The pricing
(D) The scheduling

GO ON TO THE NEXT PAGE

**Questions 186-190** refer to the following e-mail, notice, and article.

To: akatrakis@ecodress.org
From: bmunoz@texcycle.com
Date: February 12
Subject: March Itinerary

Dear Ms. Katrakis,

This message serves as confirmation that a Textiling Recycling truck will arrive at your business the afternoon of March 26. We would greatly appreciate it if the donated clothing was already sorted to speed up our collection process. Please note that your signature will be required before payment can be made.

Textile Recycling offers market rates, which fluctuate daily, for used clothing and fabrics. Currently, the value for linens is slightly down from last month. Chiffon and leather are at an all-time low due to their decreasing usage. However, as winter comes to an end, be on the lookout for polyester, which has tripled in value since last November. A company located in Vietnam is buying as much as we can offer them in the next several months.

Thank you for your business.

Regards,

Bonnie Munoz
Textile Recycling, Customer Relations

---

## Eco-Dress

Serving the metro area since 1986, we are your number one used clothing and apparel shop. Donations are always welcome! Items should be placed in the following locations:

Basket A: Coats, jackets, and sweaters
Basket B: Pants, shirts, and shorts
Shelves: Gloves, shawls, and other accessories

The demand for certain types of insulating textiles is quite high. So, for the time being, we are also welcoming donations of thermal protectors, such as cooler carriers, winter bedding, and shoe liners through March 25.

Eco-Dress keeps our planet green through its clothing recycling program. If you need anything, just ask at the checkout counter.

HAI PHONG (October 3) — Bocat has announced a new line of specialized hiking boots, the Ultrawalk DX. This new line of footwear is ideal for extreme weather conditions, including high altitude trekking where temperatures can plunge below -55°C (-67°F). The protection these shoes provide is made possible by a newly-developed custom weave of synthetic insulation. The Ultrawalk DX is also the first high-performance footwear made of more than 70 percent recycled materials, most of which are taken from cast-off clothing. The Ultrawalk DX will be sold, starting next week, exclusively at the Bocat head store in Hanoi. While international sales will begin on October 31, Bocat will begin delivering the new shoes to retailers throughout Vietnam by October 15.

**186.** What does Ms. Katrakis most likely do?

(A) Design women's apparel
(B) Write for a fashion magazine
(C) Run a used clothing store
(D) Operate a textile factory

**187.** According to the notice, where should an item like a scarf be placed?

(A) In Basket A
(B) In Basket B
(C) At the checkout counter
(D) On the shelves

**188.** Why did Eco-Dress ask that thermal protectors be dropped off by March 25?

(A) Because a buyer will arrive the next day
(B) Because winter will end soon
(C) Because a sale will begin
(D) Because new inventory will be coming in

**189.** What is Bocat most likely using in its new hiking boots?

(A) Linen
(B) Chiffon
(C) Leather
(D) Polyester

**190.** When will the new footwear be available outside of Vietnam?

(A) October 3
(B) October 10
(C) October 15
(D) October 31

*GO ON TO THE NEXT PAGE*

**Questions 191-195** refer to the following brochure, schedule, and article.

**Knoxville Commercial Development Commission**
**Special Courses for Recent Graduates**

A series of seminars designed for recent graduates who are interested in raising funds to establish their own Internet startup companies will be held by the Knoxville Commercial Development Commission (KCDC) from January 4 to 7 in the Knoxville Riverside Conference Center.

David Michaels, an independent consultant who works with dozens of new companies every year, will speak to participants about the basics of writing a summary of a proposed business strategy. Chris O'Caroll will discuss ways to get investors' attention through online advertising. Olivia Arietta will explain how crowd-funding, or getting small amounts of money from online donations, can help get your business off to a good start. Finally, the last day will be devoted to helping participants prepare to explain their visions and goals to actual investors.

Most courses are free, but a $25 materials fee is required for the investor presentation session. Sign up by emailing courses@kcdc.org.

## KCDC PROGRAM AGENDA

### Special Courses for Recent Graduates

| Day, Date, Title | Place | Time |
|---|---|---|
| **Wednesday, January 4** | | |
| • Crafting a Sales Pitch | Conference Room B | 9:30 A.M. |
| • Business Plan Fundamentals | Conference Room C | 10:30 A.M. |
| • Individual Consultation | Room 714 | 11:30 A.M. |
| **Thursday, January 5** | | |
| • Online Promotions | Conference Room B | 10:30 A.M. |
| • Individual Consultation | Room 714 | 11:30 A.M. |
| **Friday, January 6** | | |
| • Getting Public Funding | Conference Room B | 10:30 A.M. |
| • Individual Consultation | Room 714 | 11:30 A.M. |
| **Saturday, January 7** | | |
| • Investor Presentation Practice | Meeting Hall A | 10:30 A.M. |

# KCDC Seminars a Great Success

Knoxville (January 10) — Hopeful business owners participated in four days of seminars and lectures created to help them get their own startup companies operating, all thanks to the Knoxville Commercial Development Commission (KCDC).

"The seminars provided a wealth of information related to promoting my business through the internet," explained David Weisner, who plans to start a restaurant review Web site.

Also in attendance was Mary Kim, who hopes to open a digital education company. She especially enjoyed the opportunity to practice her investor presentation, during which the main selling points of her business were assessed. "I will be able to talk to investors much more effectively thanks to the information that was provided," she explained.

Sanduk Tabin, President of the KCDC, plans to host this sort of event again in July, based on the positive feedback and high turnout.

---

**191.** According to the brochure, what is a stated purpose of the program?

(A) To hire instructors for a series of lectures
(B) To boost the reputation of KCDC
(C) To instruct graduates on getting money to launch a company
(D) To help business professionals expand their networks

**192.** What is suggested about Mr. Michaels?

(A) He gave a talk on Wednesday.
(B) He is knowledgeable about internet promotions.
(C) He manages an accounting team at KCDC.
(D) He analyzes feedback provided by participants.

**193.** What does the program schedule indicate?

(A) All events take place in the same conference room.
(B) The presentation practice begins earlier than other sessions.
(C) Attendees will get several chances to have private consultations.
(D) Each day only features one class.

**194.** What is implied about Ms. Kim?

(A) She gave advice about making short speeches.
(B) She wanted to hear Mr. Tabin speak.
(C) She appreciated Ms. Arietta's feedback.
(D) She paid a fee to the KCDC.

**195.** What is mentioned in the article about KCDC?

(A) It has been run by Mr. Tabin for many years.
(B) It provided investment funds for Mr. Weisner.
(C) It is not well-known in Knoxville.
(D) It will offer similar courses in the summer.

*GO ON TO THE NEXT PAGE*

**Questions 196-200** refer to the following e-mails and handbook page.

From: e.hassan@typeflow.com
To: m.lim@kare.edu
Date: June 30
Subject: Accounting Courses

Dear Ms. Lim,

I have just enrolled in your Accounting Professional Training Certification Program and will be starting my first classes this fall. On your Web site's Frequently Asked Questions page, it says that AC113: Accounting Compliance is a required class for certification, but I have already taken a similar class through Oklahoma State University with Professor Carolyn Smith. I would therefore appreciate it if this requirement could be waived. In addition, I'm unsure of the best order in which to take the classes. I would appreciate it if you could provide a recommendation.

Sincerely,

Elliot Hassan

---

From: m.lim@kare.edu
To: e.hassan@typeflow.com
Date: July 1
Subject: Re: Accounting Courses

Dear Mr. Hassan,

Let me begin by congratulating you on your decision to earn an accounting certificate. Unfortunately, waiving AC113 is not possible. The class provides grounding in the very latest applicable financial reporting laws and will be referenced frequently in other classes.

During the fall semester, you are required to take AC102: Accounting Fundamentals, which will be held in one of the computer labs.

As a new student, you can find a more thorough explanation of our institute's requirements and policies in the program guide. The following sections are relevant to your course:

Accounting Professional Training Certification Overview: pp. 1-5
Mandatory Accounting Classes: pp. 6-10
Optional Accounting Classes: pp. 11-12
Recommended Sequence of Classes: pp. 22-23

A copy of the guide should arrive in the mail this week. After reviewing it, please contact me with any further questions you may have.

Regards,

May Lim
Kare Institute

# Kare Institute Computer Labs

Kare faculty and students are provided with computer labs (more information below) fully equipped to meet their needs.

**General Use Lab: Room 200**
50 computers with accounting and word-processing software; may be accessed by anyone with a Kare staff or student ID.

**Accounting Lab: Room 210**
15 computers with currently-used software for general accounting purposes: may only be accessed by those enrolled in first-year classes.

**Professional Lab: Room 212**
21 computers with payroll and tax accounting software, as well as banking simulation programs, available for AC203: Corporate Tax Filings and AC215: Staff Disbursement or with faculty approval.

**Testing Lab: Room 315**
Certification testing computers with software for various accounting scenarios, available only during certification testing.

Notices in every lab give the hours they are in use for classes and when they are available for personal use. Other computers for class and public use can be found in the lounge area on the first floor and are available 24/7.

---

**196.** Why does Mr. Hassan mention the Accounting Compliance class?

(A) To check if he must take it
(B) To ask for information about the professor
(C) To see if it can be done online
(D) To inquire about the price of textbooks

**197.** What is indicated about the guide?

(A) It offers faculty contact information.
(B) It includes an audio CD.
(C) Mr. Hassan will soon receive it.
(D) Ms. Lim helped edit it.

**198.** What page numbers in the guide most likely contain the answer to Mr. Hassan's inquiry?

(A) pp. 1-5
(B) pp. 6-10
(C) pp. 11-12
(D) pp. 22-23

**199.** Where will the Accounting Compliance class most likely take place?

(A) The General Use Lab
(B) The Accounting Lab
(C) The Professional Lab
(D) The Testing Lab

**200.** What is true about the computer labs?

(A) They all offer software for accounting.
(B) They all have reservation schedules.
(C) They all offer technical support staff.
(D) They all have 24-hour access.

*GO ON TO THE NEXT PAGE*

# ST 2

# READING TEST

In the Reading test, you will read a variety of texts and answer several different types of reading comprehension questions. The entire Reading test will last 75 minutes. There are three parts, and directions are given for each part. You are encouraged to answer as many questions as possible within the time allowed.

You must mark your answers on the separate answer sheet. Do not write your answers in the test book.

# PART 5

**Directions:** A word or phrase is missing in each of the sentences below. Four answer choices are given below each sentence. Select the best answer to complete the sentence. Then mark the letter (A), (B), (C), or (D) on your answer sheet.

**101.** Monitor Shipping now has ------- with 32 major clothing retailers.

(A) contracts
(B) contract
(C) contractor
(D) contracting

**102.** Official authorization must ------- prior to utilizing Sunian Inc.'s trademark.

(A) obtain
(B) be obtained
(C) obtaining
(D) be obtaining

**103.** The Customer Service Department should employ more personnel ------- client accounts have increased by 45 percent.

(A) therefore
(B) because of
(C) even though
(D) since

**104.** Frateri Inc. lost the ------- percentage of its clients to Planter Corporation.

(A) farthest
(B) deepest
(C) greatest
(D) lightest

**105.** Ms. Kajima's ------- duties consist of organizing and calculating assets of recently acquired clients.

(A) accountable
(B) accounting
(C) accounted
(D) account

**106.** Doctors recommend putting ice over the swollen area for twenty ------- thirty minutes a day.

(A) by
(B) as
(C) to
(D) on

**107.** The HR Department at Brenn Inc. offers bonuses ------- staff productivity.

(A) stimulating
(B) stimulate
(C) to stimulate
(D) will stimulate

**108.** I have included a sample portfolio of my designs for your -------.

(A) consideration
(B) anticipation
(C) explanation
(D) participation

**109.** Even though the task took ------- five hours to finish, the employees will be compensated for a full day's work.

(A) before
(B) for
(C) only
(D) right

**110.** Before the televisions are packaged, they are ------- thoroughly to ensure they function properly.

(A) assigned
(B) selected
(C) managed
(D) inspected

**111.** ------- on the organizing committee contributed to the great success of the workshop.

(A) Whoever
(B) Everyone
(C) Each other
(D) One another

**112.** Kraven Financial has ------- an agreement to lease a larger office space.

(A) signed
(B) defined
(C) engaged
(D) involved

**113.** Scantron personal finance software can help ------- track accounts, create budgets, and process payments.

(A) yourself
(B) yours
(C) your
(D) you

**114.** Providing custom glassware to a ------- array of companies, Prezis Glazier just celebrated 150 years of doing business in Bern.

(A) widen
(B) wide
(C) width
(D) widely

**115.** All announcements must receive approval from the PR Manager before they can be released -------.

(A) largely
(B) utterly
(C) absolutely
(D) externally

**116.** The International Binders Confederation ------- the interests of book publishers worldwide.

(A) recreates
(B) represents
(C) functions
(D) contributes

**117.** Prior to your upcoming interview, please complete the ------- applicant information form.

(A) enclosing
(B) enclose
(C) enclosed
(D) enclosure

**118.** The memo concerning the proposed ------- of Heath Landscaping by Manchester Builders Ltd. has been distributed.

(A) compliance
(B) acquisition
(C) attachment
(D) document

**119.** While many financial apps transfer money only to local banks, MoneyTime can send to international ones -------.

(A) before then
(B) so far
(C) throughout
(D) as well

**120.** The Vice President has ------- the importance of gaining new clients next year.

(A) administered
(B) ordered
(C) emphasized
(D) requested

GO ON TO THE NEXT PAGE

**121.** Ms. Park has proven ------- to be a loyal and innovative member of the R&D team.

(A) herself
(B) itself
(C) it
(D) she

**122.** Ms. Talia Ghulal, representative of Quartermain Solutions, stressed her company's ------- for stricter quality standards.

(A) consciousness
(B) placement
(C) fairness
(D) support

**123.** The shop had a ------- display of the latest novel from the popular science-fiction writer.

(A) gifted
(B) default
(C) massive
(D) thankful

**124.** Demeter Technologies is attempting to upgrade the portable unit ------- next month's Renewable Energy Expo.

(A) opposite from
(B) in spite of
(C) in addition to
(D) ahead of

**125.** Both strong and secure, the storage units from Bulldog Boxing are also large ------- to be used for holding vehicles.

(A) well
(B) fully
(C) closely
(D) enough

**126.** According to Mr. Kim's -------, 300 square meters of marble tiles are required to finish the lobby floor.

(A) calculations
(B) calculated
(C) calculates
(D) calculate

**127.** Get a 40 percent discount on any chair ------- you buy an office desk at Franklin's Furniture.

(A) whenever
(B) although
(C) after all
(D) such as

**128.** Patients have been truly ------- of our efforts to lower the amount of time they have to spend waiting.

(A) appreciative
(B) appreciation
(C) appreciate
(D) appreciating

**129.** The scratches on the lobby floor are ------- visible now that the polishing work has been done.

(A) falsely
(B) barely
(C) correctly
(D) precisely

**130.** The shareholders have requested that Mr. Tran ------- all possible ways to lower overhead expenses at the Bangkok facility.

(A) examine
(B) is examining
(C) to examine
(D) has examined

# PART 6

**Directions:** Read the texts that follow. A word, phrase, or sentence is missing in parts of each text. Four answer choices for each question are given below the text. Select the best answer to complete the text. Then mark the letter (A), (B), (C), or (D) on your answer sheet.

**Questions 131-134** refer to the following article.

The Kansai Park Authority this morning ------- its decision on whether or not to create
**131.**
additional hiking trails in Kansai National Forest. In a press conference today, Park

Director Lisa Hasegawa stated that more research on the environment is required -------
**132.**
the Park Authority can move forward with the project. -------. Yet, the forest has been
**133.**
attracting far more visitors since the opening of the Kansai Forest Resort. Analysts

attribute the ------- in hiking activities to the resort. According to Ms. Hasegawa, the
**134.**
Park Authority will discuss the matter again after four months.

**131.** (A) questioned
(B) confirmed
(C) approved
(D) delayed

**132.** (A) once
(B) after
(C) before
(D) during

**133.** (A) Ms. Hasegawa advises that all hikers bring protective gear.
(B) The Park Authority is looking to hire experienced tour guides.
(C) There are currently only three trails available to guests.
(D) Kansai recently introduced new environmental laws.

**134.** (A) increase
(B) advertisement
(C) disappointment
(D) plateau

*GO ON TO THE NEXT PAGE*

**Questions 135-138** refer to the following e-mail.

From: Shirley Watanabe
To: All Employees
Date: August 12
Subject: System update

Today, all employee computers will be upgraded to the latest version of our security software. -------. You will still be able to access your programs while the installation is
      **135.**
being performed, but you might ------- that your system is not running as fast as it
      **136.**
should. Once the installation is done, you will have to reboot your computer. -------, if
      **137.**
you are working on something, you can complete the process at a more convenient
time. We apologize in advance for any -------.
      **138.**

135. (A) We are working towards revising our
     security guidelines.
     (B) Our security office is open until 8
     P.M. today.
     (C) The upgrade will automatically start
     at 1 P.M.
     (D) This upgrade will only work on
     certain computer models.

136. (A) remember
     (B) notice
     (C) persuade
     (D) criticize

137. (A) In fact
     (B) In particular
     (C) Consequently
     (D) However

138. (A) interruptive
     (B) interrupt
     (C) interruptions
     (D) interrupted

**Questions 139-142** refer to the following article.

For the last four decades, Ernest Fong has been designing and selling tables and cabinets in Hertzfield. At the end of this month, he will ------- bid farewell to his loyal
**139.**
customers and start a new position at the local community college. -------. "I've spent
**140.**
years perfecting my craft, and now, I'd like to share my passion and skills with my younger colleagues," he commented. Before Mr. Fong permanently closes his shop, he is planning to hold a sale for his remaining merchandise. Several unique ------- items
**141.**
will be sold at reduced prices. Some previously-owned tables and cabinets will -------
**142.**
be available for purchase. The event will take place next Saturday at 2 P.M.

**139.** (A) finalize
(B) finally
(C) final
(D) finale

**140.** (A) Mr. Fong will be teaching classes as well as mentoring a successor.
(B) Mr. Fong worked part-time at a home décor company in Asia during college.
(C) His products are displayed at conventions every year.
(D) His store offers the most affordable prices in the city.

**141.** (A) painting
(B) electronics
(C) clothing
(D) furniture

**142.** (A) instead
(B) rarely
(C) also
(D) simply

GO ON TO THE NEXT PAGE

**Questions 143-146** refer to the following memo.

From: Calvin Newton, President of TW Electronics
To: All TW Electronics employees
Date: March 12
Subject: Acquisition update

As you are probably aware, on May 2 our acquisition of Wasserman Tech will be finalized. From that date -------, we will be called TWW Electronics Corporation. This
                                    **143.**
purchase will make us the biggest ------- of consumer electronics in the country.
                                    **144.**

You are probably wondering how this acquisition will impact you. Fortunately, your job title, duties, and salary will all remain as specified in your current employee agreement with TW Electronics. -------.
                                    **145.**

Nevertheless, you will see many changes in the coming months. ------- will be
                                                               **146.**
discussed at our next quarterly meeting on April 3 at 9:00 A.M. in the Main Auditorium. We will make sure to address all of your questions at that time.

**143.** (A) aside
(B) later
(C) until
(D) forward

**144.** (A) supplier
(B) supplies
(C) supplying
(D) supplied

**145.** (A) We will begin looking for a suitable candidate to replace the current president.
(B) Your specific job duties may vary to some extent.
(C) New agreements will be sent to you confirming the changes.
(D) Actually, the company is considering creating more positions.

**146.** (A) We
(B) Either
(C) These
(D) It

# PART 7

**Directions:** In this part you will read a selection of texts, such as magazine and newspaper articles, e-mails, and instant messages. Each text or set of texts is followed by several questions. Select the best answer for each question and mark the letter (A), (B), (C) or (D) on your answer sheet.

**Questions 147-148** refer to the following job advertisement.

## Aspengrove

Aspengrove is hiring clerks, housekeepers, concierge agents, and maintenance staff for its newest location, which opens its doors on May 31 across from the Lennox Convention Center. Clerks should have more than two years' experience in customer relations, while concierge agents should have a year or more of experience. For housekeepers and maintenance staff, prior experience is a plus, but we will train entry-level staff. Interviews are being held next week on May 22 and 23. Candidates should bring a résumé and other relevant documentation. To find out more, visit www.aspengrove.com.

**147.** What type of business is Aspengrove?

(A) A hotel chain
(B) A manufacturing plant
(C) A landscaping company
(D) A conference facility

**148.** What is suggested about the advertised positions?

(A) Prior experience is required for most of them.
(B) All of them must be filled by May 23.
(C) Candidates can apply for them at any company location.
(D) They all provide paid training.

*GO ON TO THE NEXT PAGE*

**Questions 149-150** refer to the following text message chain.

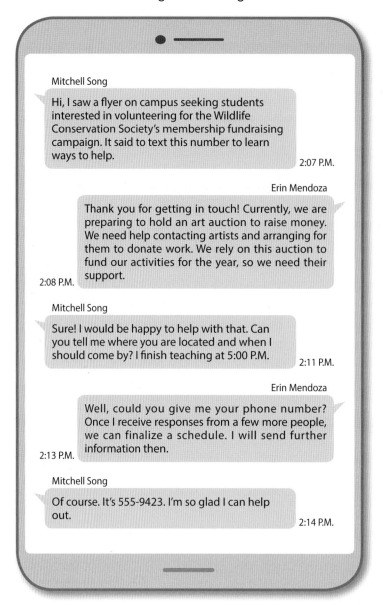

**Mitchell Song**

Hi, I saw a flyer on campus seeking students interested in volunteering for the Wildlife Conservation Society's membership fundraising campaign. It said to text this number to learn ways to help.

2:07 P.M.

**Erin Mendoza**

Thank you for getting in touch! Currently, we are preparing to hold an art auction to raise money. We need help contacting artists and arranging for them to donate work. We rely on this auction to fund our activities for the year, so we need their support.

2:08 P.M.

**Mitchell Song**

Sure! I would be happy to help with that. Can you tell me where you are located and when I should come by? I finish teaching at 5:00 P.M.

2:11 P.M.

**Erin Mendoza**

Well, could you give me your phone number? Once I receive responses from a few more people, we can finalize a schedule. I will send further information then.

2:13 P.M.

**Mitchell Song**

Of course. It's 555-9423. I'm so glad I can help out.

2:14 P.M.

**149.** Why did Mr. Song contact Ms. Mendoza?

(A) To donate some money
(B) To give feedback on a class
(C) To inquire about a volunteer position
(D) To reserve an exhibition booth

**150.** At 2:11 P.M., what does Mr. Song most likely mean when he writes, "I finish teaching at 5:00 P.M."?

(A) He worries he will be late for a meeting.
(B) He plans to call Ms. Mendoza later.
(C) He has time to help out in the evenings.
(D) He would like a ride from Ms. Mendoza.

**National Association of Museum Curators**
August 15-17, Cornell University
Ithaca, New York
10th Annual Conference

Dining Options

Welcome to the National Association of Museum Curators' 10th annual conference. Attendees are encouraged to purchase prepaid meal cards upon check-in at the registration tables in Olive Tjaden Hall. Meal cards cover breakfast, lunch, and dinner, and are $20 and $55 for one and three days, respectively. Conference passes will be issued at the same time and should be worn at all times. Meal cards are optional, but without one, conference participants will be required to pay the full price of $10 per meal. Please be aware that meal cards are only valid on the university campus.

On-campus cafeterias open at 6 A.M. and close at 9 P.M. Buffet-style meals are available in Risley Hall and Appel Commons, which also has a coffee house. Global selections, including Asian, Middle Eastern, and Latin American dishes, are offered in Willard Straight Hall. Please refer to the campus map included in the conference program to locate an eatery that matches your tastes.

There are many off-campus dining options near the conference venues as well, including the Jersey Mac Grill, Crispin's Bistro, and Empire State Pizza.

**151.** What is suggested about the National Association of Museum Curators?

(A) Its participants registered online.
(B) It is hosting a special dinner for guests.
(C) Its first professional gathering was held a decade ago.
(D) It is attended by international curators.

**152.** Where will conference attendees NOT be served lunch?

(A) In Olive Tjaden Hall
(B) In Risley Hall
(C) In Willard Straight Hall
(D) In Appel Commons

**153.** What is true about places to eat outside the conference site?

(A) They will not accept conference-issued meal cards.
(B) They charge $10 for lunch.
(C) They are shown on the map included in the conference program.
(D) They all close at 9 P.M.

GO ON TO THE NEXT PAGE

**Questions 154-155** refer to the following letter.

**Lockhead Laboratories**

2 April

Dear Mr. Reddington,

We have read your e-mail dated 31 March regarding the research assistant position here at Lockhead Labs. As stated in our job advertisement, we cannot accept applications after 14 March. There were many qualified candidates, and we have offered the position to one of them. However, your qualifications are impressive, and I will keep your information on file. I am especially interested in your current position as a research assistant at Hanborough Scientifics, as their work is similar to ours.

Thank you for expressing an interest in Lockhead Labs. I will contact you if we have another research assistant opening at the company.

Kind regards,

*Elizabeth Van Horrens*
Elizabeth Van Horrens
Laboratory Manager

**154.** Why was the letter written?
(A) To confirm an interview date
(B) To provide details about the duties of a job
(C) To request a work sample
(D) To explain that a job vacancy has been filled

**155.** What is indicated about Mr. Reddington?
(A) He is currently employed.
(B) His application was submitted before the deadline.
(C) He is applying for a lab manager position.
(D) He has limited work experience.

**Questions 156-157** refer to the following e-mail.

**To:** m.luciano@californiacatering.com
**From:** r.hall@fshie.org
**Date:** June 27
**Subject:** Food Services and Hospitality Expo

Dear Ms. Luciano,

We were delighted that you attended the Food Services and Hospitality Expo last year. However, to date, we have yet to receive your registration for this year's event. Early registration for a reduced fee of €225 is only available until the end of the month. After June 30, the price will increase to €300.

Included in the conference fee are the following:

- Reserved seating at the welcome buffet on Tuesday, October 7
- Access to all expo events
- A ticket to the closing ceremony on Thursday, October 9

The following is not included in the registration fee:

- Association Members' dinner on Wednesday, October 8. (Transportation to the event's location will be provided. A separate payment must be made directly via the Food Industry Association Web site, if you would like to participate.)

We look forward to seeing you again this year.

Sincerely,

Roberta Hall

**156.** Why did Mr. Hall send the e-mail to Ms. Luciano?

(A) To advise her of an upcoming deadline
(B) To encourage her to speak at an exposition
(C) To request that she revise a schedule
(D) To acknowledge that a payment was received

**157.** What is indicated about the event on October 8?

(A) It will feature some important guests.
(B) It can be attended at an additional cost.
(C) It will take place in the expo's facilities.
(D) It does not have many spots left.

GO ON TO THE NEXT PAGE

**Questions 158-160** refer to the following information in a library catalog.

---

http://www.parliamentarylibrary.co.uk/archivesdatabase

**Parliamentary Library Archives Database**

This database is designed to help you find historical Parliamentary records. It includes hundreds of thousands of legislative documents dating back to the 1600s, many of which are not available anywhere else. —[1]—. Listings are searchable by author or by the date of the document's creation. Each includes a synopsis of its contents. A new version, allowing for searches by location, will be available this spring. Materials marked "offline" may, in some cases, be viewed at the Archives Office. To gain access to these, you must receive approval from one of our employees. —[2]—.

[SAMPLE ENTRY]

**Rowlandson-Lloyd Letters**

A collection of letters exchanged over a hundred years ago between Peter Rowlandson and Paul George. —[3]—. Seven of the eight letters referred to have been preserved. They include discussions of proposed tax rates and Rowlandson's personal reflections. Also, they contain a partial draft of George's 29 April House of Commons address, with a number of handwritten revisions. —[4]—.

---

**158.** What is indicated about materials in the Parliamentary Library Archives Database?

(A) They are organized alphabetically.
(B) They are all available electronically.
(C) Some of them require approval to access.
(D) Some of them can be taken home.

**159.** What is true about the Rowlandson-Lloyd letters?

(A) They were written more than a century ago.
(B) They include images of old tax documents.
(C) They were restored by library employees.
(D) They will be uploaded to a Web site.

**160.** In which of the positions marked [1], [2], [3], and [4] does the following sentence best belong?

"Because of their age, many of these documents are quite fragile and may only be viewed online."

(A) [1]
(B) [2]
(C) [3]
(D) [4]

**Questions 161-164** refer to the following letter.

McAllister High School
3455 S. 18th Terrace
Miami, FL 33125
786-555-6623

October 10

Ms. Jeri Cooper
Cooper's
1452 Hardaway Dr.
Mirada, CA 90638

Dear Ms. Cooper,

I wanted to let you know how much the Music Department at McAllister High School appreciates your generosity. The twenty brass instruments your organization donated, as well as the sheet music and recordings, have helped us a great deal. —[1]—. Our school now has enough instruments to instruct 32 pupils at a time. When we last spoke, you were curious about how the students would share the equipment. We currently allow three students to use each instrument during the course of the school day. For students requiring their own mouthpieces, they pay just $25. At the beginning of the school year, a sign-up sheet is provided for everyone to choose an instrument. —[2]—.

Also, the funds you donated made it possible to hire two part-time teachers for after-school music activities. The music room is open for practice until 6:00 P.M., Monday to Friday, which has increased participation among students whose parents work. —[3]—. Some students have even started a band with one of the new teachers. If you have time, please come to one of our events and hear them play! —[4]—.

In the future, we hope to add an orchestra section to the McAllister auditorium so that we can feature live music in our theater productions. If this initiative is of interest to you, we would certainly appreciate the support. I will keep you informed about our plans for this.

Once again, thank you for supporting McAllister's aspiring musicians.

Sincerely,

*Daniel O'Malley*

Daniel O'Malley
McAllister High School, Principal

161. Why was the letter written?

(A) To invite Ms. Cooper to a music audition
(B) To thank Ms. Cooper for a contribution
(C) To profile a new teacher
(D) To request help with a performance

162. What is suggested about McAllister High School?

(A) It has recruited more staff.
(B) It is considering adding a concert hall.
(C) It will be raising class fees.
(D) It is going to open a new theater.

163. What is mentioned about the instruments at McAllister High School?

(A) They were ordered by Mr. O'Malley.
(B) They have to be repaired.
(C) They are shared by several students.
(D) They are for after-school activities only.

164. In which of the positions marked [1], [2], [3], and [4] does the following sentence best belong?

"Also, for those who cannot take a music class during the school day, this provides a chance to do so despite a full schedule."

(A) [1]
(B) [2]
(C) [3]
(D) [4]

GO ON TO THE NEXT PAGE

**Questions 165-168** refer to the following text message chain.

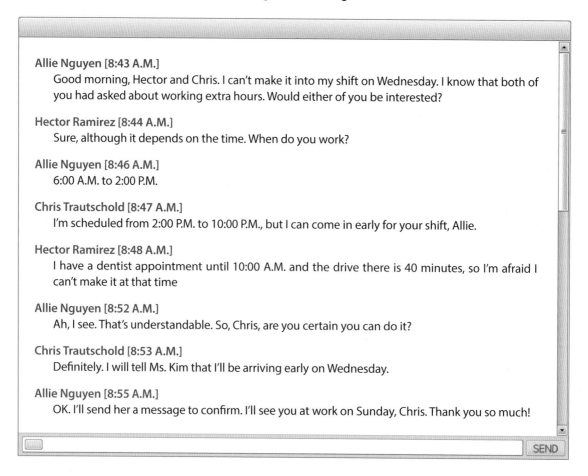

Allie Nguyen [8:43 A.M.]
Good morning, Hector and Chris. I can't make it into my shift on Wednesday. I know that both of you had asked about working extra hours. Would either of you be interested?

Hector Ramirez [8:44 A.M.]
Sure, although it depends on the time. When do you work?

Allie Nguyen [8:46 A.M.]
6:00 A.M. to 2:00 P.M.

Chris Trautschold [8:47 A.M.]
I'm scheduled from 2:00 P.M. to 10:00 P.M., but I can come in early for your shift, Allie.

Hector Ramirez [8:48 A.M.]
I have a dentist appointment until 10:00 A.M. and the drive there is 40 minutes, so I'm afraid I can't make it at that time

Allie Nguyen [8:52 A.M.]
Ah, I see. That's understandable. So, Chris, are you certain you can do it?

Chris Trautschold [8:53 A.M.]
Definitely. I will tell Ms. Kim that I'll be arriving early on Wednesday.

Allie Nguyen [8:55 A.M.]
OK. I'll send her a message to confirm. I'll see you at work on Sunday, Chris. Thank you so much!

SEND

---

**165.** Why did Ms. Nguyen contact her coworkers?

(A) To check the status of their assignments
(B) To instruct them to log their extra hours
(C) To instruct them to submit vacation requests
(D) To check if they can work in her place

**166.** What is suggested about Mr. Trautschold?

(A) He recently trained Ms. Nguyen on some tasks.
(B) He is scheduled to work with Ms. Nguyen on the weekend.
(C) He typically works overtime.
(D) He often comes to work early for his shift.

**167.** At 8:52 A.M., what does Ms. Nguyen most likely mean when she writes, "That's understandable"?

(A) She accepts Mr. Ramirez's explanation.
(B) She believes that Mr. Trautschold is dependable.
(C) She heard about Mr. Ramirez's appointment beforehand.
(D) She is familiar with a traffic situation.

**168.** What is most likely true about Ms. Kim?

(A) She drives to the office.
(B) She is trying to work extra hours.
(C) She is scheduled to work on Sunday.
(D) She manages the employees' schedules.

**Questions 169-171** refer to the following letter.

---

## The Alberta News

Dear Ms. Shen,

Thank you for continuing to support *The Alberta News*. You'll be pleased to know that we will now be offering a weekend edition, which will include an event calendar with listings of upcoming festivals and performances in the province, and a section for film and theater reviews. It will also contain discount coupons for entertainment venues, restaurants, and other local businesses.

As a special courtesy to our long-time customers, we offer this edition to you at no cost for one month. Your free trial will start on Monday, September 1, and will end on Tuesday, September 30. If you wish to continue receiving the edition after that time, you will only have to pay $7.50 more each month.

We also invite you to try using our referral program by introducing our newspaper to family members and friends. If any of your family members or friends subscribe to *The Alberta News*, you will receive our newspaper for free for one whole month!

Please send any questions or concerns to customerservice@albertanews.com.

Sincerely,

*Sasha Ringwald*
Customer Service Representative

---

**169.** What is the purpose of the letter?

(A) To request a customer to make a payment
(B) To offer discounts to entertainment venues
(C) To promote newspaper advertising to local businesses
(D) To explain a new service to an existing customer

**170.** What will NOT be included in the weekend edition of *The Alberta News*?

(A) Recipes for traditional dishes
(B) Listings of future events
(C) Reviews of movies and plays
(D) Discounts to local restaurants

**171.** What will happen if Ms. Shen chooses to continue receiving the weekend edition after September?

(A) The fees for advertising will be lowered.
(B) Her family and friends will be eligible for a discount.
(C) The cost of the edition will be added to her monthly bill.
(D) She will be given free tickets to performances.

*GO ON TO THE NEXT PAGE*

**Questions 172-175** refer to the following notice.

## White Owl Industries

Attention All Staff

We're making progress with our Corporate Environmental Program! Here are some of the latest details:

Our board has voted to boost funding to reduce the amount of waste our office produces.

Management is pleased that many of you have decided to participate in the Bike to Work initiative. More than half of our employees ride their bicycles at least three times a week.

We have achieved great results by switching to energy-efficient office lighting. We now use 45 percent less electricity, but employees are still reminded to power down appliances, lights, and computers when not in use.

Bins for materials you plan to discard are located in each department's office area:

• Regular garbage should be put in the blue trash cans.
• Materials that can be recycled should be placed in the correct trash can according to their material type. Deposit metal items in the red trash cans. (This includes cans of any size, paper clips, and foil wrap.) Put paper into the green trash cans. Please ensure that all sensitive documents are shredded before being discarded.
• The blue trash cans are emptied every day. All other trash cans are taken out every other evening.

A recent company poll indicated that employees would like to recycle plastic products as well. We are looking into this and will let you know more at Friday's meeting.

Together we can make a difference!

Sincerely,

Anwar al Falasi
Director of Maintenance

**172.** Why did Mr. al Falasi write the notice?

  (A) To give an update about a program
  (B) To announce an upcoming
     inspection
  (C) To discuss responses to a poll
  (D) To ask for a bigger budget

**173.** What is suggested as an additional way
to save resources?

  (A) Riding a bicycle twice a week
  (B) Turning unused electronics off
  (C) Ensuring that discarded paper is
     shredded
  (D) Bringing recyclable products to the
     office

**174.** How often are recyclable materials
removed?

  (A) Every day
  (B) Every other day
  (C) Once a week
  (D) Once a month

**175.** What is NOT currently being recycled at
the company?

  (A) Plastic bottles
  (B) Paper
  (C) Paper clips
  (D) Small cans

GO ON TO THE NEXT PAGE

**Questions 176-180** refer to the following Web page and e-mail.

| About Us | Our Services | Location & Contact | Programs & Outreach |

# Business Marketing Seminars
## Sponsored by Benton Advertising and the Adorado Chamber of Commerce

Benton Advertising and the Adorado Chamber of Commerce (ACC) are pleased to offer a new series of marketing seminars. These sessions are presented at no cost to our members by professionals in the field of marketing who will provide instruction on a range of issues. Please note that registration for each seminar is limited to 100 attendees and must be completed at the ACC's downtown location on Broadhurst Ave. Participants will receive travel mugs with the ACC logo.

| Topic | Time | Date | Location | Instructor |
|---|---|---|---|---|
| The Value of Social Media Ads | 1:00 P.M. - 5:00 P.M. | June 3 | ACC Auditorium | Alyssa Vazquez |
| The Right Way to Advertise Your New Business | 10:00 A.M. - 1:00 P.M. | June 8 | ACC Auditorium | Enrique Perez |
| Big Data for Small Business | 3:30 P.M. - 6:00 P.M. | June 15 | ACC Auditorium | Andrea Fernandez |
| Billboards Are Out, Pop-ups Are In | 6:00 P.M. - 7:30 P.M. | June 29 | ACC Auditorium | Jose Martin |

From:       info@adoradocc.org
To:          ajohns@ihat.com
Date:        June 2
Subject:    Seminar registration
Attachment:  Johns.rtf

Dear Ms. Johns,

We applaud your decision to join us for our business marketing seminar. We are sure that you will gain valuable knowledge about how to promote the opening of your store. You will be able to apply everything you learn immediately.

Attached with this e-mail is acknowledgement of your seminar registration. Visit our Web site to view a map to the event facility. Be sure to sign in at the front desk to get a visitor's badge. From there, signs will guide you to the auditorium.

Thank you for your contribution as a member of the Adorado Chamber of Commerce.

Alejandro de las Torres
Adorado Chamber of Commerce

**176.** According to the Web page, what is being offered?

(A) Private face-to-face meetings with professionals
(B) A computer program to help analyze information
(C) A chance to increase marketing knowledge
(D) Teaching opportunities at a local business school

**177.** What is NOT indicated about the seminars?

(A) They are hosted by Benton Advertising and the ACC.
(B) They are held in a different location every year.
(C) They are offered to ACC members.
(D) They can fit only up to a certain number of guests.

**178.** Who will lead the event Ms. Johns is planning to attend?

(A) Ms. Vazquez
(B) Mr. Perez
(C) Ms. Fernandez
(D) Mr. Martin

**179.** In the e-mail, the word "apply" in paragraph 1, line 2, is closest in meaning to

(A) inquire
(B) use
(C) spread
(D) place

**180.** What file is attached to the e-mail?

(A) An attendee's confirmation
(B) A certificate of completion
(C) A list of seminar topics
(D) Directions to a venue

GO ON TO THE NEXT PAGE

**Questions 181-185** refer to the following memo and e-mail.

To: All Staff
From: HR Department
Date: February 3
Subject: Announcement

At the beginning of the year, Sinor Tech added a new policy, Rule 31-4. It introduces dress code guidelines in the office. Please refrain from wearing exercise-related attire (e.g. hooded track jackets or tight leggings) and clothing with graphic elements (e.g. large logos or images) while at work. Also, please avoid wearing hats or sneakers.

We appreciate your attention to the updated policy. Rule 31-4 will help us maintain a professional office environment.

**From:** HR Department
**To:** Staff List
**Date:** February 12
**Subject:** Poll: Appropriate Office Attire

Attention Staff:

On Friday, Glassoffice researcher Stan Johnson will pay a visit to Sinor Tech to talk with volunteers about their opinions and experiences with casual office attire and the rules in place prohibiting it. He will present research showing that casual dress standards reduce morale as staff complaints to HR occur more frequently.

Mr. Johnson will also be adding to his research by giving an online questionnaire to our staff. The questionnaire should only require five minutes to complete and is optional. Sinor Tech staff who choose to participate won't be asked for any information that could be used to identify them, and all names will be removed from any published results.

You can fill out the questionnaire by visiting https://www.glassoffice.com/questionnaire.

We value everyone's input.

**181.** Why was the memo sent?

(A) To give an update on an upcoming product launch
(B) To explain a revised benefits package
(C) To remind staff of a company regulation
(D) To announce a new corporate logo

**182.** What is the purpose of Mr. Johnson's visit?

(A) To discuss marketing techniques
(B) To demonstrate a device
(C) To introduce a new type of fabric
(D) To share research on dress codes

**183.** According to Mr. Johnson's research, what will Rule 31-4 most likely reduce?

(A) Staff absences
(B) Employee complaints
(C) Shipping errors
(D) Clothing sales

**184.** What is indicated about the questionnaire?

(A) It can be accessed through Sinor Tech's Web site.
(B) It has only five questions.
(C) It will be led by the Sinor Tech advertising team.
(D) Participants will not be identified.

**185.** In the e-mail, the word "value" in paragraph 4, line 1, is closest in meaning to

(A) appreciate
(B) assess
(C) profit
(D) charge

GO ON TO THE NEXT PAGE

**Questions 186-190** refer to the following e-mail, list, and article.

**To:** wjenkins@photoshoot.biz
**From:** esmythe@aspentree.com
**Date:** May 3
**Subject:** Aspentree Country Club's Community Appreciation Day

Dear Mr. Jenkins,

As a long-time member of Aspentree Country Club, it would be a pleasure to see you at our Community Appreciation Day on Sunday, May 31. We are excited to welcome you, as we are planning to host many different activities to promote the benefits of participating in sports. If you reply to this e-mail message before May 10, we will mail you a voucher to receive a special gift.

Eric Smythe
Outreach Director, Aspentree Country Club

### Aspentree Country Club's Community Appreciation Day, May 31

### Roles and Tasks

- Outreach coordinator: Eric Smythe

- Sponsorship liaison: Lena Goldstein

- Speakers: Ji-hye Lee (Swimming), Scott McAllister (Tennis)

- Children's Badminton Contest: Antonio de Velazquez

- Sports and Arts Instruction / Trainers: Hillary von Teesdale, Mitchell Yorke, Shirley Thorncleft

# Appreciation Bash at Aspentree Country Club

by Erin Keelstone, June 2

Last Sunday, Aspentree Country Club held an exciting Community Appreciation Day. In addition to celebrating 35 years in operation, the occasion was a way to thank the community for its support. The facility opened its doors to members and the public alike during this well-attended event.

Participants were able to listen to top athletes give talks, and T-shirts, notebooks, and pens were handed out by business sponsors. Attendees with a special voucher were able to play a complimentary round of golf with our professional instructors.

Throughout the day, a significant number of people gathered for Mitchell Yorke's presentations. "I had intended to find out more about the tennis and swimming classes, but I did not expect to be so entertained by Mr. Yorke's demonstration on how to step to the rhythm of Latin music," said Wally Jenkins.

Without a doubt, the presentation that gathered the biggest crowd was Olympic champion Ji-hye Lee's talk on taking lessons at the club's pool when she was growing up. The audience, which included more than 70 students, was clearly fascinated by the stories of her swimming career. She stayed much longer than scheduled, answering questions and signing autographs.

The badminton competition featuring both singles and doubles matches made all the young attendees very happy. There were treats and ribbons presented by the staff member supervising the games. Aspentree Country Club was so pleased with the turnout that they may make the event a yearly one.

---

**186.** What is Mr. Jenkins encouraged to do?

(A) Attend an event
(B) Fill out a questionnaire
(C) Meet with Mr. Smythe
(D) Plan an event

**187.** How did some attendees likely get a free golf lesson?

(A) By replying to Mr. Smythe's e-mail
(B) By entering a contest
(C) By listening to Ms. Thorncleft's talk
(D) By showing up early to an event

**188.** What does Mr. Yorke most likely specialize in?

(A) Tennis
(B) Dance
(C) Swimming
(D) Badminton

**189.** What is indicated about the presentation on swimming?

(A) It drew a lot of interest.
(B) It was canceled.
(C) It was shown on television.
(D) It was given by a country club director.

**190.** Who most likely distributed ribbons?

(A) Eric Smythe
(B) Hillary von Teesdale
(C) Antonio de Velazquez
(D) Scott McAllister

*GO ON TO THE NEXT PAGE*

**Questions 191-195 refer** to the following Web page, e-mail, and notice.

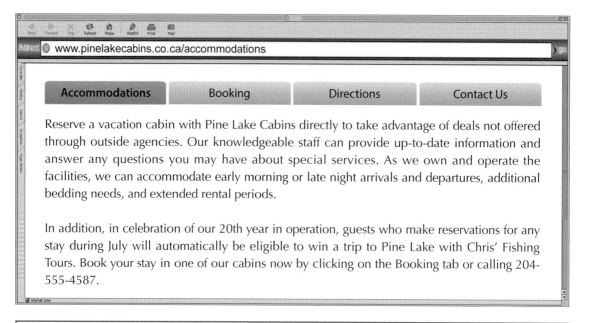

**Accommodations** | Booking | Directions | Contact Us

Reserve a vacation cabin with Pine Lake Cabins directly to take advantage of deals not offered through outside agencies. Our knowledgeable staff can provide up-to-date information and answer any questions you may have about special services. As we own and operate the facilities, we can accommodate early morning or late night arrivals and departures, additional bedding needs, and extended rental periods.

In addition, in celebration of our 20th year in operation, guests who make reservations for any stay during July will automatically be eligible to win a trip to Pine Lake with Chris' Fishing Tours. Book your stay in one of our cabins now by clicking on the Booking tab or calling 204-555-4587.

---

**To:** Marcia_Weissblum@friendlymail.com
**From:** cabins@pinelakecabins.co.ca
**Date:** 12 June
**Subject:** Reservation Successful

Dear Ms. Weissblum,

We appreciate your reservation of a cabin through Pine Lake Cabins' Web site. Information regarding your stay is listed below.

Pine Lake Cabins
Pine Lake, BC V0L1C0
Canada

| Cabin | Pink Chalet |
|---|---|
| Rate/Night | $215.00 |
| Additional Charges | 3 inflatable kayaks ($30/day each) |
| Check-in | Thursday, 20 July |
| Check-out | Saturday, 22 July |
| Confirmation Code | #759J34 |

A valid form of identification must be presented upon check-in, along with a 20 percent security deposit. The remainder of your total will be due upon check-out. For recommendations on local activities or tickets to events, please contact the manager on duty.

We hope you enjoy your stay at Pine Lake Cabins.

Sincerely,

Anna Hooper
Pine Lake Cabins

**Attention Guests**

During your stay, please note the following:

• Jemore Bistro, our on-site facility, is undergoing maintenance and will be closed July 20 through July 24. Please ask one of our receptionists for other great options in town.

• Due to damage from recent storms, our dock is being rebuilt during the week of July 23. Our neighbors, Pine Lake Condos, will provide a place to keep your boat. The usual $25 daily fee applies.

We apologize in advance for any inconvenience that this may cause.

Pine Lake Cabins Rental Management

**191.** According to the Web page, what is true about Pine Lake Cabins?

(A) Residents are offered reduced rates.
(B) It is frequently booked by travel agencies.
(C) Customers can make special arrangements.
(D) It is currently hiring additional employees.

**192.** According to the e-mail, what must Ms. Weissblum do on July 20?

(A) Respond to an email
(B) Make a deposit
(C) Bring a coupon
(D) Return some equipment

**193.** What is implied about Pine Lake Cabins?

(A) It has no vacancy in July.
(B) It is mainly used by families.
(C) It processed Ms. Weissblum's reservation over the phone.
(D) It has entered Ms. Weissblum in a contest.

**194.** According to the notice, what information can guests obtain from a receptionist?

(A) What eateries are nearby
(B) How to contact cleaning staff
(C) When community events will be held
(D) Where tourist attractions are located

**195.** What is indicated about Ms. Weissblum?

(A) She will not be able to reserve additional kayaks.
(B) She would prefer to check in earlier in the day.
(C) She would prefer to upgrade her cabin.
(D) She cannot dine at a restaurant on the cabin premises.

*GO ON TO THE NEXT PAGE*

**Questions 196-200** refer to the following letter and e-mails.

October 6

Desiree Sinor
Valiant Manufacturing Ltd.
Marketing Division
Wickham Building

Ms. Sinor,

On November 11, you are invited to attend the safety training session. Company policies and procedures for workplace health and safety will be covered, and a contact list of local emergency services will also be distributed.

Be aware that all full-time staff members are required to attend the event. It will be held in the Northrup Building's event hall from 9 A.M. to 12 P.M. Afterward, a catered meal will be provided across the street in the Camlan Building's dining hall.

To prepare for the training, please read the company manual that was given to you, as it covers some of the content that will be discussed during the session. In the event that you are unable to participate, you will need to alert your team leader and your department's designated personnel associate, David Symonds, right away. Mr. Symonds can be contacted at dsymonds@valiantltd.co.uk or by dialing #432 on your office phone.

We hope to see you at the session.

Sincerely,

Brian Arthur
Head of Personnel
Valiant Manufacturing Ltd.

| | |
|---|---|
| **From:** | Desiree Sinor |
| **To:** | David Symonds |
| **Date:** | November 12 |
| **Subject:** | Safety training |

Mr. Symonds,

I was scheduled to participate in the safety training session on November 11. Unfortunately, I had a severe cold in the early morning and went to the hospital that day. I have a confirmation note written by my doctor and can provide it if required. Please advise if there are any additional actions I should take to resolve the situation.

Regards,

Desiree Sinor

| From | David Symonds |
|------|---------------|
| To | Desiree Sinor |
| Date | November 12 |
| Subject | RE: Safety training |

Hello Ms. Sinor,

I'm sorry to hear you didn't feel well. Please bring me a copy of the doctor's note, and I will add it to your records. I work in the Personnel Department, in suite 407 of the Shalott Building. You are also welcome to send it to me via company e-mail. This is all that we require, as your supervisor has told us that he is aware of the situation.

An additional training event has been scheduled for December 2. It will take place from 3 P.M. to 6 P.M. due to other meetings being held earlier in the day. No meal will be provided, but coffee and light snacks will be available. Refer to the original invitation you received if you need more details.

Sincerely,

David Symonds
Personnel Associate
Valiant Manufacturing Ltd.

**196.** According to the letter, what is true about the training session?

(A) It is held every two weeks.
(B) It is only open to Personnel employees.
(C) Full-time staff will not be asked to participate.
(D) Staff should review some materials beforehand.

**197.** Where is Mr. Arthur's office located?

(A) In the Wickham Building
(B) In the Northrup Building
(C) In the Camlan Building
(D) In the Shalott Building

**198.** Why did Ms. Sinor send the e-mail to Mr. Symonds?

(A) To request a detailed timetable of a workshop
(B) To get directions to the Personnel Department's office
(C) To suggest a revision to some safety guidelines
(D) To find out how to make up for a missed event

**199.** What will Ms. Sinor probably do next?

(A) Provide a document to the Personnel Department
(B) Ask for a new invitation letter
(C) Complete and upload a file to the company Web site
(D) Speak to a supervisor about her problem

**200.** What is indicated about the session on December 2?

(A) Attendees will receive a meal voucher.
(B) It will be led by Mr. Symonds.
(C) Some emergency contact information will be given.
(D) It will take place during the morning.

GO ON TO THE NEXT PAGE

TES

# READING TEST

In the Reading test, you will read a variety of texts and answer several different types of reading comprehension questions. The entire Reading test will last 75 minutes. There are three parts, and directions are given for each part. You are encouraged to answer as many questions as possible within the time allowed.

You must mark your answers on the separate answer sheet. Do not write your answers in the test book.

# PART 5

**Directions:** A word or phrase is missing in each of the sentences below. Four answer choices are given below each sentence. Select the best answer to complete the sentence. Then mark the letter (A), (B), (C), or (D) on your answer sheet.

**101.** They have not ------- reserved a room for the monthly meeting.

(A) soon
(B) much
(C) yet
(D) less

**102.** In order to file an auto insurance claim, the policy holder must provide ------- from at least two repair shops.

(A) reservations
(B) associations
(C) comprises
(D) estimates

**103.** Since ------- combined with NW Catch, our market share of the North American salmon industry has expanded.

(A) it
(B) we
(C) its
(D) us

**104.** The MacGregor Oil Field, which produced ------- 400,000 barrels of oil per day last month, has been purchased by a Norwegian company.

(A) toward
(B) across
(C) nearby
(D) over

**105.** For the last six months, the Rader Company ------- on an ad campaign for its newly designed model, the R40 motorbike.

(A) has focused
(B) are focused
(C) focusing
(D) focuses

**106.** In spite of a production ------- in the third quarter, unit numbers are still under the monthly target projected in the schedule.

(A) increased
(B) increase
(C) to increasing
(D) increasing

**107.** Blackbriar NGO's representatives are ------- to the board of directors.

(A) accounting
(B) account
(C) accountable
(D) accountability

**108.** Since the parking garage is currently being repaired, guests may reach Prentiss Business Center more ------- by riding the bus.

(A) apparently
(B) accurately
(C) extensively
(D) conveniently

**109.** Ms. Zhang in the HR Department will call ------- applicants to schedule appointments.

(A) selected
(B) selects
(C) selecting
(D) selection

**110.** The recent merger means that ------- of SW Corporation's and DC, Inc.'s departments will combine to cut costs.

(A) several
(B) which
(C) range
(D) another

**111.** The 1.5 million square meter Greun Botanical Garden was ------- the largest park in Barterton.

(A) neither
(B) once
(C) apart
(D) that

**112.** The responsibility for running GMS Ltd.'s Web site has been ------- to Mr. Reece.

(A) updated
(B) provided
(C) delegated
(D) responded

**113.** Ten books, five of ------- were over 100 years old, were recently found on the property.

(A) what
(B) which
(C) them
(D) these

**114.** Less than one year after it ------- bankruptcy, Colby Kitchen Supplies' stock is trading well.

(A) faced
(B) face
(C) facing
(D) faces

**115.** *Practical Investment Strategies* contains helpful ------- for inexperienced stock traders.

(A) advisable
(B) advisor
(C) advises
(D) advice

**116.** Despite performing ------- analysis, the engineers were unable to determine the cause of the problem with the new solar panel.

(A) exhaust
(B) exhausted
(C) exhaustedly
(D) exhaustive

**117.** The study's organizers will consult with universities ------- across the nation.

(A) at
(B) from
(C) in
(D) then

**118.** Textbooks are ------- shipped to the campus by an assistant in our main warehouse.

(A) greatly
(B) timely
(C) harshly
(D) typically

**119.** As of this morning, all finalists ------- of their results both by e-mail and by text message.

(A) notified
(B) have been notified
(C) will notify
(D) are notifying

**120.** ------- the head receptionist is on leave, her assistant will be temporarily promoted to fill her position.

(A) Rather
(B) Instead
(C) While
(D) Yet

*GO ON TO THE NEXT PAGE*

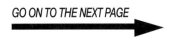

TEST 3

**121.** Review Fashion accepts ------- clothes, which are repurposed and donated to local charities.

(A) willing
(B) careless
(C) announced
(D) unwanted

**122.** Welmarch National Park guests who opt to go on the self-guided walking tour can explore the trails at their own -------.

(A) stability
(B) style
(C) action
(D) pace

**123.** The publishing company is seeking to hire an editorial assistant capable of ------- various tasks at once.

(A) manage
(B) manager
(C) manages
(D) managing

**124.** The Ballins Supermarket manager instructed that all display stands be arranged by Friday night in ------- for the weekend sale.

(A) return
(B) preparation
(C) result
(D) compensation

**125.** To allow enough time to edit, we ------- that articles be emailed at least a week before the publication date.

(A) transmit
(B) recognize
(C) recommend
(D) assure

**126.** ------- the Morriston City Council, house purchases in the city increased by 20 percent over the previous year.

(A) Regarding
(B) Rather than
(C) While
(D) According to

**127.** The records archive was reorganized ------- to enable clerks to locate customer data without difficulty.

(A) commonly
(B) considerably
(C) carelessly
(D) consecutively

**128.** Because of the ------- of car rental agencies in Huntsville, taxi drivers have been making huge profits during the expo.

(A) shortest
(B) shortage
(C) short
(D) shortening

**129.** Newly released guides often contain glossaries of ------- terms for those unfamiliar with the topic.

(A) relevant
(B) damaged
(C) eventual
(D) constant

**130.** Ms. Tran will ------- train tickets for all employees taking part in the seminar.

(A) book
(B) accept
(C) authorize
(D) vend

# PART 6

**Directions:** Read the texts that follow. A word, phrase, or sentence is missing in parts of each text. Four answer choices for each question are given below the text. Select the best answer to complete the text. Then mark the letter (A), (B), (C), or (D) on your answer sheet.

**Questions 131-134** refer to the following article.

---

**Housing Sales Increasing**

The Housing Authority anticipates that by the end of this year new home purchases will exceed 2,000 transactions. This number is 20 percent higher than the ------- year's
                                                           **131.**
figure and exceeds the all-time record set two years ago. The Housing Authority believes that this increase has occurred for various reasons, ------- the availability of
                                                          **132.**
special loans to first-time buyers. Contrary to the demand for residential properties, the commercial real estate market has shown almost no ------- during the past decade
                                                      **133.**
despite the city's effort to attract new businesses to the area. -------.
                                                     **134.**

---

**131.** (A) previous
    (B) present
    (C) following
    (D) overall

**132.** (A) particular
    (B) particularly
    (C) particulars
    (D) particularity

**133.** (A) competition
    (B) advantage
    (C) cost
    (D) improvement

**134.** (A) Some office complexes will actually be demolished in the coming year.
    (B) Another reason is the reputation of the local school district.
    (C) This effort has been successful thanks to support from the community.
    (D) Companies are drawn to the city by low taxes and excellent infrastructure.

*GO ON TO THE NEXT PAGE*

**Questions 135-138** refer to the following information.

Your Denizli beverage dispenser will be an important addition to your business. -------, **135.** making sure that the dispenser is working properly will be an essential part of your daily operations. Here are several important things to remember to keep your machine in good condition. First, use Denizli-certified -------, especially Denizli water filters. **136.** Second, be cautious when changing tanks and hoses. Reviewing the user guide will help you to avoid leaks and spills. Third, stick to the recommended cleaning schedule. -------. Last of all, if your dispenser requires maintenance, we recommend that you **137.** choose a ------- repair specialist. If you keep these four things in mind, your beverage **138.** dispenser should last you a long time.

**135.** (A) Therefore
(B) Despite this
(C) Basically
(D) In that case

**136.** (A) connection
(B) power
(C) workers
(D) parts

**137.** (A) The beverage dispenser can be operated continuously.
(B) Make sure to use only sterilized equipment and cleaning solutions approved by Denizli.
(C) If urgent repairs are required, call the number on the back of the machine.
(D) Certain drinks are served in much larger volumes than others.

**138.** (A) qualify
(B) qualified
(C) qualifying
(D) qualification

**Questions 139-142** refer to the following memo.

From: S. Pers, Zoo Superintendent
To: All Staff
Date: 15 August
Subject: Animal Show Policy

This memo is to let all employees know about an update to the ------- policy for our
                                                                **139.**
animal shows, which goes into effect today. We have received a number of same-day

requests from ticket holders who ask to sit next to the aisle due to the extra space.

Effective immediately, we will allow such changes ------- on the day the reservations are
                                                  **140.**
made. Going forward, attendees ------- more leg room are encouraged to sit in the back
                               **141.**
rows, as they often have spots available. -------. This change should reduce distractions
                                          **142.**
while the shows are being held.

139. (A) seating
     (B) parking
     (C) camera
     (D) payment

140. (A) more
     (B) only
     (C) late
     (D) well

141. (A) they require
     (B) required
     (C) having required
     (D) who require

142. (A) The view is not that great, but it is
         much more comfortable there.
     (B) The dolphin show is currently one of
         the most popular attractions.
     (C) Weekends are an especially busy
         time for us.
     (D) Visitors are reminded not to touch or
         feed the animals at any time.

GO ON TO THE NEXT PAGE

**Questions 143-146** refer to the following press release.

Coscia Manufacturing, a plastic production company in Lenexa, KS, has received funding from the Kansas Conservation Organization (KCO). The funding was granted based on development plans reviewed by the KCO. These plans call for redesigning Coscia's main plant as an environmentally-friendly facility.

-------. In addition, funding will be used for plant upgrades ------- air filtration and waste
 **143.**                                                                **144.**
recycling systems. Following these -------, any leftover funds will be invested in
                                    **145.**
research to develop more bio-degradable products.

Don Stecher, Vice President of Manufacturing, ------- this project in partnership with
                                               **146.**
Kathleen Valentine of the KCO.

---

**143.** (A) Environmental concerns have received much attention in the plastics industry.
(B) Mr. Stecher is reported to have conducted a similar project at his former company.
(C) One major inclusion will be solar panels to generate power for machines.
(D) Finding alternative material sources is a common goal for manufacturers.

**144.** (A) such as
(B) whereas
(C) despite
(D) so that

**145.** (A) appointments
(B) corrections
(C) advances
(D) improvements

**146.** (A) to supervise
(B) supervising
(C) will supervise
(D) were supervising

# PART 7

**Directions:** In this part you will read a selection of texts, such as magazine and newspaper articles, e-mails, and instant messages. Each text or set of texts is followed by several questions. Select the best answer for each question and mark the letter (A), (B), (C) or (D) on your answer sheet.

**Questions 147-148** refer to the following notice.

## Details for Classified Advertising

The deadline for placing a classified ad in the *Gilliam Weekly* is Thursday morning at 11:30, for publication on Friday. No changes will be accepted after you submit your text. Only Gilliam reserves the right to edit the text.

Ads are paid for in advance. Advertisements that have already been paid for to run for a month can be canceled after one week for advertising credit in the future. Send the text for your ad to adv@gilliamweekly.com. Discounts are offered for multiple ads.

Call 413-9598 for pricing.

**147.** What will happen if an advertiser submits an ad on a Friday morning?

(A) The ad will be more expensive for the advertiser.
(B) The ad will be rejected by the newspaper.
(C) The ad will be posted on the following Friday.
(D) The ad will be published on that afternoon.

**148.** According to the notice, when do advertisers receive credit?

(A) When the newspaper edits the text
(B) When they place a half-page ad
(C) When the newspaper misprints the text
(D) When they cancel an ad

*GO ON TO THE NEXT PAGE*

**Questions 149-150** refer to the following online chat discussion.

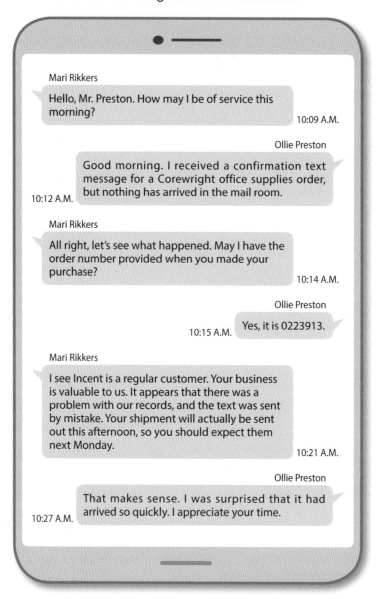

Mari Rikkers

Hello, Mr. Preston. How may I be of service this morning?

10:09 A.M.

Ollie Preston

Good morning. I received a confirmation text message for a Corewright office supplies order, but nothing has arrived in the mail room.

10:12 A.M.

Mari Rikkers

All right, let's see what happened. May I have the order number provided when you made your purchase?

10:14 A.M.

Ollie Preston

10:15 A.M. Yes, it is 0223913.

Mari Rikkers

I see Incent is a regular customer. Your business is valuable to us. It appears that there was a problem with our records, and the text was sent by mistake. Your shipment will actually be sent out this afternoon, so you should expect them next Monday.

10:21 A.M.

Ollie Preston

That makes sense. I was surprised that it had arrived so quickly. I appreciate your time.

10:27 A.M.

**149.** What is suggested about Incent?

(A) It is interviewing Mr. Preston next week.

(B) It is a major shipping firm.

(C) It has just updated some customer records.

(D) It has bought from Corewright before.

**150.** At 10:27 A.M., what does Mr. Preston most likely mean when he writes, "That makes sense"?

(A) He understands why a delivery did not arrive.

(B) He forgot to respond to a text message.

(C) He discovered that a payment was not processed.

(D) He did not go to the right mail room.

## North American Loggers Conference (NALC)

For more than a decade, the NALC has attracted the biggest industry names and thousands of attendees. This year promises to be another big event. It begins with a keynote speech by Alan Luciano, CEO of Westfalls Logging, and continues throughout the week with workshops, seminars, and lectures given by business leaders in the industry. This year's main topic is on the sustainable future of responsible forestry and how paperless offices will affect future growth.

Participating in the NALC guarantees you insider knowledge in today's competitive market. Sign up before April 15 to receive a promotional discount at www.nalc.org.

**151.** What is indicated about the NALC?

(A) It features talks by business leaders.
(B) It is sponsored by international companies.
(C) It includes product demonstrations.
(D) It is hosted by Westfalls Logging.

**152.** What event detail is NOT included in the advertisement?

(A) The main topic
(B) A promotion deadline
(C) The location
(D) A guest speaker's job title

**Questions 153-154** refer to the following Web page.

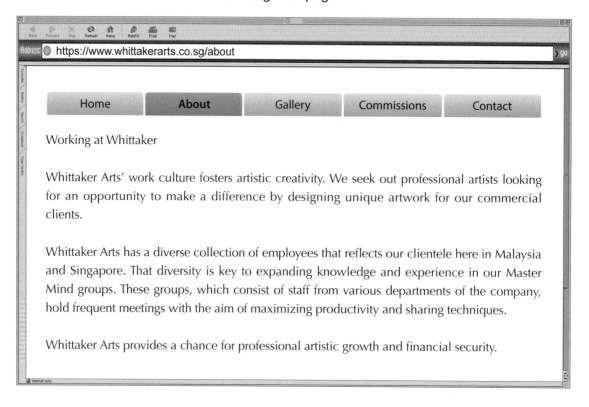

https://www.whittakerarts.co.sg/about

| Home | About | Gallery | Commissions | Contact |

Working at Whittaker

Whittaker Arts' work culture fosters artistic creativity. We seek out professional artists looking for an opportunity to make a difference by designing unique artwork for our commercial clients.

Whittaker Arts has a diverse collection of employees that reflects our clientele here in Malaysia and Singapore. That diversity is key to expanding knowledge and experience in our Master Mind groups. These groups, which consist of staff from various departments of the company, hold frequent meetings with the aim of maximizing productivity and sharing techniques.

Whittaker Arts provides a chance for professional artistic growth and financial security.

**153.** What is mentioned about Whittaker Arts' staff?

(A) They are hired by a job placement firm.
(B) They like collaborating with other artists.
(C) They worked for multiple companies.
(D) They are from various backgrounds.

**154.** What is a purpose of Whittaker Arts' Master Mind groups?

(A) Discussing potential solutions
(B) Recruiting new workers
(C) Contacting potential clients
(D) Providing financial advice

**Questions 155-157** refer to the following e-mail.

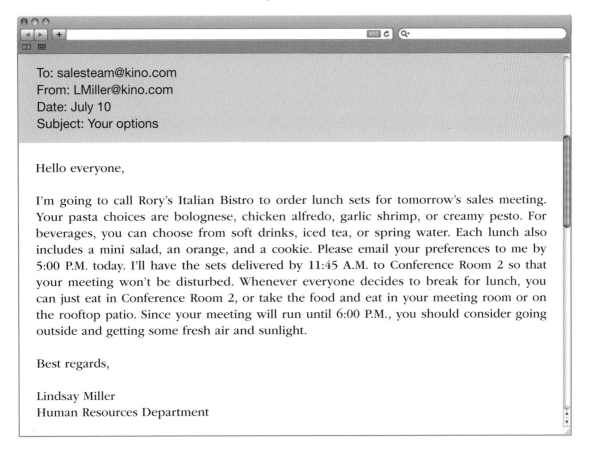

To: salesteam@kino.com
From: LMiller@kino.com
Date: July 10
Subject: Your options

Hello everyone,

I'm going to call Rory's Italian Bistro to order lunch sets for tomorrow's sales meeting. Your pasta choices are bolognese, chicken alfredo, garlic shrimp, or creamy pesto. For beverages, you can choose from soft drinks, iced tea, or spring water. Each lunch also includes a mini salad, an orange, and a cookie. Please email your preferences to me by 5:00 P.M. today. I'll have the sets delivered by 11:45 A.M. to Conference Room 2 so that your meeting won't be disturbed. Whenever everyone decides to break for lunch, you can just eat in Conference Room 2, or take the food and eat in your meeting room or on the rooftop patio. Since your meeting will run until 6:00 P.M., you should consider going outside and getting some fresh air and sunlight.

Best regards,

Lindsay Miller
Human Resources Department

**155.** What is the purpose of the e-mail?

(A) To inform staff members of a meeting location
(B) To organize the details of a meal
(C) To announce the opening of a new restaurant
(D) To request reimbursement for food expenses

**156.** What is indicated about the lunch sets?

(A) They include a piece of fruit.
(B) They are offered at a discounted price.
(C) They will be delivered on July 10.
(D) They will be served outdoors.

**157.** What is suggested about the meeting?

(A) It is held once a year.
(B) It will not stop for lunch at a set time.
(C) It will discuss food and drink sales.
(D) It will take place in Conference Room 2.

*GO ON TO THE NEXT PAGE*

**Questions 158-160** refer to the following e-mail.

**From:** Erin Sui
**To:** All Staff
**Date:** March 29
**Subject:** Information

Hello,

Beginning Wednesday, Sencomp Electronics will begin requiring the use of a new ID verification system. Customers paying in cash or by credit card will not notice a change upon checkout, but the procedure for customers paying with checks will be different.

Customers will still be able to use checks for their purchases. However, the cashier will also be required to scan the customer's ID with the new scanner located next to each cash register, which will compare the ID to the information printed on the check and issue an "approved purchase" stamp on every receipt.

These new precautions will be instituted in every store nationwide. Customers using voucher slips issued by domestic banks are exempt from this requirement. Please refer to chapter 10 in the employee handbook if you have any questions.

Sincerely,

Erin Sui
CFO
Sencomp Electronics

**158.** Why was the e-mail written?

(A) To explain the results of a survey
(B) To follow up on a recent order
(C) To suggest a plan to increase sales
(D) To describe a new process

**159.** What does Ms. Sui indicate about Sencomp Electronics?

(A) It will require identification for some purchases.
(B) It is selling a new line of scanners.
(C) It plans to update its employee handbook.
(D) It will close early on Wednesdays.

**160.** Who will receive an approval stamp when paying?

(A) Customers paying with cash
(B) Customers paying with a credit card
(C) Customers paying with a check
(D) Customers paying with a voucher slip

Chao and Tzao Advertising plans on expanding their staff. Company representative George Chao confirmed that at least 150 more workers will be hired to keep up with the changing industry.

"Broadcast advertising has been steadily declining, while digital advertising has been growing at a rapid pace," commented Chao. —[1]—. "Therefore, there has been a growing need for qualified professionals who possess not only creative and editorial skills, but also technical knowledge." —[2]—.

In order to expand its pool of applicants, Chao and Tzao Advertising will be participating in local career fairs. The next fairs in Hong Kong are scheduled on November 28 at the Waterfront Convention Center and on December 9 at City University of Hong Kong. —[3]—. Those seeking employment but unable to attend these job fairs can email Yunna Kim at YKim@chaotzaoad.com for more information. —[4]—.

**161.** What does Mr. Chao indicate about digital advertising?

(A) It is cheaper than traditional advertising methods.
(B) It requires companies to seek employees with multiple skills.
(C) It is a popular subject for university study.
(D) It will replace conventional forms of advertising.

**162.** According to the article, what is Chao and Tzao Advertising planning to do?

(A) Raise the salaries of its workers
(B) Open a new location
(C) Take part in events held in Hong Kong
(D) Modify its training procedure

**163.** Who most likely is Ms. Kim?

(A) A Human Resources specialist
(B) A company sales representative
(C) A university professor
(D) A building manager

**164.** In which of the positions marked [1], [2], [3], and [4] does the following sentence best belong?

"In particular, the agency is looking for graphic designers, copy editors, technical advisors, and salespeople."

(A) [1]
(B) [2]
(C) [3]
(D) [4]

*GO ON TO THE NEXT PAGE*

**Questions 165-167** refer to the following Web page.

**Sierra Theater**

**A Theater for Performing Arts Showcasing Local and National Productions**
**We are pleased to present the play, *The Frontier's Cry***

Performances of this musical production will begin on September 15 as part of the theater's *American Greats* series. Theater members may reserve tickets in advance of the show. It features classic and modern songs about life on the frontier.

Allison Lindy, the director of the show, brings more than two decades of experience to the production, which is to run for seven weeks. Before joining the theater's management staff in January of this year, Ms. Lindy was the director of productions at SRO Theater in Boston for seven years; she also spent four years teaching Performing Arts at the Franklin School of the Arts, located in Chicago.

*The Frontier's Cry* uses state-of-the-art lighting, special effects, and pyrotechnics, as well as historical clothing, hairstyles, and props from America's pioneer days. The performers will hold acting seminars on several dates in October. The price for the workshop is $20 in addition to the normal ticket price and includes free costume rental.

**165.** What is indicated about *The Frontier's Cry*?

(A) It plays both old and new music.
(B) It will be shown through the end of September.
(C) It is based on recent events.
(D) It is the first performance in the *American Greats* series.

**166.** Who is Ms. Lindy?

(A) A theater employee
(B) A famous performer
(C) An arts critic
(D) A history professor

**167.** According to the Web page, what can theater visitors do for an extra fee?

(A) Receive a souvenir
(B) Join an acting workshop
(C) Tour a facility
(D) Watch an exclusive show

**Questions 168-171** refer to the following online chat discussion.

---

**Woojung Bae [1:09 P.M.]**
I hope you all had a good lunch. I wanted to see where we are on the marketing presentation for our client meeting on Thursday.

**Connie Julius [1:10 P.M.]**
It's almost completed, but we still need to add the company introduction video.

**Woojung Bae [1:11 P.M.]**
I believe Jay is in charge of making the video.

**Jay Perkins [1:12 P.M.]**
Well, I finished filming all of the content. However, I'm having some issues with the video editing software. I can't seem to save my work.

**Woojung Bae [1:14 P.M.]**
That's not good. Have you tried talking to someone from the IT team?

**Jay Perkins [1:15 P.M.]**
Yes, I talked to Tim Stowe yesterday, but he wasn't familiar with the program.

**Connie Julius [1:17 P.M.]**
Have you tried talking to the software's manufacturer? They may be able to provide you with a solution.

**Jay Perkins [1:18 P.M.]**
Why didn't I think of that? OK, I'll do that right now.

**Woojung Bae [1:20 P.M.]**
Jay, please let me know once you get that resolved. By the way, Connie, did you make sure we have the conference room for this Thursday?

**Jay Perkins [1:21 P.M.]**
Of course.

**Connie Julius [1:22 P.M.]**
I'll contact the HR Manager and check with him.

---

SEND

---

**168.** What is indicated about the presentation?

(A) Its deadline has been extended.
(B) It is missing some materials.
(C) Its content needs to be revised.
(D) It will include a product demonstration.

**169.** What department does Mr. Stowe most likely work in?

(A) Marketing
(B) Information Technology
(C) Editorial
(D) Human Resources

**170.** At 1:18 P.M., what does Mr. Perkins mean when he writes, "Why didn't I think of that"?

(A) He did not know about a technical issue.
(B) He wished he provided a better solution.
(C) He should have contacted a business.
(D) He will consider meeting Mr. Stowe.

**171.** What is Ms. Julius asked to do next?

(A) Confirm a reservation
(B) Interview a candidate
(C) Submit an application
(D) Review a document

*GO ON TO THE NEXT PAGE*

# COGISTICS OPENS LARGE FACILITY

Porto Velho [10 October] — Cogistics Agricorp, the Brazilian coffee producer headquartered in our city, has begun construction of a new processing facility located in Mixco, Guatemala, which is due to open on 7 January. This plant, to be one of the largest in the country, will be managed exclusively by local employees.

The plant will help the company make greater inroads into North American markets. "Roasting our farmers' coffee in Mixco will help us produce fresher, better products. —[1]—. This should make us one of the top players in a competitive industry," explained Cogistics CEO Marcela Sousa. Ms. Sousa and the rest of the board will lead the inaugural ceremony of the Mixco facility.

Cogistics began offering its products to North American vendors three years ago. —[2]—. This was also where its newest blends of coffee were first introduced. —[3]—. However, regional sales figures have faltered, slumping from a high of $5.1 million in its first year to $3.4 million this year. The company believes that the facility's closer proximity to markets will improve product quality and lead to increased sales.

Cogistics' three other roasting facilities are located in the Brazilian cities of Jaru and Sorocaba and in Cochabamba, Bolivia. —[4]—. Ms. Sousa has also stated that negotiations for a plant located in the Mexican state of Chiapas are underway with government officials there. She believes that a deal will be reached soon.

**172.** What is mentioned about Cogistics Agricorp?

(A) It plans to increase its business in North America.
(B) It will merge with a competing North American company.
(C) It plans to relocate its headquarters.
(D) It began its operations three years ago.

**173.** What is suggested about Ms. Sousa?

(A) She will visit Guatemala in January.
(B) She travels to North America frequently.
(C) She will become Mixco's first plant manager.
(D) She is satisfied with the profits from the newest coffee blends.

**174.** Where will Cogistics Agricorp most likely build its next roasting facility?

(A) In Brazil
(B) In Guatemala
(C) In Mexico
(D) In Bolivia

**175.** In which of the positions marked [1], [2], [3], and [4] does the following sentence best belong?

"At 9,000 tons of coffee annually, its production goal for this facility is ambitious."

(A) [1]
(B) [2]
(C) [3]
(D) [4]

*GO ON TO THE NEXT PAGE*

**Questions 176-180** refer to the following notice and e-mail.

## The Pine Oak Hiking Club
## What's on the September Agenda?

- **September 9** – Red Deer Trail

  Guide: Nora Bryson
  Difficulty: Easy
  Total length: 5 kilometers
  Trail conditions: Few obstacles; you may encounter strong winds in open areas.

  Meet in front of the Pine Oak Center at 11:00 A.M. Bring water and snacks, and make sure to dress warmly.

  ----------------------------------------------------------------

- **September 16** – Sequoia Nature Trail

  Guide: Zachary Quinn
  Difficulty: Moderate
  Total length: 7.5 kilometers
  Trail conditions: Some uneven and rocky paths

  Bring water and snacks. We recommend walking sticks.

  ----------------------------------------------------------------

- **September 23** – No hikes scheduled

  ----------------------------------------------------------------

- **September 30** – Appalachian Blaze Trail

  Guide: Cooper Hayden
  Difficulty: Moderate to Difficult
  Total length: 11 kilometers
  Trail conditions: Trail grade is steep initially. The rest of the paths are moderate. Two streams must be crossed.

  Pack lunch and water. A camera is recommended to capture some of the breathtaking views. Wear waterproof shoes.

  ----------------------------------------------------------------

Unless otherwise stated, all hikes will start in front of the Pine Oak Center at 9 A.M. To register or for more information, contact Sydney Brennan at sbrennan@pineoakhike.com.

If you have any questions or want to volunteer to lead a hike, let Sydney know.

| From | Sydney Brennan <sbrennan@pineoakhike.com> |
|------|---------------------------------------------|
| To | Julian Griffin <jgriffin@lac.net> |
| Date | Wednesday, September 14 |
| Subject | Sunday's Hike |

Hello Julian,

You signed up for the hike that Zachary Quinn was scheduled to lead. Unfortunately, Zachary has been suddenly called away on a business trip, so he will not be able to lead that hike. Therefore, we will reschedule the hike for mid-October and also replace the trail with the Plateau View Trail, which is always popular. Its length and difficulty level are similar to that of the Sequoia Nature Trail. I will be personally leading this one. We will meet in the main parking lot of the Fair Creek Hotel and walk to the trailhead together. If you would like to join this hike, please email me by 8 A.M. tomorrow.

Regards,

Sydney

**176.** What is the purpose of the notice?

(A) To announce changes to club policies
(B) To compare similar types of trails
(C) To request assistance with upcoming club activities
(D) To inform people about hiking opportunities

**177.** Who most likely is Mr. Quinn?

(A) A club volunteer
(B) A hotel receptionist
(C) A club president
(D) A professional photographer

**178.** What trail is probably most challenging?

(A) Red Deer Trail
(B) Sequoia Nature Trail
(C) Appalachian Blaze Trail
(D) Plateau View Trail

**179.** What is true about the hike on September 16?

(A) It requires waterproof shoes.
(B) It has been postponed.
(C) It was originally supposed to be led by Ms. Brennan.
(D) It is perfect for beginners.

**180.** What is indicated about the Plateau View Trail?

(A) The trail crosses several streams.
(B) The trail is exposed to strong winds.
(C) It has not been hiked by the group.
(D) It is about 7.5 kilometers long.

GO ON TO THE NEXT PAGE

**Questions 181-185** refer to the following e-mail and receipt.

From: lfernandes@musemarketers.com
To: customersupport@officepoint.com
Date: January 11
Subject: Shipment
Attachment: Invoice

To Whom It May Concern:

I bought a variety of products from OfficePoint, which arrived yesterday. While the online catalog said the order would take 7 to 10 days to ship, it arrived in just four. However, I was surprised by the low quality of the items. The binders don't close properly; the misalignment of the three inside rings causes the plastic sleeves to fall out. The electric staplers are difficult to turn on. I used the glossy paper to print some brochures, but the coating wasn't as bright as I expected. And although I did not open the box of the matte printer paper, I'll just go for another brand.

I plan to return items 1, 2, 4, and 5 as listed on the attached invoice. I would appreciate it if you could send a package label at your earliest convenience. Our company had no issues with our last purchase through your catalog and left a positive comment on the Web site. Unfortunately, based on our experience this time, we are quite dissatisfied.

Sincerely,

Lionel Fernandes

---

**OfficePoint**
www.officepoint.com
**The Professional's Choice in Office Supplies**

| Item | Amount | Price |
|---|---|---|
| 1. Glossy printer paper (box of 5 reams) | 2 @ $40.25 | $80.50 |
| 2. Matte printer paper (box of 5 reams) | 3 @ $29.50 | $88.50 |
| 3. Paperclips (box of 100) | 50 @ $2.99 | $149.50 |
| 4. Binder with clear sleeves (3 pack) | 25 @ $1.99 | $49.75 |
| 5. Stapler (electric) | 5 @ $14.99 | $74.95 |

Subtotal: $443.20

Promo Code: OFFICE10 − $15.00

Tax (7.5%): $32.12

Shipping and Handling:
(standard 7-10 business days) $20.00

Total: $480.32

**Returns:** Most unopened or unused products can be returned within three months of delivery with credit to your account for the amount of the purchase. Products that have been opened or used are not covered by this policy and may not be returned under any circumstances. A product of equal value may be ordered in situations where a product is deemed defective.

**181.** What is indicated about Mr. Fernandes' order?

(A) It was delivered earlier than anticipated.
(B) It contained ten electric staplers.
(C) It included damaged merchandise.
(D) It had an extra item.

**182.** What does Mr. Fernandes mention in the e-mail?

(A) His company has done a marketing campaign for OfficePoint.
(B) He has called OfficePoint's Customer Support.
(C) He received a package label from OfficePoint.
(D) His company has ordered from OfficePoint before.

**183.** In the e-mail, the phrase "go for" in paragraph 1, line 6, is closest in meaning to

(A) move
(B) rush
(C) reach
(D) choose

**184.** Which item will Mr. Fernandes most likely have to keep?

(A) The glossy printer paper
(B) The matte printer paper
(C) The binders
(D) The staplers

**185.** What does OfficePoint offer to its customers?

(A) Credit for items that have been returned
(B) Discounts for large orders
(C) IT support for office equipment
(D) Complimentary shipping for defective items

GO ON TO THE NEXT PAGE

| From | Sean Kim |
|------|----------|
| To | Danica Tomasi |
| Date | Friday, 7 June, 10:48 A.M. |
| Subject | Advertisement |

Dear Ms. Tomasi,

Good morning from headquarters!

Our Marketing Manager in Beijing, Gwan-yun Yu, has said that the Mandarin translation of our Engage to Exercise Program advertisement can be done by Tuesday, as scheduled, in order for it to be sent out to Mandarin-speaking regions where we conduct business.

However, Mr. Yu recommended that the descriptions accompanying the images be reduced in length. He said most Chinese news agencies request that ads do not contain more than 200 words. He added that the ad will have a higher chance of being published if it's shorter. (I will send you his text message in a moment.) As such, it may be a good idea to make some changes. Please respond when you and your team have decided what to do.

Regards,

Sean Kim
Community Outreach Supervisor
Spectranova, Inc.

---

**From:** Danica Tomasi
**To:** Sean Kim
**Date:** Friday, 7 June, 3:25 P.M.
**Subject:** RE: Advertisement
**Attachment:** New_program.doc

Good afternoon Sean,

It is good to hear from you. I have applied Mr. Yu's suggestion. Please send it to him for translation and distribution after looking it over to ensure that it is error-free. In addition to our media contacts, please remind him that a number of advertisements should be printed and provided to program participants.

Sincerely,

Danica Tomasi
Media Relations Manager
Spectranova, Inc.

## Spectranova Reaches Out with New Program

Spectranova, Inc. moves forward with its Engage to Exercise Program. The company is committed to putting $40 million towards athletic clothing and equipment for schools in countries where it conducts business in order to get more children involved in sports, playing a role in promoting healthy activities among the youth. By partnering with school districts and educational outreach organizations, a variety of fitness techniques will be taught to professional educators and academic administrators. Educational institutions will use their facilities to host events, and teachers will coach individual teams to create a greater sense of pride and accomplishment in students' lives. More information about the program can be found online at www.spectranova.co.au/eep.

Spectranova, Inc. is an athletic sporting goods company based in Sydney, with branches in Singapore, Beijing, Taipei, and Los Angeles.

**186.** What is most likely true about Mr. Yu?

(A) He knows much about news formats in China.
(B) He used to live in Los Angeles.
(C) He is in charge of the Engage to Exercise Program.
(D) He is meeting with Mr. Kim next week.

**187.** What did Ms. Tomasi do recently?

(A) She went on a business trip to Sydney.
(B) She visited several schools.
(C) She updated some content.
(D) She translated an advertisement.

**188.** What is one reason for the program?

(A) To invest in factories producing athletic products
(B) To train teachers on fitness activities
(C) To open new educational institutions
(D) To help students learn about national sports teams

**189.** What is mentioned in the press release?

(A) The type of sports events held at Spectranova
(B) The annual profit that Spectranova generates
(C) The application requirements for Spectranova's program
(D) The market in which Spectranova specializes

**190.** Where does Mr. Kim most likely work?

(A) In Sydney
(B) In Singapore
(C) In Taipei
(D) In Los Angeles

*GO ON TO THE NEXT PAGE*

**Questions 191-195** refer to the following Web page, form, and forum post.

### Worldwide Butterfly Forum Rules

- Discussions should relate to butterfly identification only. While there is no limit to the length of a post, off-topic posts such as those related to collecting and breeding butterflies, or equipment sales will be removed.
- Topic lines should be written in the following format: "location, butterfly appearance." Please keep in mind that because posts are made by members from around the world, this information is critical. For example, an acceptable topic line would be: "Gagauzia, Orange, tan, black spots." "I require some assistance" on the other hand is unacceptable.
- Please include high-resolution images of the butterfly as well as information related to the date, time, and temperature of your sighting. The less information you provide, the harder it is to make an accurate identification.
- Because of this Web site's popularity, administrators take around three to five days to comment on a post. Therefore, we ask that members limit themselves to one post per day.

---

### Worldwide Butterfly Forum
## Sign up to Become a Member!

**Full name:** William Hermann

**E-mail address:** whermann@openmail.net

**\* Background in insect-related fields:** Master's Degree in Botany, research focus on flowering bushes

**\* Most recent employer:** Merricut College

\* not required but helps our members identify expert sources of information in posted comments.

**Would you like to subscribe to our monthly publication delivered to your inbox?**
Yes ☑   No ☐

**Member consent agreement:**
I agree that the Worldwide Butterfly Forum may use content posted by its users for promotional or advertising purposes. Members' private information will never be sold to other parties.
I agree ☑   I don't agree ☐

**New Topic Post**

Member: William Hermann
Topic line: Need help with ID
Time: 07/24 2:35 P.M.

I'm on a year-long research trip in Romania where I have encountered this copper and blue butterfly in the field near my worksite. I believe that it is a long-tailed blue butterfly, but want to double-check. A former research assistant of mine said that it is quite destructive to broom plants, which I am here to study. Before I attempt to remove them, I'd like a positive identification. Attached is a photo I took yesterday.

copper_blue_0723.jpg

**191.** What does the Web page indicate about the forum?

(A) It requires a membership fee to view.
(B) It removes a post after 24 hours.
(C) It allows users to promote their merchandise.
(D) It is used by international participants.

**192.** What does the Worldwide Butterfly Forum promise its members?

(A) It offers a weekly online newsletter.
(B) It checks work references of new members.
(C) It keeps private information secure.
(D) It will respond to a post within one day.

**193.** Why did Mr. Hermann post on the forum?

(A) To provide professional advice on a topic
(B) To confirm an assumption
(C) To reply to a post made by another member
(D) To ask for butterfly breeding assistance

**194.** How did Mr. Hermann break the forum rules?

(A) His topic line is not detailed.
(B) His post does not contain an image.
(C) He advertised an item for sale.
(D) He wrote a post that is too long.

**195.** What is most likely true about Mr. Hermann?

(A) He is a Web site administrator.
(B) He is applying for a research grant.
(C) He recently published an article in a scientific journal.
(D) He used to do research at a college.

*GO ON TO THE NEXT PAGE* ➡

**Questions 196-200** refer to the following Web page, online review, and e-mail.

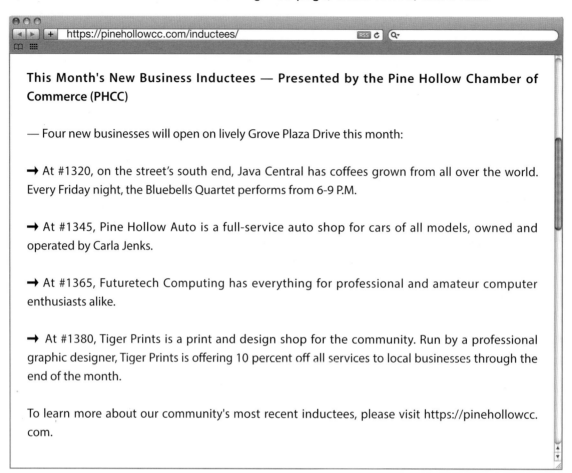

https://pinehollowcc.com/inductees/

**This Month's New Business Inductees — Presented by the Pine Hollow Chamber of Commerce (PHCC)**

— Four new businesses will open on lively Grove Plaza Drive this month:

→ At #1320, on the street's south end, Java Central has coffees grown from all over the world. Every Friday night, the Bluebells Quartet performs from 6-9 P.M.

→ At #1345, Pine Hollow Auto is a full-service auto shop for cars of all models, owned and operated by Carla Jenks.

→ At #1365, Futuretech Computing has everything for professional and amateur computer enthusiasts alike.

→ At #1380, Tiger Prints is a print and design shop for the community. Run by a professional graphic designer, Tiger Prints is offering 10 percent off all services to local businesses through the end of the month.

To learn more about our community's most recent inductees, please visit https://pinehollowcc.com.

---

Pine Hollow Online Gazette—Business Section

### Java Central Opens Doors to Sleepy Town

By Tammy Smith

Java Central's doors opened yesterday to wake the sleepy residents of Pine Hollow. Owner Gary Jeffers served more than half the town's population in just hours after opening. The highlight of the day was when Mr. Jeffers began handing out free cappuccinos to every customer in the store. For those not familiar with coffee drinks, like the Cinnamon Mocha Twirl, colorful pictures of each drink are framed on the walls. Next month, Mr. Jeffers will also be adding a small bakery, right next to Java Central, to complement his coffee shop.

Java Central would like to thank Ed Brown for making the beautiful pictures of their different beverages. His store is located at #1380 Grove Plaza Drive.

| To | Ed Brown <edbrown@sendanemail.com> |
|---|---|
| From | Carla Jenks <c.jenks@phauto.com> |
| Date | Wednesday, April 13 |
| Subject | Request |

Hi Ed,

This is Carla from over at Pine Hollow Auto. We met briefly at the Chamber of Commerce ceremony about two weeks ago. I read the *Pine Hollow Online Gazette*'s article about Java Central and saw the beautiful pictures. I was wondering if you could help me make 500 posters. Let me know how long it will take you to complete my order. If possible, I'd like them to arrive at my shop by next Friday. I need my order by this date because I am preparing for an upcoming trade show at Berkenshire. The event will last from April 25 to April 27. Oh, and I'd like to know if I'm able to take advantage of your promotion.

Thank you so much,
Carla

**196.** What is suggested about Grove Plaza Drive?

(A) Its rental costs have gone up.
(B) Its businesses will provide discounts to local residents.
(C) A new store will open near its southern end.
(D) The PHCC's main office is located there.

**197.** In the review, the word "highlight" in paragraph 1, line 2, is closest in meaning to

(A) spot
(B) feature
(C) peak
(D) point

**198.** What is most likely true about Ms. Jenks?

(A) She is a member of the Pine Hollow City Council.
(B) She will sell her office space to Mr. Jeffers next month.
(C) She plans to meet Mr. Brown at an opening ceremony.
(D) She wants Tiger Prints to design some promotional material.

**199.** Where would Ms. Jenks like her order to be delivered to next Friday?

(A) At 1320 Grove Plaza Drive
(B) At 1345 Grove Plaza Drive
(C) At 1365 Grove Plaza Drive
(D) At 1380 Grove Plaza Drive

**200.** According to the e-mail, what will happen on April 25?

(A) Mr. Brown will hold a special sale.
(B) Ms. Jenks will relocate her shop.
(C) A convention will begin at Berkenshire.
(D) A new bakery will open on Grove Plaza Drive.

*GO ON TO THE NEXT PAGE*

# READING TEST

In the Reading test, you will read a variety of texts and answer several different types of reading comprehension questions. The entire Reading test will last 75 minutes. There are three parts, and directions are given for each part. You are encouraged to answer as many questions as possible within the time allowed.

You must mark your answers on the separate answer sheet. Do not write your answers in the test book.

# PART 5

**Directions:** A word or phrase is missing in each of the sentences below. Four answer choices are given below each sentence. Select the best answer to complete the sentence. Then mark the letter (A), (B), (C), or (D) on your answer sheet.

**101.** Vienna Bakery ------- certified organic ingredients to elevate the quality of its pastries.

(A) uses
(B) sets
(C) spends
(D) allows

**102.** Your responsibilities as a market researcher are essentially the same as -------.

(A) his
(B) himself
(C) he
(D) him

**103.** All guests will experience outstanding service at our ------- renovated resort on Crystal Cay.

(A) readily
(B) widely
(C) newly
(D) yearly

**104.** Aberdeen Footwear offers a complete ------- of boots tailored for a variety of indoor and outdoor conditions.

(A) kind
(B) range
(C) fashion
(D) method

**105.** Please inform the guests that ------- business suites are fully furnished and have wireless internet.

(A) each
(B) all
(C) every
(D) whole

**106.** Please send ------- for the amount on the utility bill by next Friday.

(A) paid
(B) pays
(C) paying
(D) payment

**107.** ------- you are unable to locate the information you require, feel free to email us at notfaqs@dgmail.com.

(A) If
(B) As
(C) So
(D) Or

**108.** The Samson Architects Awards Board introduced a new ------- for designs constructed with eco-friendly materials.

(A) superiority
(B) recruitment
(C) category
(D) engagement

**109.** A confident presenter is more likely to move around the stage or remain ------- the stand rather than behind it.

(A) against
(B) after
(C) beside
(D) into

**110.** Ms. Martinez figured that the orientation session ------- three hours, but the talks ran longer than expected.

(A) to last
(B) would last
(C) is lasting
(D) has lasted

**111.** The receptionist should ------- you with the list of documents you need to enroll in the course.

(A) provide
(B) suggest
(C) explain
(D) outline

**112.** Providing images of athletes wearing the clothing makes any sportswear campaign more -------.

(A) effectiveness
(B) effectively
(C) effective
(D) effect

**113.** The science fiction graphic novel *Season of the Trickster* is being transformed into a miniseries ------- Rachel Stonewall and Selena Vasquez.

(A) stars
(B) star
(C) starred
(D) starring

**114.** After a lengthy debate, the proposal to construct a second bridge across Mohican River was ------- declined.

(A) formerly
(B) finally
(C) densely
(D) hardly

**115.** The merger cannot be ratified ------- next month because the contract will not be delivered over the public holiday.

(A) among
(B) notwithstanding
(C) following
(D) until

**116.** Stockbroker Cali Dufresne acknowledges her ability to make ------- trades to skills she learned from her mother.

(A) profited
(B) profiting
(C) profitable
(D) profits

**117.** Ms. Hwang, the new HR Director, has just ------- the scheduling conflicts that had led to many complications last quarter.

(A) resolved
(B) reminded
(C) finished
(D) offered

**118.** Mr. Park has been a dependable member of Holcroft & Associates ------- interning during university.

(A) while
(B) since
(C) on
(D) were

**119.** Ms. Katagara found presenting at the Osaka Tech Convention ------- easy.

(A) comparatively
(B) comparing
(C) comparable
(D) compared

**120.** Direton businesses are being requested to strictly limit their electricity ------- during the heat wave.

(A) usable
(B) usage
(C) user
(D) useful

*GO ON TO THE NEXT PAGE*

**121.** The budget for the technology conference is firmly -------, leaving no possibility for discussion.

(A) establishing
(B) have established
(C) establish
(D) established

**122.** Holiday donations ------- by the Hartford City Council will be distributed to charities throughout the city.

(A) collect
(B) collected
(C) have collected
(D) are collecting

**123.** The cabins on the newest cruise ship in the Moonlight Tour fleet have been ------- designed for comfort on long voyages and stormy seas.

(A) instantly
(B) extremely
(C) approximately
(D) intentionally

**124.** ------- its attractive membership package, Accusure Tax Preparers sees little client turnover.

(A) In support of
(B) Inside
(C) Due to
(D) Regarding

**125.** Notebook manufacturer Portability confirmed this morning that its ZPC-2050 is already in ------- and will be available in stores by the end of the year.

(A) recession
(B) perception
(C) production
(D) management

**126.** The Accounting Department requires all staff members ------- payment slips by Thursday at 6 P.M.

(A) submitting
(B) had submitted
(C) to submit
(D) submitted

**127.** Hermes & Associates' lawyers are ------- permitted to speak to the media during a trial.

(A) hard
(B) high
(C) distant
(D) seldom

**128.** ------- Mr. Tartus can do to improve the mobile application would be welcomed.

(A) Much
(B) That
(C) Anything
(D) Almost

**129.** Periodic updates made to member files by Curtis Medical Group are completely ------- and ensures patients' safety and confidentiality.

(A) secure
(B) authentic
(C) definite
(D) dedicated

**130.** Over the last decade, the maintenance of facilities in the park ------- by the New Jersey Recreation Department.

(A) was managed
(B) has been managed
(C) had managed
(D) would have managed

# PART 6

**Directions:** Read the texts that follow. A word, phrase, or sentence is missing in parts of each text. Four answer choices for each question are given below the text. Select the best answer to complete the text. Then mark the letter (A), (B), (C), or (D) on your answer sheet.

**Questions 131-134** refer to the following press release.

*Market Tracker*, hosted by Tony Calabrese and Josephine Gargano, is a local television show offering the latest updates on the economy ------- investment-related news.
**131.**
*Market Tracker* was first broadcast a decade ago, with Calabrese giving the updates.

It became one of the most highly-regarded programs in New England after Calabrese

------- Gargano five years later. Over time, the partners ------- to broaden the range of
**132.**                                                 **133.**
program topics to include advice about investment-related matters. -------.
                                                              **134.**

*Market Tracker* is on once a week, after the stock market closes on Friday afternoon.

---

**131.** (A) therefore
(B) along with
(C) additionally
(D) in regard

**132.** (A) referred
(B) transferred
(C) joined
(D) hired

**133.** (A) agreeing
(B) agreement
(C) agreed
(D) agreeable

**134.** (A) The shows often feature talks by successful money managers.
(B) Financial journalism has become a very competitive field over the decade.
(C) Investors can do research on their own by using the internet.
(D) Most advisors recommend owning a wide variety of investments to reduce risk.

GO ON TO THE NEXT PAGE

**Questions 135-138** refer to the following information.

---

### GreenPlus Hotel

Frequently Asked Questions

**How can I confirm that my hotel reservation has been processed?**

-------. If you do not receive this notification, contact your financial institution. If no
  **135.**
payment has been made to our resort, it is ------- that your transaction was not
                                                **136.**
completed. -------, please call us at 800-555-1212 so that we may assist you with the
                **137.**
problem.  This number is toll-free if you are calling from inside the country, but -------
                                                          **138.**
that you may be charged for calls made from foreign locations.

---

**135.** (A) Please note that we will never
contact you about payments via
e-mail.
(B) We offer several convenient online
booking options for overseas
guests.
(C) Visitors who arrive without
reservations are accommodated
when possible.
(D) You should receive your room
information via e-mail within 24
hours.

**136.** (A) likely
(B) simple
(C) necessary
(D) appropriate

**137.** (A) However
(B) Furthermore
(C) In this event
(D) In conclusion

**138.** (A) remember
(B) remembers
(C) remembered
(D) remembering

**Questions 139-142** refer to the following memo.

To: All Marley Supplements staff
From: Edgar Marley
Date: December 3
Subject: Survey Findings

At today's board meeting, a decision was made that will increase company profits and also improve our firm's reputation.

The Strategy Department ------- findings from their survey at the meeting. They also
        **139.**
showed how purchasing locally-raised agricultural products to support the area's economy would reduce our shipping expenses.

The survey revealed that customers prefer to buy from companies that invest in the local economy. Accordingly, ------- will replace our present overseas partners with
        **140.**
nearby producers.

Furthermore, the Shipping Department will begin working with several companies here in town for storage and delivery services that create jobs for the people of this community. Our drivers, warehouse workers, and other valued employees will be hired from the immediate vicinity.

-------. In the long run, these changes should have a ------- impact on both our
**141.**                                   **142.**
profitability and our image in the community.

**139.** (A) will have shared
    (B) will share
    (C) shared
    (D) is sharing

**140.** (A) we
    (B) it
    (C) your
    (D) her

**141.** (A) This is because there simply are too few qualified candidates in this area.
    (B) Current employees should be given the opportunity to apply first for any such opening.
    (C) An announcement will be posted on our Web site to inform the public about these exciting plans.
    (D) Some board members were unable to attend because of prior commitments.

**142.** (A) supplementary
    (B) reduced
    (C) favorable
    (D) foreign

*GO ON TO THE NEXT PAGE* →

**Questions 143-146** refer to the following letter.

Josephine Lucchese
Trujillo Systems
9822 W. 95 St.
Overland Park, KS 66212

Dear Ms. Lucchese,

-------. Trujillo Systems' product sorting machine has been extremely helpful to us in the
**143.**
six months since we installed it. Our factory ------- reliable and accurate methods of
**144.**
inspecting and sorting large shipments of agricultural materials. Now that we are using
Trujillo Systems' product, we can evaluate the quality of materials better and quickly
organize them in our plant. Due to its customizable features, workers are able to
configure the machine to their ------- settings. Since the machine has allowed us to
**145.**
reduce time spent on projects, we have achieved major ------- in efficiency. We
**146.**
continue to be very impressed with your product, and we fully expect to attain even
better results thanks to Trujillo Systems as time goes on.

Best regards,

*David Benavides*

David Benavides
Vice President, AgroSur Industries

---

**143.** (A) We thank you for considering a career at AgroSur Industries.
(B) Your business has been a loyal client of AgroSur Industries.
(C) AgroSur Industries needs to purchase a new product sorting machine soon.
(D) I am happy to provide input as a representative of AgroSur Industries.

**144.** (A) will lack
(B) are lacking
(C) lack
(D) used to lack

**145.** (A) final
(B) desired
(C) extra
(D) useful

**146.** (A) instructions
(B) separations
(C) improvements
(D) answers

# PART 7

**Directions:** In this part you will read a selection of texts, such as magazine and newspaper articles, e-mails, and instant messages. Each text or set of texts is followed by several questions. Select the best answer for each question and mark the letter (A), (B), (C) or (D) on your answer sheet.

**Questions 147-148** refer to the following information.

---

### Take Citywide Info

Don't have time to go to the post office? We guarantee that our bike messengers can complete urgent deliveries anywhere in town in under an hour, at any time of day or night.

Just log on to our Web site to find out how much you have to pay for delivery. Your quote will be based on how much your package weighs.

After our messenger takes your parcel, you will be provided with a special code that allows you to track its progress in real time, with a constantly-updated arrival time.

---

**147.** What is included in the information?

(A) Short distance deliveries are discounted.
(B) Large parcels must be sent out by regular mail.
(C) Customers can calculate a price online.
(D) Bike messengers will call recipients before departing.

**148.** What is the purpose of the special code?

(A) To change an order's destination
(B) To view a delivery's progress
(C) To receive a cost estimate
(D) To estimate a package's size

GO ON TO THE NEXT PAGE

**Questions 149-150** refer to the following e-mail.

**To:** Liam Daniels
**From:** Eilana Guedes
**Date:** May 29
**Subject:** Remerton branch

Dear Mr. Daniels,

Last November, your application to relocate to the Remerton branch was not approved because there was no availability there during that time. The Remerton branch director contacted me today, however, and said that he's looking for an experienced assistant store manager. In addition, he is considering internal applicants first, so I wanted to give you priority. If you are still interested in this opportunity, please inform me by this Thursday. If you would like to just stay at your current branch, I'll go ahead and post the opening on our company's announcement board. I await your response.

Sincerely,
Eilana Guedes

**149.** Why was the e-mail written?

(A) To request feedback on a computer program
(B) To introduce a new assistant store manager
(C) To forward directions to an office
(D) To announce an open position

**150.** What will Ms. Guedes wait to do?

(A) Speak with a branch director
(B) Hold a training session
(C) Respond to an e-mail
(D) Publish an ad

**Questions 151-152** refer to the following text message chain.

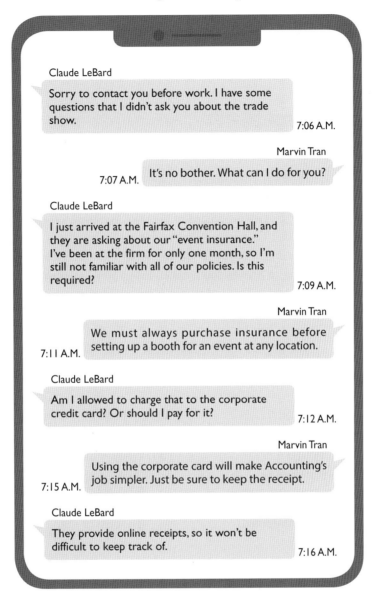

Claude LeBard

Sorry to contact you before work. I have some questions that I didn't ask you about the trade show.

7:06 A.M.

Marvin Tran

7:07 A.M. It's no bother. What can I do for you?

Claude LeBard

I just arrived at the Fairfax Convention Hall, and they are asking about our "event insurance." I've been at the firm for only one month, so I'm still not familiar with all of our policies. Is this required?

7:09 A.M.

Marvin Tran

We must always purchase insurance before setting up a booth for an event at any location.

7:11 A.M.

Claude LeBard

Am I allowed to charge that to the corporate credit card? Or should I pay for it?

7:12 A.M.

Marvin Tran

Using the corporate card will make Accounting's job simpler. Just be sure to keep the receipt.

7:15 A.M.

Claude LeBard

They provide online receipts, so it won't be difficult to keep track of.

7:16 A.M.

**151.** At 7:07 A.M., what does Mr. Tran mean when he writes, "It's no bother"?

(A) He thinks that Mr. LeBard should not purchase additional insurance.
(B) He welcomes Mr. LeBard's inquiries.
(C) Mr. LeBard is able to submit an online receipt.
(D) Mr. LeBard can easily find information about booth setup.

**152.** What is indicated about Mr. LeBard?

(A) He requires reimbursement for his meals.
(B) He has signed up for a new credit card.
(C) He needs help preparing for a presentation.
(D) He has recently joined a new company.

GO ON TO THE NEXT PAGE

**Questions 153-154** refer to the following memo.

**MEMO**

FROM: Garett Jacotey
TO: Ciao Down Employees
DATE: June 3
SUBJECT: Sign update

This is to provide further information about our recently purchased electronic display which our restaurant's owner has said will be placed at the front entrance.

The new screen will feature images of daily specials along with Ciao Down's regular options, although we are still waiting to finalize the graphic design work. We will make our decision in the next several days, and then finalize the sign. Hopefully, it will be set up by the beginning of July.

If you have questions regarding this matter, please get in touch with me.

Garett Jacotey

**153.** What is indicated about the sign?

(A) It will have a digital display.
(B) It will show new items each week.
(C) It has been set up recently.
(D) It requires additional materials.

**154.** What information will the sign include?

(A) An employee directory
(B) A seating chart
(C) A profile of the restaurant's owner
(D) A list of menu items

**Questions 155-157** refer to the following article.

June 5—The Delaney Bay Cultural Association (DBCA) announced yesterday that Janice Sullivan won the Eighth Annual Amateur Photography Contest. Her award-winning entry, titled *Peace*, along with the entries of the other twelve finalists, will be shown from August 1 to August 10 at the DBCA Arts Center. On August 11, there will be an award ceremony where Ms. Sullivan will be presented with a $2,000 cash prize in honor of her achievement by DBCA President Phillip Gonzales. While admission to the exhibition is free any financial contributions are welcome to support the DBCA's work.

This will be the first time that the DBCA will be featuring the works of this year's competitors on its Web site. "The online gallery will allow more people to view and enjoy selected works by some of our city's most talented photographers," said Mr. Gonzales.

It is important to note that the arts center won't be open from August 12 to August 31 due to its yearly summer break. The center will reopen for its fall season on Monday, September 1, with a special lecture on different types of jazz music presented by local musicologist Dr. Miriam Katano.

**155.** What is NOT indicated about exhibition?

(A) It will end on August 10.
(B) It is only open to professional photographers.
(C) It does not charge an entrance fee.
(D) It will feature Ms. Sullivan's work.

**156.** What is indicated about Ms. Sullivan?

(A) She will judge a photography competition in June.
(B) She is a member of a cultural organization.
(C) She is a music professor at a university.
(D) She will be attending an event on August 11.

**157.** What does the article imply about the arts center?

(A) It offers art courses to the public.
(B) It has recently attracted more visitors.
(C) The winning entry from last year is available online.
(D) The photography exhibit will be the last show of the season.

*GO ON TO THE NEXT PAGE*

**Questions 158-160** refer to the following advertisement.

## Doiron Financial

Doiron Financial provides excellent investing and wealth management services. It was started 25 years ago by Allan Doiron, who came to New Haven after working as a successful banker for many years in Hartford.

Originally focused on individuals wishing to prepare for retirement or invest in stocks, the company built up a sound reputation locally. That helped it to get small- and medium-sized business clients that needed services beyond just basic investments. Allan's daughter became the company's CEO six years ago and began working with many high-profile corporations across the state, including Delta-U Pharmaceuticals and Avytech Electronics, and opened new offices in Hartford and Bridgeport.

While the markets have had their ups and downs, and competition is fierce, the company has a reputation for providing long-term strategies that stand the test of time and help corporate and individual clients meet their objectives.

For financial assistance you can rely on, look no further than Doiron Financial. Information and services are provided on our Web site at www.doironfinancial.com.

**158.** Where would the advertisement most likely appear?

(A) At an electronics convention
(B) In a city newspaper
(C) At a job fair
(D) In a travel magazine

**159.** What is most likely true about Doiron Financial?

(A) It is planning to purchase a rival firm.
(B) It is a family-run company.
(C) Its clients are mostly retirees.
(D) Its main office is in Hartford.

**160.** What is NOT stated as a change Doiron Financial has experienced?

(A) An update to its security policies
(B) An appointment of a new executive
(C) An expansion into other cities
(D) An increase to its customer base

**Questions 161-164** refer to the following online chat discussion.

---

**Julia Cassel [2:09 P.M.]**
Good afternoon, Sora and Kevin. I'm wondering if a package was dropped off. Some documents are supposed to be delivered to me today, but I'm concerned they may have been sent to another building. They're from Ortlieb Marketing and should have a label that says "priority."

**Sora Johnson [2:10 P.M.]**
We haven't received anything at the reception desk. I think you should go to the Security Office in the main lobby.

**Kevin Lee [2:12 P.M.]**
I see a large envelope from Ortlieb Marketing, here in the HR office, but I can't find the recipient's name.

**Julia Cassel [2:13 P.M.]**
That is probably mine. Do you mind checking the package's label again?

**Kevin Lee [2:14 P.M.]**
I apologize. I see your name now. It was written underneath the address.

**Julia Cassel [2:16 P.M.]**
Wonderful. I need that package sent over to my office right away, please.

**Kevin Lee [2:17 P.M.]**
Sure. I was about to go to the 3rd floor anyway.

**Julia Cassel [2:20 P.M.]**
Thank you so much.

---

SEND

**161.** Why did Ms. Cassel start the online chat discussion?

(A) She is preparing a sales report.
(B) She is waiting for some important documents.
(C) She sent a package to the wrong address.
(D) She is expecting some clients to arrive soon.

**162.** What does Ms. Johnson recommend doing?

(A) Contacting Ortlieb Marketing
(B) Visiting another area
(C) Checking the receptionist desk
(D) Moving a meeting location

**163.** At 2:14 P.M., what does Mr. Lee most likely mean when he writes, "I apologize"?

(A) He did not read a label correctly.
(B) He needs Ms. Cassel to provide clearer directions.
(C) He is unable to arrive at the office on time.
(D) He cannot find a shipping invoice.

**164.** What will Mr. Lee probably do with the package?

(A) Review its contents
(B) Give it a receptionist
(C) Take it to the post office
(D) Bring it to Ms. Cassel

*GO ON TO THE NEXT PAGE*

## ANDREA SARCHET'S RETURN

The Operations Oversight Division is pleased to welcome back senior corporate counsel Andrea Sarchet. —[1]—. For six weeks, Andrea has been in New York City participating in a professional workshop on Corporate Legal Requirements. Legal policy training enables companies to ensure that they obey the latest regulations. Andrea is a part of an increasing number of executives who have finished this challenging program. —[2]—. As a member of the National Committee of Corporate Legal Counselors (NCCLC), Andrea was recognized for playing a role in writing a set of guidelines to help companies avoid lawsuits. —[3]—. Fantastic job, Andrea! —[4]—.

**165.** What is suggested about Andrea Sarchet?

(A) She was recently promoted.
(B) She works as a lawyer.
(C) She often goes on business trips.
(D) She lives in New York City.

**166.** What is NOT indicated about the workshop?

(A) It lasted for six weeks.
(B) It provided training on corporate regulations.
(C) It was organized by the NCCLC.
(D) It has been attracting more executives.

**167.** In which of the positions marked [1], [2], [3], and [4] does the following sentence best belong?

"Several participants are CEOs from well-known corporations."

(A) [1]
(B) [2]
(C) [3]
(D) [4]

---

### Work Continues at Local Parks

MIDDLETON (September 6) – The town of Middleton is currently expanding and renovating 15 of its 30 parks. These improvements so far have cost the town €4.1 million, which is equivalent to the annual amount spent by the Middleton Parks Department (MPD) on operating and maintaining the park's facilities. An extra €1.5 million will also be spent before all the renovation work is finished next month, which brings the total cost to approximately €5.6 million.

However, this renovation project will not burden the town's budget, as it is funded by the MPD. Over the last few years, the local parks have drawn more and more visitors from outside of town.

This has helped lead to a strong growth in profits, which come from parking fees, equipment rental fees, sales at snack shops, and events held at the parks. In fact, last year's figures show that the MPD generated €6.6 million in profit, making it one of the few Parks Departments in the country that can be considered financially independent.

The renovation project is the result of extensive research done last June by the MPD that mainly focused on the conditions of the town's parks. As part of the research, a survey was administered to 2,000 local residents who regularly frequent the town's parks. One of the main things the participants were asked to do was to evaluate the quality of the facilities and to make any suggestions. The compiled data and project proposal were then submitted to the Town Council. After careful review, the council decided to approve the MPD's renovation project.

---

**168.** How much does it cost the Middleton Parks Department each year to manage the town's parks?

(A) €1.5 million
(B) €4.1 million
(C) €5.6 million
(D) €6.6 million

**169.** What is expected to happen in October?

(A) Renovations will be completed.
(B) A park will be closed.
(C) Survey forms will be distributed.
(D) A new town official will be appointed.

**170.** How is the Middleton Parks Department different from other similar agencies?

(A) It provides a wide variety of activities.
(B) It operates the largest park system in the country.
(C) It mostly relies upon donations.
(D) It supports itself from the revenue it generates.

**171.** Who was consulted for suggestions before the current project began?

(A) Middleton residents
(B) International tourists
(C) Economics professors
(D) Landscape architects

GO ON TO THE NEXT PAGE

**Questions 172-175** refer to the following e-mail.

| | |
|---|---|
| **From:** | Lupe Cantu |
| **To:** | Dylan Amano; Stephan Mendoza; Kira Goldstein; Melissa Ahn |
| **Date:** | September 19 |
| **Subject:** | Company program |
| **Attachments:** | Class_goals; Policies_Code_of_conduct; Press_Release_Template |

Hello everyone,

Thank you all for agreeing to create a new hire training program in anticipation of opening our second office in Calgary on December 3. —[1]—. Like we discussed during last week's planning session, five classes will need to be designed. —[2]—. I am assigning the following responsibilities to each of you; please note the dates by which each task should be completed. —[3]—.

**Dylan Amano:** Make detailed summaries about what will be covered for each class by October 21. (Refer to the attached class goals.)

**Stephan Mendoza:** Create presentation slides with the guidelines and policies to be taught. (See attached HR document.)

**Dylan Amano:** Upload training materials to the employee Web page. (Send this information to Seth Adalja in IT.)

**Kira Goldstein:** Contact all new hires about the training class schedule. (A list of names will be emailed next month.)

**Melissa Ahn:** Create a press release announcing our second office's opening and the new training courses. (Complete the attached press document and send it to Wren Torea in Marketing by November 19.)

—[4]—. Our next planning session will be held on October 18 to review our progress. Until that time, if you have any problems or questions please let me know.

Lupe Cantu
Personnel Manager

**172.** When are the class descriptions due?

(A) On October 18
(B) On October 21
(C) On November 19
(D) On December 3

**173.** Who does NOT need to use one of the e-mail attachments?

(A) Mr. Amano
(B) Mr. Mendoza
(C) Ms. Goldstein
(D) Ms. Ahn

**174.** What does Mr. Cantu ask the recipients to do before the next meeting?

(A) Inspect a new workplace
(B) Submit their assignments to him
(C) Work in pairs on all tasks
(D) Inform him of any issues

**175.** In which of the positions marked [1], [2], [3], and [4] does the following sentence best belong?

"There are plenty of things to do until then."

(A) [1]
(B) [2]
(C) [3]
(D) [4]

GO ON TO THE NEXT PAGE

**Questions 176-180** refer to the following Web page and e-mail.

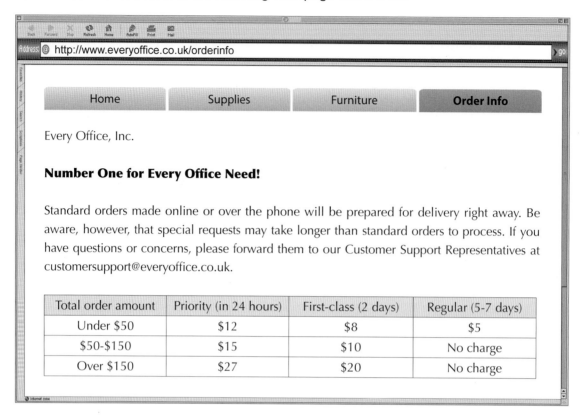

http://www.everyoffice.co.uk/orderinfo

| Home | Supplies | Furniture | **Order Info** |

Every Office, Inc.

**Number One for Every Office Need!**

Standard orders made online or over the phone will be prepared for delivery right away. Be aware, however, that special requests may take longer than standard orders to process. If you have questions or concerns, please forward them to our Customer Support Representatives at customersupport@everyoffice.co.uk.

| Total order amount | Priority (in 24 hours) | First-class (2 days) | Regular (5-7 days) |
|---|---|---|---|
| Under $50 | $12 | $8 | $5 |
| $50-$150 | $15 | $10 | No charge |
| Over $150 | $27 | $20 | No charge |

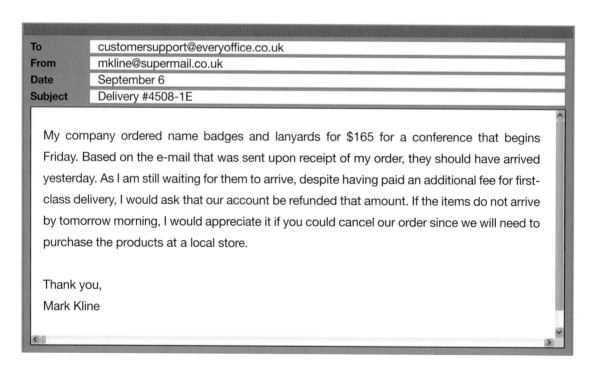

| To | customersupport@everyoffice.co.uk |
|---|---|
| From | mkline@supermail.co.uk |
| Date | September 6 |
| Subject | Delivery #4508-1E |

My company ordered name badges and lanyards for $165 for a conference that begins Friday. Based on the e-mail that was sent upon receipt of my order, they should have arrived yesterday. As I am still waiting for them to arrive, despite having paid an additional fee for first-class delivery, I would ask that our account be refunded that amount. If the items do not arrive by tomorrow morning, I would appreciate it if you could cancel our order since we will need to purchase the products at a local store.

Thank you,

Mark Kline

**176.** In the Web page, what is indicated about Every Office, Inc.'s shipping?

(A) Regular shipping for orders less than $50 is complimentary.
(B) Shipping fees are based on the weight of the items.
(C) Local orders may receive a discount.
(D) Some orders may take seven days to be delivered.

**177.** On the Web page, the word "forward" in paragraph 1, line 3, is closest in meaning to

(A) ship
(B) push
(C) expedite
(D) submit

**178.** What is the purpose of the e-mail?

(A) To report some damaged merchandise
(B) To indicate a delivery issue
(C) To inquire about a custom order
(D) To obtain directions to a local supplier

**179.** How much did Mr. Kline pay for shipping?

(A) $5
(B) $12
(C) $20
(D) $27

**180.** According to the e-mail, why might Mr. Kline decide to visit a local store?

(A) He must have his items before a specific date.
(B) He wants to choose from a wider selection of products.
(C) He prefers to do business with local retailers.
(D) He hopes to buy the items at a cheaper price.

TEST 4

*GO ON TO THE NEXT PAGE*

**Questions 181-185** refer to the following Web page and e-mail.

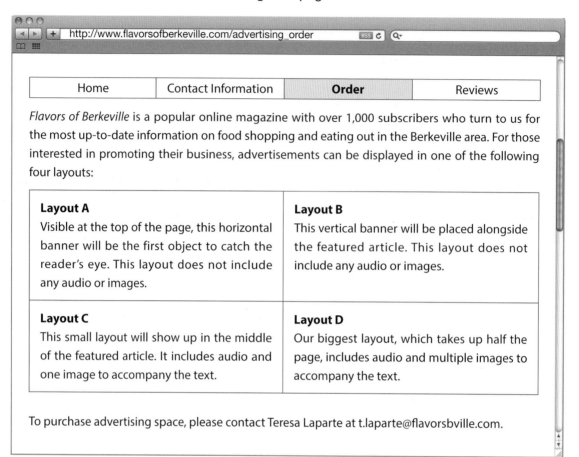

http://www.flavorsofberkeville.com/advertising_order

| Home | Contact Information | **Order** | Reviews |

*Flavors of Berkeville* is a popular online magazine with over 1,000 subscribers who turn to us for the most up-to-date information on food shopping and eating out in the Berkeville area. For those interested in promoting their business, advertisements can be displayed in one of the following four layouts:

**Layout A**
Visible at the top of the page, this horizontal banner will be the first object to catch the reader's eye. This layout does not include any audio or images.

**Layout B**
This vertical banner will be placed alongside the featured article. This layout does not include any audio or images.

**Layout C**
This small layout will show up in the middle of the featured article. It includes audio and one image to accompany the text.

**Layout D**
Our biggest layout, which takes up half the page, includes audio and multiple images to accompany the text.

To purchase advertising space, please contact Teresa Laparte at t.laparte@flavorsbville.com.

| From | Benjamin Kane <b.kane@bruebistro.com> |
| To | Teresa Laparte <t.laparte@flavorsbville.com> |
| Date | October 24 |
| Subject | Advertisement for Brue Bristo |

Dear Ms. Laparte,

I was hoping to post another advertisement with *Flavors of Berkeville*. I'd like to go with the large advertisement layout again. Please go ahead and use the same audio and text as before, but this time I will give you three new photos of my recently remodeled restaurant. I'll leave it up to your design artists to decide where to place the photos in the advertisement. Could you tell me the size requirements for submitting images?

Sincerely,

Benjamin Kane
Owner,
Brue Bistro

**181.** Where does Ms. Laparte work?

(A) At a local restaurant
(B) At a food-related publisher
(C) At a Web design firm
(D) At a food manufacturing company

**182.** What is stated about Layout A?

(A) It is easily noticed.
(B) It is affordable.
(C) It can be made very quickly.
(D) It includes the most text.

**183.** In what advertisement layout is Mr. Kane most likely interested?

(A) Layout A
(B) Layout B
(C) Layout C
(D) Layout D

**184.** What is suggested about Brue Bistro?

(A) It will be closed during renovations.
(B) It is being remodeled by a famous design artist.
(C) It has been advertised in *Flavors of Berkeville* before.
(D) It was recently nominated for an award.

**185.** What does Mr. Kane ask about the photos?

(A) How much does it cost to print them
(B) How big they should be
(C) Where they should be sent
(D) How many are allowed

*GO ON TO THE NEXT PAGE*

**Questions 186-190** refer to the following article, Web page, and e-mail.

Toronto (November 23) — Starting next week, Wayne McAllister, award-winning reporter and founder of the decade-old Ontario Online, will give a series of seminars on issues currently facing journalism.

Mr. McAllister will speak at Vancouver's Main Street Auditorium on December 1 and 2. He will speak at Quebec City's Oiseau Convention Hall on December 4. On December 6, he will give a talk in Winnipeg's Downtown Auditorium. On December 8, he will head to Toronto's Metro Conference Center. And on December 9, he will wrap up with a talk at Montreal's Commons Library.

Seats are selling out fast. For more information and to purchase tickets, visit www.ontarioonline.co.ca.

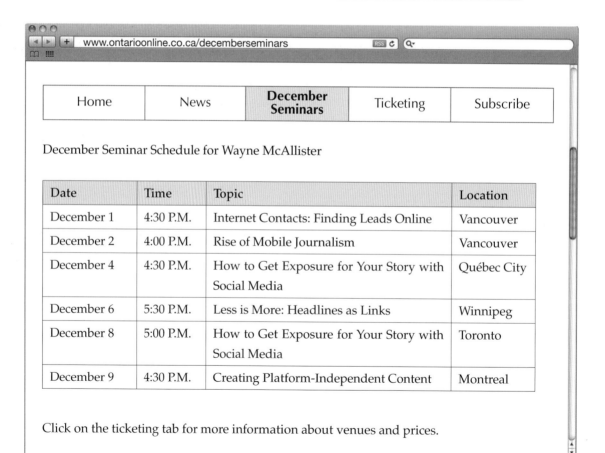

www.ontarioonline.co.ca/decemberseminars

| Home | News | **December Seminars** | Ticketing | Subscribe |

December Seminar Schedule for Wayne McAllister

| Date | Time | Topic | Location |
|------|------|-------|----------|
| December 1 | 4:30 P.M. | Internet Contacts: Finding Leads Online | Vancouver |
| December 2 | 4:00 P.M. | Rise of Mobile Journalism | Vancouver |
| December 4 | 4:30 P.M. | How to Get Exposure for Your Story with Social Media | Québec City |
| December 6 | 5:30 P.M. | Less is More: Headlines as Links | Winnipeg |
| December 8 | 5:00 P.M. | How to Get Exposure for Your Story with Social Media | Toronto |
| December 9 | 4:30 P.M. | Creating Platform-Independent Content | Montreal |

Click on the ticketing tab for more information about venues and prices.

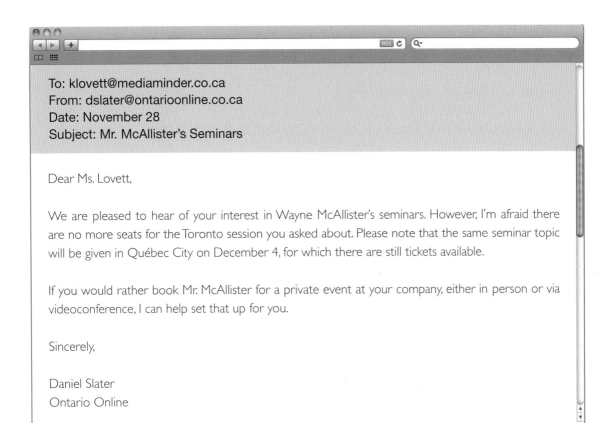

To: klovett@mediaminder.co.ca
From: dslater@ontarioonline.co.ca
Date: November 28
Subject: Mr. McAllister's Seminars

Dear Ms. Lovett,

We are pleased to hear of your interest in Wayne McAllister's seminars. However, I'm afraid there are no more seats for the Toronto session you asked about. Please note that the same seminar topic will be given in Québec City on December 4, for which there are still tickets available.

If you would rather book Mr. McAllister for a private event at your company, either in person or via videoconference, I can help set that up for you.

Sincerely,

Daniel Slater
Ontario Online

**186.** What is indicated about Mr. McAllister?

(A) He opened a business 10 years ago.
(B) He lives in Québec City.
(C) He regularly gives free seminars at convention halls.
(D) He tours Canada every December.

**187.** Where will the talk regarding headlines be given?

(A) The Main Street Auditorium
(B) The Downtown Auditorium
(C) The Oiseau Convention Hall
(D) The Commons Library

**188.** What is the purpose of the e-mail?

(A) To announce a scheduling delay
(B) To accept an invitation
(C) To book a private speaking engagement
(D) To reply to an inquiry

**189.** What event date was Ms. Lovett originally interested in?

(A) December 2
(B) December 4
(C) December 6
(D) December 8

**190.** What most likely is Mr. Slater's occupation?

(A) Company CEO
(B) Web site developer
(C) Administrative specialist
(D) News reporter

*GO ON TO THE NEXT PAGE*

TEST 4

*Business Partners: Issue 34*

## TEN MOBILE PROGRAMS TO BOOST YOUR BOTTOM LINE

1. Tripfolio provides an easy way to track all your business vehicle expenses. Perfect for staff who spend a lot of time on the road, it puts all of your expenditures in one convenient location and organizes them with an interface that is user-friendly.

When you get behind the wheel with your mobile device running Tripfolio, it will track where you go with the device's navigation function and upload it. Each trip is put in a virtual log, creating an exact record of your route. Access the log to add trip details like fuel expenses or to comment on traffic conditions.

You can access new features to display traffic conditions, parking availability, or time-saving shortcuts. One popular use of this is to optimize trips that happen regularly, like deliveries, weekly client meetings, and airport shuttling.

Every route is backed up on the application's server. The app's price covers usage, storage, and ongoing development costs. A Personal plan is priced at $5 per month and comes with 20 virtual logs for the month. More expensive plans come with a larger number of virtual logs.

---

Thank you for downloading the Tripfolio mobile app!

To get started, please fill out the information below. Once completed, you can start your first virtual log. Don't forget that subscription upgrades are available. If you need more logs, visit www.tripfolioapp.com/accounts. Drive safely!

**User Details:**
Name: William Burke
E-mail: williamb@sunkitsales.com
Mobile number: 702-555-6813
How frequently do you travel? 11-14 times weekly
Do you ever visit other cities: Yes
Frequent destinations: Los Angeles, Phoenix, Santa Fe, Albuquerque

**Select a Plan:**
Personal: $5.00/month ☐
Small Business: $15.00/month ☐
Medium Business: $30.00/month ☑
Large Business: $50.00/month ☐

| To: | williamb@sunkitsales.com |
| --- | --- |
| From: | support@tripfolioapp.com |
| Date: | November 27 |
| Subject: | User notice |

Greetings Tripfolio user,

A change will be made to our subscription package prices beginning next year. This will enable us to provide valuable updates to our service, like including more expense recording features and providing two additional language options. Also, Medium and Large Business subscribers will be able to purchase new special packages, which include printed log records and route maps when phone service is unavailable. Revised pricing, which will be effective January 1, is as follows:

| Plan | Monthly Price | Virtual Log Capacity |
| --- | --- | --- |
| Personal | $5 | 30 logs |
| Small Business | $15 | 50 logs |
| Medium Business | $30 | 100 logs |
| Large Business | $60 | 300 logs |

Medium and Large Business subscribers will be given a complimentary travel bag. Get in touch if you have any questions!
support@tripfolioapp.com

**191.** According to the article excerpt, what does the Tripfolio mobile app allow users to do?

(A) Record customer purchases
(B) Book international flights
(C) Reserve rental vehicles
(D) Store route details

**192.** What is implied about the Tripfolio mobile app?

(A) It has won several awards for its design.
(B) It requires access to a device's functions.
(C) It is only compatible with the latest smart devices.
(D) It is more expensive than competing applications.

**193.** Why is Mr. Burke eligible to receive a travel bag?

(A) He purchased a Tripfolio subscription as a gift.
(B) He entered a community contest.
(C) He has been to many local attractions.
(D) He is a Medium Business plan subscriber.

**194.** What is NOT mentioned in the e-mail as a reason for the change in price?

(A) Offering new special packages
(B) Providing more ways to record expenses
(C) Allowing more countries to access the app
(D) Adding new language options

**195.** What specific change is being made to the Personal plan?

(A) Driving directions are being updated.
(B) Payment methods are being improved.
(C) Some unnecessary security features are being removed.
(D) The virtual log capacity will increase.

*GO ON TO THE NEXT PAGE*

**Questions 196-200** refer to the following advertisement, form, and letter.

## Looking for Full-time Web Programmer

MediaMark, an award-winning IT company, has served Chicago businesses since 1992. We are looking for a Web programmer to design select aspects of our online payment programs, under the guidance of the head software developer. Qualified candidates should have either a Master's Degree in Computer Science or one year of programming experience. Applicants will need to display proven ability to create high-tech Web sites and keep them secure.

Visit www.mediamark.com/jobs to apply.

---

www.mediamark.com/jobs/web_programmer/

**Name:** Danica Kovac
**Phone Number:** 650-555-7835
**E-mail:** dkovac@lightningmail.com

**Education:** Bachelor's Degree in Computer Science from Westport University

**Current Employer:** Datalock Security
**Position:** Web programmer
**Time Worked:** 3 months

**Past Employer:** Lancet Coders
**Position:** Programmer
**Time Worked:** 12 months

**Past Employer:** iNet Connect
**Position:** Junior Software Developer
**Time Worked:** 2 months

**Attached Documents:**
CV
references

**Cover Letter:** I would like to apply for the full-time Web programmer position at MediaMark. I have been working as a Web programmer for a security company that maintains protected databases. As the company is a startup, I am responsible for programming work on nearly all projects. I was formerly employed at an international software firm, Lancet Coders, working under the world-renowned Dave Moss. Also, my instructor and advisor, Gina Romano, will confirm that I can design Web sites using the latest technology. As a matter of fact, while studying in university, I received a $200 cash prize for my project to make an online store, and it is currently used as an example for other university students.

## Submit Form

## WESTPORT UNIVERSITY
## School of Computer Science

Liam Appleton
MediaMark
2992 Berkeley Ave.
Menlo Park, CA 94025

Dear Mr. Appleton,

This letter is in regard to Danica Kovac's job application. As Ms. Romano is out on leave for the remainder of the term, she requested that I write this letter in her place. Ms. Kovac's strong programming skills and an ability to quickly solve difficult problems earned her a place at the top of her class. She was given an opportunity to continue working part-time by her supervisor and notable industry leader, Philip Zhou, after a two-month internship. I am certain Ms. Kovac will be a valuable addition to your staff.

Regards,

*Joshua Rhodes*

Joshua Rhodes
Dean of Westport College of Engineering

**196.** What is indicated about the Web programmer position?

(A) It includes traveling to different countries.
(B) It will only be for one year.
(C) It involves designing a limited number of application features.
(D) It requires working during weekends.

**197.** What is true about Ms. Kovac?

(A) She has the same mentor as Mr. Moss.
(B) She works in a retail store.
(C) She has sent applications to several companies.
(D) She is qualified to fill a job opening.

**198.** Who is Ms. Romano?

(A) A business software developer
(B) A computer science instructor
(C) A university administrator
(D) An engineering student

**199.** What is implied about Westport University?

(A) It invites industry leaders to give lectures.
(B) It provides software demonstrations.
(C) It offers monetary awards.
(D) It is looking to hire a new professor.

**200.** Where does Mr. Zhou most likely work?

(A) MediaMark
(B) Datalock Security
(C) Lancet Coders
(D) iNet Connect

*GO ON TO THE NEXT PAGE*

# ST 5

# READING TEST

In the Reading test, you will read a variety of texts and answer several different types of reading comprehension questions. The entire Reading test will last 75 minutes. There are three parts, and directions are given for each part. You are encouraged to answer as many questions as possible within the time allowed.

You must mark your answers on the separate answer sheet. Do not write your answers in the test book.

# PART 5

**Directions:** A word or phrase is missing in each of the sentences below. Four answer choices are given below each sentence. Select the best answer to complete the sentence. Then mark the letter (A), (B), (C), or (D) on your answer sheet.

---

**101.** To be entered into the contest, your ------- must be received by June 10.

(A) submission
(B) submit
(C) submitted
(D) submitter

**102.** New tenants ------- get their apartment keys after they pay their security deposit.

(A) usually
(B) previously
(C) constantly
(D) annually

**103.** Nordic Angler hires sales clerks that are ------- about fishing so that they can get customers excited about purchasing items.

(A) pleasant
(B) courteous
(C) enthusiastic
(D) logical

**104.** In recognition of our continued business, the Berkford Office Supplies sent our company a ----- for $100.

(A) balance
(B) certificate
(C) way
(D) receipt

**105.** Thorndon Café invites customers to sample its array of beverages ------- locally sourced ingredients.

(A) contain
(B) contains
(C) contained
(D) containing

**106.** Should your plans change, you may ------- reschedule your reservation dates or request a partial refund.

(A) whether
(B) either
(C) except
(D) during

**107.** We have printed enough information packets to distribute ------- of how many guests attend.

(A) instead
(B) much
(C) regardless
(D) within

**108.** T&G Associates is happy to ------- that Lee's Fitness is relocating to a larger facility on Blair Street.

(A) assemble
(B) promote
(C) report
(D) supervise

**109.** After just two months as Department Manager, Mr. Kim has attended ------- a dozen conferences.

(A) nearer
(B) near
(C) nearing
(D) nearly

**110.** The CEO gave his ------- for the merger with the Tar-Spec Corporation.

(A) aspect
(B) authorization
(C) pleasure
(D) influence

**111.** ------- open only to enrolled students, the Deacon University Legal Library can now be accessed by members of the public.

(A) Extensively
(B) Abruptly
(C) Previously
(D) Shortly

**112.** This afternoon, theater guests should be aware that the *Serene Lake* performance will be ------- by repair work on the auditorium.

(A) booked
(B) composed
(C) delayed
(D) expected

**113.** Mr. Martini will oversee the training program for new technicians since ------- became the new department head.

(A) himself
(B) his
(C) he
(D) him

**114.** ------- she missed her connecting flight, Ms. Carter arrived at the Technology Expo as scheduled.

(A) Now that
(B) Although
(C) Since
(D) As soon as

**115.** Ms. Thompson ----- her speech when the video projector stopped working during her product presentation.

(A) improvised
(B) authorized
(C) officiated
(D) reached

**116.** Due to the rain, the workers are not finished ------- the roof of the house.

(A) of
(B) from
(C) in
(D) with

**117.** Shoppers should use the bathrooms near the rear entrance of the mall while ------- by the front entrance are being repainted.

(A) each
(B) the ones
(C) that
(D) the other

**118.** This year, HD Department Store is ranked second ------- in national sales.

(A) overall
(B) jointly
(C) broadly
(D) consecutively

**119.** For exceptional quality at ------- prices, be sure to shop at the Cherry Creek Outlets in Welmington.

(A) afforded
(B) affordable
(C) afford
(D) affording

**120.** Director Chieko Mori was pleased to learn several reviewers made a ------- between her film and Kintaro Igeta's beloved *A Day in Yokohama*.

(A) difference
(B) comparison
(C) request
(D) relationship

*GO ON TO THE NEXT PAGE*

**121.** The new package tracking application indicates the current location ------- the estimated delivery date and time of the parcel.

(A) when
(B) as well as
(C) in order to
(D) in addition

**122.** Clarkson Ltd. is searching for an experienced ------- capable of managing its Southeast Asian branch.

(A) administrating
(B) administrative
(C) administrator
(D) administer

**123.** The advanced tread technology of Firelake tires provides the ------- grip possible on snowy or icy roads.

(A) firmly
(B) firmest
(C) firm
(D) firmer

**124.** Including client testimonials on the homepage will give the firm increased ------- with the public.

(A) anticipation
(B) permission
(C) objectives
(D) credibility

**125.** The opening ceremony was relocated to Geordie Stadium to ensure ------- seating for all spectators.

(A) persistent
(B) adequate
(C) whole
(D) modern

**126.** Residents ------- Haylee Carter's decades of service to the community next week at Tieri Banquet Hall.

(A) honored
(B) have honored
(C) will have been honoring
(D) will be honoring

**127.** PDL Biotech requires personnel to call the Security Office ------- if they detect any leaks or malfunctions in the lab.

(A) rather
(B) right away
(C) as
(D) not many

**128.** It is the duty of ------- leaves the office last to turn off the lights.

(A) whoever
(B) anybody
(C) all
(D) someone

**129.** WHAL, Inc. and Davidson Corp. recently ------- on an environmental campaign to clean up the city streets.

(A) collaborated
(B) instituted
(C) subsided
(D) designated

**130.** This summer, the Children's Museum of Science attracted 20 percent more visitors than it ------- during the same time last year.

(A) did
(B) does
(C) will do
(D) has done

# PART 6

**Directions:** Read the texts that follow. A word, phrase, or sentence is missing in parts of each text. Four answer choices for each question are given below the text. Select the best answer to complete the text. Then mark the letter (A), (B), (C), or (D) on your answer sheet.

**Questions 131-134** refer to the following advertisement.

With CityGolf's two-week trial membership, you'll have a chance to sample our golf facilities, lessons, and other amenities. -------. No commitment is required. To get
                                             **131.**
started, you just need a credit card and a valid form of identification, but we will not charge your account unless you keep the membership for ------- 15 days. During this
                                                                        **132.**
period, if you feel that CityGolf is not for you, ------- call our customer support center at
                                                    **133.**
1-800-555-1212. When you connect with a representative, ask to ------- your
                                                                 **134.**
membership after confirming your identity. So, what are you waiting for?

**131.** (A) Private golf classes are not offered at this time.
(B) Our customer support specialists are always available to assist you.
(C) During the trial, you don't need to make a payment or sign a contract.
(D) You must make a small deposit when you register for a membership

**132.** (A) over
(B) less than
(C) nearly
(D) not quite

**133.** (A) simply
(B) rightly
(C) constantly
(D) normally

**134.** (A) activate
(B) renew
(C) extend
(D) cancel

GO ON TO THE NEXT PAGE

**Questions 135-138** refer to the following letter.

Like all Farisys employees, you are allowed a limited number of sick days on which you may take paid leave for medical -------. To receive full payment for the day off, you
**135.**
------- submit an official doctor's letter confirming that there was a health issue. -------
**136.**                                                                              **137.**
must clearly indicate the date you sought medical attention, the fact that you are advised not to work, and the date on which you will be able to resume your duties. This information will be kept by the branch manager in your personnel file. -------. Staff
**138.**
medical files are available only to your direct supervisor and the HR Department, and will not be shared with other individuals, departments, or outside organizations.

**135.** (A) qualifications
(B) insurance
(C) equipment
(D) reasons

**136.** (A) asks
(B) are asking
(C) were asking
(D) are asked to

**137.** (A) It
(B) I
(C) These
(D) They

**138.** (A) The length of your absence could depend on a variety of circumstances.
(B) Your personal information is kept strictly confidential by Farisys.
(C) You will receive a yearly review from the Human Resources Department.
(D) You should speak to your branch manager if your job is negatively affecting your health.

**Questions 139-142** refer to the following e-mail.

---

To: ericnakagawa@xrmail.com
From: JohnKim@hartleylaboratories.com
Date: 2 October
Subject: Starting work at Hartley Labs

Dear Mr. Nakagawa,

Welcome to Hartley Laboratories. We would like to thank you for ------- the full-time
                                                            **139.**
position of assistant researcher. We are excited for your first day at the Redlands,
California facility on October 9. Please come to the main laboratory and inform the
receptionist that you are looking for Karen Bautista. She ------- you to your work
                                                                      **140.**
station. There, you will find your laboratory coat ------- all of the equipment you will
                                                              **141.**
need for your job here. As you know, due to the variety of hazardous materials we work
with, there are quite a lot of safety rules to follow. Reviewing the procedures manual will
help make you aware of the handling requirements of the different substances. -------.
                                                                           **142.**

Please let me know anytime if you have questions on any of this.

Thanks,

John Kim
Facility Manager

---

**139.** (A) applying
(B) considering
(C) posting
(D) accepting

**140.** (A) directs
(B) will direct
(C) did direct
(D) direct

**141.** (A) along with
(B) additionally
(C) also
(D) as well

**142.** (A) The requirements will change later this year.
(B) You should have received a copy via e-mail.
(C) If a material seems hazardous, you should contact a supervisor.
(D) You must inspect all equipment daily.

*GO ON TO THE NEXT PAGE*

**Questions 143-146** refer to the following article.

July 21 – ARF Controls, Inc., the nation's largest supplier of thermostats, expects its incoming orders to increase dramatically in the coming year. This ------- is based on the
**143.**
news that additional thermostat requirements will be implemented due to stricter power plant regulations. CEO Bart Pearson predicts that ARF will sell a staggering 750,000 units this quarter. -------.
**144.**
ARF purchases many of its products from smaller companies and customizes them ------- plants of all sizes. "The need for increased amounts of ------- in the industry is
**145.**                                           **146.**
allowing ARF to expand its business quickly," Mr. Pearson said. "We think that the future potential is enormous."

**143.** (A) cancellation
(B) forecast
(C) price
(D) choice

**144.** (A) Mr. Pearson has over 35 years of experience in the industry.
(B) ARF's five largest clients are major power plant manufacturers.
(C) This is the first time in the company's history it has reached such a figure.
(D) Nowadays, factory thermostats are very advanced.

**145.** (A) while
(B) for
(C) as
(D) on

**146.** (A) manufacture
(B) manufacturer
(C) manufactured
(D) manufacturing

## PART 7

**Directions:** In this part you will read a selection of texts, such as magazine and newspaper articles, e-mails, and instant messages. Each text or set of texts is followed by several questions. Select the best answer for each question and mark the letter (A), (B), (C) or (D) on your answer sheet.

**Questions 147-148** refer to the following notice.

### Welcome to Gelson Inn

We will try to make sure that your stay here is an enjoyable experience. If for any reason, you are not satisfied with your stay, please call extension 200 for housekeeping.

Breakfast is served every morning from 7:00 A.M. – 11:00 A.M. in our restaurant located to the right of the reception hall on the first floor. Please present your room card to the host when you enter the restaurant.

We are always trying to improve our services, so please call me at extension 202 if you have any suggestions or comments.

Sincerely yours,

Alex Cominta
Manager
Gelson Inn

TEST 5

**147.** What is the purpose of the notice?

(A) To communicate with hotel guests
(B) To welcome a new staff member
(C) To promote a menu
(D) To hire a housekeeping worker

**148.** How should feedback be provided?

(A) By writing an e-mail
(B) By speaking with the hotel manager
(C) By calling the front desk
(D) By filling out a questionnaire

*GO ON TO THE NEXT PAGE*

TEST 5    143

**Questions 149-150** refer to the following advertisement.

## Corky's Emporium

Everything must go from our beachside shop!

Corky's Emporium is clearing everything out from last season's inventory! Everything from brand name goggles to sandals has been marked down below warehouse prices. It's all available for 40-75% off!

This sale lasts from September 25 to October 3. Don't miss out!

Hours of operation: 9:30 A.M. to 8:00 P.M., open 7 days a week. Find us on the northeast corner of Main Street and Highrise Drive, or shop online at www. corkysemporium.co.ca.

**149.** Who most likely posted this notice?

(A) A shoe designer
(B) A warehouse supervisor
(C) A marketing director
(D) A business owner

**150.** What is implied about Corky's Emporium?

(A) It was recently opened.
(B) It provides coupons frequently.
(C) It is located near a body of water.
(D) It holds weekly promotional events.

**Questions 151-152** refer to the following text message chain.

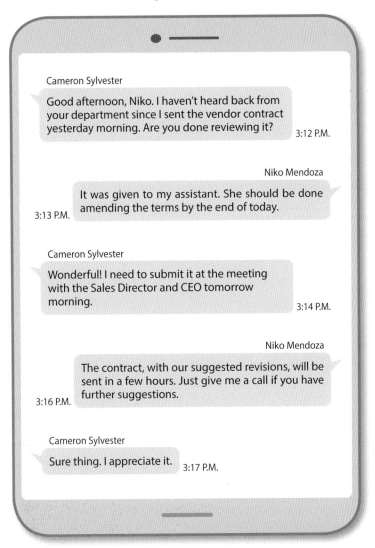

Cameron Sylvester

Good afternoon, Niko. I haven't heard back from your department since I sent the vendor contract yesterday morning. Are you done reviewing it? 3:12 P.M.

Niko Mendoza

It was given to my assistant. She should be done amending the terms by the end of today. 3:13 P.M.

Cameron Sylvester

Wonderful! I need to submit it at the meeting with the Sales Director and CEO tomorrow morning. 3:14 P.M.

Niko Mendoza

The contract, with our suggested revisions, will be sent in a few hours. Just give me a call if you have further suggestions. 3:16 P.M.

Cameron Sylvester

Sure thing. I appreciate it. 3:17 P.M.

**151.** For which department does Ms. Mendoza most likely work?

(A) Finance
(B) Personnel
(C) Sales
(D) Legal

**152.** At 3:17 P.M., what does Mr. Sylvester most likely mean when he says, "Sure thing"?

(A) He will take notes over the phone.
(B) He will email a finalized contract to a vendor.
(C) He will deliver some documents to the CEO.
(D) He will let Ms. Mendoza know about any changes.

*GO ON TO THE NEXT PAGE*

**Questions 153-154** refer to the following memo.

To: All staff
From: Stephen Monteroy
Date: May 17
Subject: Overtime work

Good morning,

June and July are traditionally the busiest months for taxi drivers. Therefore, we expect a need for 30 percent more working hours than usual. Before posting job ads, I wanted to see if any current employees would be interested in taking on some overtime work. Drivers will be paid their regular hourly rate plus 10 percent for each extra hour worked. If this interests you, please inform me by 4:00 P.M. on May 17. Also, if you are taking days off in June and July, please inform me by that date, so I can take your leave into account when planning to hire temporary drivers.

Sincerely,

Stephen Monteroy

**153.** What is the purpose of the memo?
(A) To suggest that staff take time off in July
(B) To report on a change in cab fares
(C) To request business expenses from the last two months
(D) To announce an opportunity for employees

**154.** According to the memo, what will Mr. Monteroy probably do soon after May 17?
(A) Revise the current vacation policy
(B) Resign from his position
(C) Recruit more permanent employees
(D) Post an advertisement for seasonal workers

## Contributions Are Welcomed

Willow Falls Museum's (WFM) mission is to provide the public with access to our exhibits at no cost. WFM is heavily dependent on financial contributions to create and maintain the exhibitions you now see on display. Please consider contributing by filling out a form at the front desk or on our Web site at www.willowfallsmuseum.org/support.

If you are interested in becoming a WFM Friends' Club member, please stop by the information booth or sign up online at www.willowfallsmuseum.org/sponsor. Sponsors will receive our museum's collector's guide, detailing our most notable history exhibits to date, a monthly e-mail with information about all the events at our museum, and a stylish WFM T-shirt to show your support for our museum. Sponsors are asked to give at least $180 in support annually.

**155.** Where would the flyer most likely be distributed?

(A) In a history museum
(B) In a school office
(C) In a bookstore
(D) In a government building

**156.** What is stated about the museum displays?

(A) They change once a month.
(B) They are managed by a well-known curator.
(C) They do not require an admission fee.
(D) They have been recently restored.

**157.** What is NOT mentioned as a benefit of sponsors?

(A) Sponsors receive a clothing item.
(B) Sponsors are sent a calendar of events.
(C) Sponsors' names are posted online.
(D) Sponsors get a book showcasing certain works.

**Questions 158-160** refer to the following e-mail.

**From:** Lance Pratt
**To:** Nathan Forester
**Date:** Monday, October 4
**Subject:** Rush Hills Resort

Dear Mr. Forester,

According to our records, you and your family will be arriving at Rush Hills Resort the weekend after next. —[1]—. I'm pleased that you chose us as your vacation destination.

We should mention that the Waterford Cycling Championship will be held here in two weeks' time. It's a two-day bicycle race from Waterford to Brentshire. It's fun to watch, but please note that several tourists attractions, including the Waterford Museum, will be closed during the race. —[2]—.

The highway through town will remain open, so arriving at our facility will not be a problem. —[3]—. Do expect significant delays if you plan to head into town, due to spectators here to watch the event, especially since we are so close to the starting line of the race. It may be difficult to make reservations in Waterford's restaurants due to the increased number of visitors. —[4]—.

I didn't want this event to come as a surprise upon your arrival, so I thought I should inform you of it well in advance. If you would like more information, please give us a call.

Sincerely,

Lance Pratt
General Manager, Rush Hills Resort

---

**158.** Why did Mr. Pratt send the e-mail to Mr. Forester?

(A) To offer his apologies for a reservation mistake
(B) To respond to an inquiry about the resort's services
(C) To explain the process of receiving a family discount
(D) To provide information about a scheduled event

**159.** What is implied about the Rush Hills Resort?

(A) It is not accessible from the highway.
(B) It is located in the city of Waterford.
(C) It arranges bicycle tours for its guests.
(D) It will be closed during the race.

**160.** In which of the positions marked [1], [2], [3], and [4] does the following sentence best belong?

"As you have booked to stay with us for five nights, you will have other opportunities to visit them."

(A) [1]
(B) [2]
(C) [3]
(D) [4]

**Questions 161-163** refer to the following letter.

Henry Labasse
Rue de la Louthe 911
5451 Bordeaux
France

Dear Mr. Labasse,

Due to the current global business environment being greatly interdependent and interconnected, developing professional relationships with colleagues from all over the world is becoming more crucial than ever. That is why Medic United has created a comprehensive list with details on over 50,000 medical lab researchers located in 60 countries. Join Medic United today to expand your peer network.

If you subscribe to our Silver Business Listing, you can access the name and contact information of every individual listed in our database, as well as information on other medical professionals, such as nurses, physicians, and MRI technicians. If you decide to subscribe to our Gold Business Listing, you can access all the information mentioned above along with detailed data on current medical projects and advancements.

To give you a chance to explore this service, we will offer you a free one-month trial. To sign up for this complimentary service or to become a regular subscriber, please go to our Web site, www.mcunited.com.bg/subscription.

Sincerely,

*Eleanor Renard*
Eleanor Renard
Director of Marketing

**161.** What is the purpose of the letter?

(A) To attract a new customer
(B) To request more information
(C) To schedule a check-up
(D) To recommend medical experts

**162.** Who most likely is Mr. Labasse?

(A) A laboratory researcher
(B) A physician
(C) A nurse
(D) An MRI technician

**163.** What service does Medic United offer?

(A) Recovering lost data
(B) Facilitating professional communications
(C) Providing healthcare classes
(D) Developing Web sites

*GO ON TO THE NEXT PAGE*

**Questions 164-167** refer to the following text message chain.

---

**Amy Fischer [10:09 A.M.]**
Good morning, everyone. I'm looking for Kimberly.

**Jose Navarro [10:11 A.M.]**
I just saw her a few minutes ago. Is everything OK?

**Amy Fischer [10:12 A.M.]**
Unfortunately, the projector doesn't seem to be operational, and I've tried everything.

**Jose Navarro [10:13 A.M.]**
That's awful! When does today's training session begin?

**Amy Fischer [10:15 A.M.]**
At 10:30 sharp. About 20 people have already shown up, and we're expecting 44.

**Kimberly Min [10:16 A.M.]**
I was in the storage room looking for an extra one, but I didn't have any luck. Amy and I still need to set up the speakers and arrange the information packets, and we've only got a few minutes left.

**Jose Navarro [10:17 A.M.]**
There isn't enough time to go to another branch and borrow a projector. I am going to go to Max Tech to buy a new one. It's just down the street.

SEND

---

**164.** Where most likely is Ms. Fischer?

(A) At a concert hall
(B) In a conference room
(C) In a storage facility
(D) At an electronics store

**165.** At 10:13 A.M., why does Mr. Navarro most likely say, "That's awful"?

(A) A machine is not working.
(B) A speaker will arrive late.
(C) A staff member is too busy.
(D) A meeting has been postponed.

**166.** What is implied about Ms. Min?

(A) She takes initiative.
(B) She is Mr. Navarro's supervisor.
(C) She designed a training program.
(D) She is a new employee.

**167.** What will Mr. Navarro most likely do next?

(A) Join Ms. Fischer and Ms. Min
(B) Call another branch
(C) Speak to a manager
(D) Purchase an item

**Questions 168-171** refer to the following e-mail.

| From | Martha Riva <mriva@employprospects.com> |
|---|---|
| To | Samantha Price <sprice@tmail.com> |
| Date | March 17 |
| Subject | Next step |

Dear Samantha,

Thank you for sending me your résumé and college transcript. I have added your information to Employ Prospects' database.

We have found several short-term positions that match your qualifications and experience. These include two administrative positions, an office assistant position in a law firm, and a front-desk position in a dental office. In addition, we have a permanent, full-time position available. This job will start as a three-month internship, but afterwards will lead to a permanent position as a production assistant in a broadcasting company. As you have a degree in Media and Communications, this would be an ideal match for you. However, your résumé states that you currently live in Stella Falls, which is quite far from the broadcasting company's office in Baltimore. Please let me know if you are willing to make the commute. The other openings are located within your area, but we can offer you more opportunities if you are flexible with long distances.

Before contacting any employer, we require two references from you. They must be professional references from either your former employers or university professors. Please email me their names and phone numbers by tomorrow. Once you have done this, we will set up an interview between you and one of our professional recruiting consultants. Please contact my office to schedule a convenient time.

Sincerely,

Martha Riva
Employ Prospects

**168.** What is the purpose of the e-mail?

(A) To confirm a reservation
(B) To request further information
(C) To announce an interview result
(D) To give driving directions

**169.** What is indicated about Ms. Price?

(A) She works for Employ Prospects.
(B) She has sent some documents to Ms. Riva.
(C) She is an experienced producer.
(D) She recently received her degree.

**170.** What is true about the front-desk position?

(A) It has a flexible work schedule.
(B) It is for a law firm.
(C) It is a permanent position.
(D) It is located near Stella Falls.

**171.** What has Ms. Riva NOT asked Ms. Price to do?

(A) Complete and return a form
(B) Confirm her willingness to travel
(C) Provide references
(D) Arrange a meeting

*GO ON TO THE NEXT PAGE*

**Questions 172-175** refer to the following schedule of events.

---

### Mexico City Global Marketing Convention
### November 15-18 ★ Necaxa Business Center ★ Mexico City, Mexico

**Program of Events**
**Monday, November 15**

**Search Engine Toolkit**
7:45 A.M. to 8:30 A.M. Lecture Hall C

Elizabeth Lee, columnist for *Marketing Today*, is here to talk about industry changes, answer questions, and promote her new book, *Search Engine Toolkit*.

**Web Design Introduction**
8:45 A.M. to 9:30 A.M. Anahuac Pavilion

Web designers Mary Ellen Torres and Rick Garcia guide participants through several easy, hands-on lessons on creating effective Web pages.

**Online Advertising Seminar**
9:45 A.M. to 10:30 A.M. Jacaranda Theater

Marketing to clients on the internet.
Presenters: Jose Hernandez, i-Promote's Advertising Director, and Susan Karre, Manager of Social Media Campaigns for MarketTrue. Study materials for the session will be on sale by the entrance to the theater on the day of the seminar.

**Consumers in the 21st Century**
10:45 A.M. to 11:30 A.M. Conference Room 403

Panelists Roy Sinor and Bernard Diaz lead a discussion on what current patterns tell us about future marketing trends.
• Accommodations near the business center can be booked though our Web site, www.gmconf.mx. Meals are available at the center's food court or at any of the many nearby restaurants.
• A one-day ticket valid for these or any other convention events can be purchased for 1,100 pesos online or in-person.
• To ensure you have a seat, please show up early as no reservations can be made ahead of time. Please be aware that while photos are permitted, video and audio recordings of any kind are prohibited.

**172.** What is suggested about the opening day of the Mexico City Global Marketing Convention?

(A) Attendance is anticipated to be lower on that day.
(B) Ms. Lee will discuss ideas for a new book.
(C) No events are scheduled in the afternoon.
(D) It has been planned by a marketing publication.

**173.** Where will marketing convention attendees be able to participate in interactive activities?

(A) In Lecture Hall C
(B) In the Anahuac Pavilion
(C) In the Jacaranda Theater
(D) In Conference Room 403

**174.** What is mentioned about the seminar's study materials?

(A) They should be ordered on the last day.
(B) They must be requested from the speaker.
(C) They can be bought at the venue.
(D) They are included in the ticket price.

**175.** What are marketing convention attendees encouraged to do?

(A) Contact organizers with questions
(B) Take a shuttle to the business center
(C) Arrive early for the events
(D) Take photos after a session ends

*GO ON TO THE NEXT PAGE*

**Questions 176-180** refer to the following schedule and letter.

**One-A Corporation**

Morning Seminar at Rosedale Community Center
8:30 A.M. to 12:15 P.M., Friday, 30 June

**Schedule**

**8:15 A.M.** One-A staff arrive to check in and receive name tags

**8:30 A.M. Session:** My First Year as a Manager in the Accounting Department

**9:15 A.M. Session:** How to Manage Customer Support Employees That Need Assistance

**10:00 A.M. Session:** Inspiring Sales Staff for Top Performance

**10:30 A.M.** Meet and greet with the speakers; refreshments

**11:00 A.M. Session:** Taking a Career in IT Management to the Next Level

**11:30 A.M.** Closing address

---

14 July

Mr. David Sheppard
Clay Enterprises
88 Sidney Street
Cambridge CB2 3ND
UK

Dear Mr. Sheppard,

You may remember that we met two weeks ago during the seminar I attended with my colleagues from One-A. The sessions that you and your co-presenters gave were informative and helpful. I appreciated Ella Larsson's discussion on supervising customer support employees and Andrew Giano's talk on how to motivate team members to produce better results.

Your session was particularly interesting, however, as I will soon take on an executive role at my company. Listening to your experience on managing a large team of specialists, I learned a lot about a path I hope to follow. I am hoping that you could share more information about the techniques and resources that you have found effective in your role as Chief Technology Officer. I would be very grateful of any guidance you could provide that would help me realize my future goals.

I sincerely thank you for your time and feedback. I look forward to speaking with you again soon, at a time convenient for you.

Sincerely,

*Lisa Takeda*

Lisa Takeda

**176.** Why was the seminar organized?

(A) To invite employees to volunteer at a community center
(B) To teach staff management skills
(C) To encourage workers to obtain a marketing degree
(D) To train new personnel on security policies

**177.** In what department does Mr. Sheppard most likely work?

(A) Accounting
(B) Marketing
(C) Customer Service
(D) Information Technology

**178.** When did Mr. Giano most likely give his presentation?

(A) At 8:30 A.M.
(B) At 9:15 A.M.
(C) At 10:00 A.M.
(D) At 11:00 A.M.

**179.** In the letter, the word "realize" in paragraph 2, line 6, is closest in meaning to

(A) earn
(B) appreciate
(C) distinguish
(D) achieve

**180.** What did Ms. Takeda do in her letter to Mr. Sheppard?

(A) Requested a recommendation letter
(B) Thanked him for his input
(C) Made changes to an agenda
(D) Asked for a new contract

GO ON TO THE NEXT PAGE

**Questions 181-185** refer to the following e-mails.

From: victoriaf@brightpecan.com
To: all-employees@brightpecan.com
Date: January 27
Subject: System upgrade

Hello all,

We will be upgrading the systems on all office computers on Friday, January 31. Every company-owned machine will be updated. In particular, members of the Personnel, Accounting, and Customer Support Divisions should make sure they are ready for this, as the work might adversely affect some of the programs they are currently using.

It is very important that you save and make backups of all your important files, since we will be rebooting the computers once the upgrade is done. Users with software that runs processes continuously are cautioned that the upgrade might accidentally delete some files. So we strongly suggest that routine tasks on the date of the changeover be performed ahead of time or postponed. Any employee out of the office on vacation or business on Friday will need to make sure that their files are safely backed up before then.

Victoria Fleury

| From | mjarvi@brightpecan.com |
|------|------------------------|
| To | klao@brightpecan.com |
| Date | January 28 |
| Subject | Payments |

Ms. Lao,

This e-mail is in regard to a potential issue processing employee paychecks. Currently, my computer program is set up to transmit that information to the bank on Friday afternoon. However, considering Ms. Fleury's e-mail yesterday, the pay date for this month may need to be adjusted to accommodate the change. I will be participating in a seminar on Accounting Regulations tomorrow and Thursday. I could perform the process this afternoon, but that means we may need to postpone payments to some of our suppliers until next week. Or we could push payday forward to next Monday, February 3. That may be unacceptable for some employees, especially if they have payments to make on Saturday, February 1. I will need your permission one way or the other, and will then take the appropriate course of action.

Sincerely,
Martin Jarvi

**181.** What is the purpose of the first e-mail?

(A) To prepare staff for potential software issues
(B) To describe the process of installing a new program
(C) To request that advance notice be given for business trips
(D) To give a possible resolution to a payment problem

**182.** In what division does Ms. Fleury most likely work?

(A) Information Technology
(B) Accounting
(C) Personnel
(D) Customer Support

**183.** Why most likely does Mr. Jarvi need to reschedule a task?

(A) His computer is broken.
(B) A project deadline has changed.
(C) He wants to avoid losing data.
(D) He has not paid his credit card bill.

**184.** According to Mr. Jarvi, what is a possible date for the task to be rescheduled?

(A) January 27
(B) January 28
(C) January 31
(D) February 1

**185.** What is Mr. Jarvi planning to do on January 29?

(A) Deposit some extra paychecks
(B) Go on a holiday
(C) Meet with a supervisor
(D) Participate in a professional meeting

*GO ON TO THE NEXT PAGE*

Questions 186-190 refer to the following advertisement, form, and letter.

## Transform Your Restaurant into a Successful Business

Does your restaurant offer high-quality food and service, but still struggle to turn a profit? Join the Restaurant Management Resource Association (RMRA) and get comprehensive training on monitoring and managing the financial side of your business! The bottom line is that the professional help is a must in this age. We have helped restaurant owners all over the country achieve their financial goals for over a decade. Here is a brief summary of what the RMRA offers.

**Access to Informative Resources** – An extensive collection of articles, reviews, and reports written by industry experts that focus on helping restaurant proprietors achieve sustained profitability. These resources are updated each week to provide our members with the most up-to-date information.

**Customized Templates** – A wide selection of free downloadable forms, worksheets, and report templates that can be modified to meet your business' specific requirements.

**Connect with the Community** – Join the RMRA Network, our online discussion forum, and share insights and ideas with thousands of network members who know the challenges and demands of the industry.

**Specialized Lectures** – Participate in various online courses covering strategies ranging from controlling food costs and pricing menus to managing overall expenses.
Note: This feature is only available with a gold membership.

Get access to the RMRA now with a one-time registration fee of $80 plus a membership fee of $100 (basic) or $150 (gold) per year.

## RMRA Inductee Information

First Name: Gary
Last Name: Hansen
Name of Business: Hansen's Pizzeria
Telephone Number: 206-318-4336
Street: 18744 Garden Ln.
City: Seattle
State: Washington
Postal Code: 98102
Email Address: ghansen@hansenpizzeria.com
Create Username: ghansen99
Create Password: *******
Verify Password: *******
Choose Membership Type: [√] Basic  [ ] Gold

The RMRA promises to provide the skills and knowledge necessary to attain long-term financial success. If your business' finances have not improved after one year as an RMRA member, we will reimburse half of your RMRA membership fee.
Note: This feature is only available with a gold membership.

Gary Hansen
Hansen's Pizzeria
18744 Garden Lane
Seattle, WA 98102

Dear Mr. Hansen,

We are sorry to hear that your business has not taken off, even after enrolling in our service. Unfortunately, we cannot issue you a refund.

Our policy clearly states that the refund is only available for gold members. And as you have enrolled in basic service, you do not qualify for the refund. However, what I can do for you is provide you with six more months of our service, free of charge. Please let me know if you are interested.

Best regards,

Benjamin Kim
Manager of Customer Service at RMRA

**186.** In the advertisement, the word "sustained" in paragraph 2, line 3, is closest in meaning to

(A) credited
(B) supported
(C) consistent
(D) saved

**187.** What is suggested about Mr. Hansen?

(A) He is not interested in taking online classes.
(B) He plans on expanding his business to another city.
(C) He recently renovated his store.
(D) He has replied to a letter from Mr. Kim before.

**188.** How much did Mr. Hansen pay for his RMRA membership?

(A) $100
(B) $150
(C) $180
(D) $230

**189.** When does the RMRA provide a refund?

(A) When businesses receive a damaged product
(B) When a lecture is canceled
(C) When a client is unhappy with the quality of a lecture
(D) When a service fails to create a positive outcome

**190.** What does Mr. Kim offer to do?

(A) Track a delivery
(B) Extend a service
(C) Mail a product catalog
(D) Review an order

*GO ON TO THE NEXT PAGE*

**Questions 191-195** refer to the following article, letter, and e-mail.

## Safety Audits to Increase

SAN DIEGO [FEBRUARY 27] – The city council has passed new regulations related to safety audits for all schools. Effective right away, private schools must be audited bimonthly rather than once a quarter, and public schools must be audited monthly rather than once a year when school is in session. Audits will cover emergency preparedness and security procedures. Council member Dean Yoo, who was elected last year, is responsible for creating the Be Alert initiative. "Ensuring the well-being of our children is important to all of us," said Mr. Yoo. The city will contact school administrators directly to explain the updated rules and to schedule audits. The public can contact Ben Michaels of the Department of Public Safety at (858) 555-9823.

---

March 21

Carolyn Kilday
Xavier Preparatory School

Dear Ms. Kilday,

Private schools will be audited more often due to updated city regulations. A check of our office records indicates that your school's most recent safety audit was passed on November 10. It is now overdue under the new rules. We have scheduled an auditor to arrive at your institution on March 28 at 9 A.M. Should you need to change this appointment for any reason, we request that you contact Mr. Ben Michaels of the Department of Public Safety either by e-mail at b.michaels@sandiego-dps.gov or by calling (858) 555-9823.

Yvonne Grimm
Department of Public Safety

To: Ben Michaels <b.michaels@sandiego-dps.gov>
From: Carolyn Kilday <c.kilday@xavierprep.edu>
Date: March 23
Subject: Safety audit

Dear Mr. Michaels,

This is in regard to a letter I received alerting me to a pending safety audit here at Xavier Preparatory School. This needs to be delayed. The school has purchased new smoke detectors to replace older ones that have become defective with age. The installation specialist responsible for the upgrades has said that this will take approximately five days to complete, and an additional day to fully test. I would like to reschedule the audit for the week following the one that was originally scheduled. I look forward to hearing back from you.

Sincerely,

Carolyn Kilday
Headmaster, Xavier Preparatory School

**191.** Who is Mr. Yoo?

(A) A local journalist
(B) A school administrator
(C) A repair technician
(D) A town official

**192.** How often will Xavier Preparatory School be inspected in the future?

(A) Every month
(B) Every other month
(C) Once a quarter
(D) Once a year

**193.** In the letter, the word "check" in paragraph 1, line 1, is closest in meaning to

(A) mark
(B) control
(C) review
(D) stop

**194.** Why did Ms. Kilday send the e-mail?

(A) To file a complaint about a new regulation
(B) To postpone a city employee's visit
(C) To confirm a service appointment
(D) To request an invoice for a renovation project

**195.** What is implied about Xavier Preparatory School's smoke detectors?

(A) They were purchased at an affordable rate.
(B) They began malfunctioning after November 10.
(C) They are in the wrong locations.
(D) They were installed by Ms. Kilday.

*GO ON TO THE NEXT PAGE*

**Questions 196-200** refer to the following e-mails and quote.

---

From:      Lawrence McGill <lmcgill@createadate.com>
To:          Wendy Song <wsong@minnesota.edu>
Date:      Thursday, June 2
Subject:   Venue quote
Attachment:  quote.rtf

---

Dear Ms. Song,

I appreciated your call in regard to the Minnesota State Educators Awards Brunch here in Minneapolis. I have included the details for a variety of venues that suit your needs.

As per your request, an Italian restaurant has been included. While we have never hosted an event there, it comes strongly recommended by a colleague.

To lock in the rates quoted, your full payment must be submitted by Friday, June 10. I look forward to working further with you in preparation for your event.

Regards,
Lawrence McGill

---

## Quotes for Dining Venues

Client: Minnesota State Educators
Guest count: 36
Meal type: Brunch buffet
Set date: August 8

| Restaurant | Cuisine | Extra Features | Price per Guest* | Total Cost |
|---|---|---|---|---|
| Riverbend | Mexican | Live music entertainment available on request | $25 | $900 |
| Gemelli Bistro | Italian | Courtyard area available | $30 | $1080 |
| Wishing Tree | Vietnamese | Personalized menus available for catering | $35 | $1260 |
| Chez Neuf | Cajun | 3-minute walk to nearest subway stop | $40 | $1440 |
| Oyster Platter | Seafood | Seating for groups of up to 50 | $45 | $1620 |

*Prices are all-inclusive, parking off-site, however, may incur additional fees.

| From | Wendy Song <wsong@minnesota.edu> |
|------|----------------------------------|
| To | Lawrence McGill <lmcgill@createadate.com> |
| Date | Tuesday, June 7 |
| Subject | Deposit |

Dear Mr. McGill,

I appreciate all the work you've done on the brunch arrangements. The full payment has been made through your online payment system. The option to have musical entertainment was tempting, but the highest priority for our members is a venue with access to public transportation.

Since the event location has been chosen, what I need now is a recommendation for a shop from which to order the award plaques. I would also like to present a brief slideshow during the event, but let's discuss that when we get together on June 23. Additionally, at that meeting, I will require your assistance in finalizing the design of the invitations and selecting a print shop.

Sincerely,
Wendy Song

**196.** What is indicated about Mr. McGill?

(A) He is a restaurant critic.
(B) He owns a catering company.
(C) He works near an Italian restaurant.
(D) He is planning a meal.

**197.** What restaurant did Mr. McGill include based on Ms. Song's request?

(A) Riverbend
(B) Gemelli Bistro
(C) Wishing Tree
(D) Chez Neuf

**198.** What is suggested about Wishing Tree?

(A) It is the cheapest option available.
(B) It provides outdoor seating.
(C) Changes can be made to its menu.
(D) Parking is complimentary in the evening.

**199.** How much did Ms. Song most likely pay?

(A) $1080
(B) $1260
(C) $1440
(D) $1620

**200.** According to the second e-mail, what will Ms. Song do next?

(A) Mail some invitations
(B) Order award plaques
(C) Rehearse a presentation
(D) Book a meeting room

*GO ON TO THE NEXT PAGE*

# READING TEST

In the Reading test, you will read a variety of texts and answer several different types of reading comprehension questions. The entire Reading test will last 75 minutes. There are three parts, and directions are given for each part. You are encouraged to answer as many questions as possible within the time allowed.

You must mark your answers on the separate answer sheet. Do not write your answers in the test book.

## PART 5

**Directions:** A word or phrase is missing in each of the sentences below. Four answer choices are given below each sentence. Select the best answer to complete the sentence. Then mark the letter (A), (B), (C), or (D) on your answer sheet.

**101.** The ability to speak multiple languages is a crucial skill in today's rapidly ------- global economy.

(A) evolver
(B) evolve
(C) evolving
(D) evolves

**102.** All of the speakers will have finished their talks at the seminar ------- we arrive at the conference center.

(A) in a similar way
(B) only when
(C) by the time
(D) as early as

**103.** At Nemo International, the maximum ------- for shipping containers is 30 metric tons.

(A) weighing
(B) weight
(C) weigh
(D) weighted

**104.** While Ms. Lim is on vacation, please contact Mr. Moreau regarding any ------- matters that occur.

(A) urgent
(B) correct
(C) substitute
(D) deleted

**105.** The trainers at Nine Muses Academy helped Carolyn McMurphy improve ------- singing voice noticeably.

(A) hers
(B) herself
(C) she
(D) her

**106.** Due to seasonal demand, processing orders may take a day ------- than usual.

(A) longer
(B) longest
(C) length
(D) long

**107.** When sending blueprints to a company client, keep such documents ------- by using this courier service.

(A) securely
(B) securing
(C) secure
(D) security

**108.** CPS Motors asserts that its newest electric car runs quieter and more ------- than any other vehicle on the market.

(A) currently
(B) mainly
(C) abruptly
(D) efficiently

**109.** Despite the distributor's ------- that the shipment would be located, Ms. Park is thinking about ending their contract.

(A) assuredly
(B) assurance
(C) assure
(D) assured

**110.** A ------- briefcase is an essential item for sales representatives who travel frequently to visit clients.

(A) vigorous
(B) comparable
(C) meticulous
(D) durable

**111.** Gryphon Security will reply within one day to all customer complaints ------- through the company Web site.

(A) filed
(B) file
(C) files
(D) filing

**112.** Mr. Ramirez carefully measured the dimensions of the office ------- determining how many desks could fit in the room.

(A) but also
(B) before
(C) in fact
(D) instead

**113.** Both Mr. Mason's credit history and the amount ------- on his mortgage will be factors in approving his request for refinancing.

(A) occupied
(B) rented
(C) involved
(D) owed

**114.** Industry ------- stipulate that all employees must wear appropriate protective gear while on the factory floor.

(A) expenditures
(B) topics
(C) opinions
(D) regulations

**115.** The security deposit for the rental car will be returned ------- the vehicle is inspected upon being returned.

(A) only
(B) once
(C) neither
(D) although

**116.** To guarantee fairness, Mr. Palmer will ------- choose an employee to use the parking spot in front of the building.

(A) greatly
(B) randomly
(C) entirely
(D) proportionately

**117.** Matsuda Kitchen Appliances ------- as a leader in the Asian market.

(A) were to continue being seen
(B) will continue seeing
(C) to continue to see
(D) continues to be seen

**118.** Starting June 6, Jean Renault will ------- all questions regarding current projects at Alterman Laboratories.

(A) dedicate
(B) comply
(C) reply
(D) handle

**119.** Mr. Nguyen is a ------- team member with an impressive ability to design attractive advertisements.

(A) resourced
(B) resourceful
(C) resourcefully
(D) resourcefulness

**120.** Computer programming is among the highest-paying ------- in the South Asian region.

(A) devices
(B) industries
(C) sources
(D) situations

*GO ON TO THE NEXT PAGE*

**121.** The shuttle buses will not be running while routine maintenance ------- place.

(A) has taken
(B) taking
(C) is taking
(D) took

**122.** The historian has verified that this piece is a ------- Renaissance painting from the 1400s.

(A) genuine
(B) descriptive
(C) correct
(D) temporary

**123.** The Vice President is satisfied with how smooth the ------- of the two departments has been after restructuring.

(A) consolidates
(B) consolidate
(C) consolidation
(D) consolidated

**124.** The critically-acclaimed documentary *Deep Deception* advocates awareness ------- environmental issues related to water and energy conservation.

(A) at
(B) of
(C) by
(D) to

**125.** Kimduk Tech was ------- purchased for approximately $400 million.

(A) reporting
(B) reportedly
(C) reports
(D) reporter

**126.** The quarterly schedule for the R&D Department lists six ------- to be accomplished over the next three months.

(A) competitors
(B) objectives
(C) conclusions
(D) clients

**127.** -------, management allows employees to wear casual clothing in the office for a special occasion.

(A) Once in a while
(B) At this point
(C) By this time
(D) In a moment

**128.** The full title of the manual is *Revised Regulations for Laboratory Experiments*, but it is usually ------- as *The Regulations*.

(A) assembled
(B) referred to
(C) expanded on
(D) compared

**129.** Even though most restaurants in the area offer catering services, ------- provide the extensive list of menu items that we do.

(A) any
(B) all
(C) neither
(D) few

**130.** Adding more flight routes would probably have a ------- impact on travel bookings.

(A) substantial
(B) multiple
(C) biggest
(D) cooperative

# PART 6

**Directions:** Read the texts that follow. A word, phrase, or sentence is missing in parts of each text. Four answer choices for each question are given below the text. Select the best answer to complete the text. Then mark the letter (A), (B), (C), or (D) on your answer sheet.

**Questions 131-134** refer to the following e-mail.

From: service@campersdepot.co.uk
To: hendricks1577@mugremail.co.uk
Date: April 22
Subject: Re: Campers Depot Login Information

Dear Valued Customer,

This message was sent because you ------- a password reset for your Campers' Depot
**131.**
account. Accordingly, we have updated your account, and you have been issued a

temporary password: I23bon18. Keep in mind that it will be ------- until midnight on
**132.**
April 23. Before that, use the password to log in to the members-only section on our

Web site. To finalize the reset procedure, enter the necessary information -------
**133.**
prompted.

We at Campers' Depot are committed to protecting your personal information. -------.
**134.**

Best regards,

Campers' Depot Online Services

**131.** (A) would request
(B) requesting
(C) requested
(D) request

**132.** (A) secured
(B) accessible
(C) open
(D) valid

**133.** (A) from
(B) over
(C) when
(D) upon

**134.** (A) Customers who register for our online service will receive 10 percent off their purchases in the first year.
(B) You will find a number of upgrades to the members-only section of our Web site.
(C) If you were not the one to initiate the reset process, please call Tech Support right away.
(D) We offer top-quality camping supplies and safety equipment for all of your outdoor adventures.

*GO ON TO THE NEXT PAGE*

**Questions 135-138** refer to the following advertisement.

---

**Now Accepting Tenants**

Campus Towers Apartment Complex is hosting its annual Pool Party and Open House event on July 15-16. This comfortable lifestyle can be -------! Our apartments -------
**135.** **136.**
convenient access to Glenfield University's campus. You'll love our fully-furnished rooms, with state-of-the-art kitchens. Every renter also has access to our fitness center and reading room. -------, you might not want to stay home too often! Campus Towers
**137.**
Apartment Complex is right in the heart of the city, and you have various dining and entertainment options, right outside your door.

Our rental consultants are available seven days a week, from 9 A.M. to 6 P.M. -------.
**138.**
Give us a call to arrange a tour of our units now!

Karl Niemann (858) 555-5512

---

**135.** (A) most
(B) theirs
(C) yours
(D) mine

**136.** (A) offer
(B) offering
(C) have offered
(D) offered

**137.** (A) Likewise
(B) Accordingly
(C) Apparently
(D) However

**138.** (A) After-hours appointments can be scheduled with prior notice.
(B) We will extend these hours during the summer season.
(C) We are considering hiring more maintenance workers for this project.
(D) Several commercial units will be available for rent next month.

**Questions 139-142** refer to the following comment card.

---

I am very happy with the Ekmekci 500. It bakes delicious food quickly and evenly. And it's much ------- than a conventional oven. It is able to cook a pizza in just three
**139.**
minutes. The Ekmekci 500 features a variety of helpful functions that are simple to
------- . For instance, you can bake up to three different items at one time, just by
**140.**
pushing a few buttons on top of the machine. ------- . Better yet, the ingenious space-
**141.**
saving design makes it easy to store ------- use.
**142.**

---

**139.** (A) cheaper
(B) faster
(C) stronger
(D) neater

**140.** (A) operate
(B) copy
(C) extend
(D) install

**141.** (A) I bake desserts almost every day now.
(B) A special sensor prevents overcooked or burned food.
(C) I did not find it easier to cook with this device.
(D) The Ekmekci Company also makes special bread-making appliances.

**142.** (A) after
(B) while
(C) once
(D) with

GO ON TO THE NEXT PAGE

**Questions 143-146** refer to the following article.

The number of businesses in the Rancho Penasquitos district has risen dramatically in the last year. Results from a recent survey show that the number ------- 20 percent—
**143.**
more than four times the rate of adjacent neighborhoods. The area currently lacks office space to accommodate this growth. As a -------, proposals have been accepted to
**144.**
build three new business parks. -------. At the moment, Rancho Penasquitos only has
**145.**
one—the North County Office Complex. The new business parks will create a -------
**146.**
1,500 offices.

**143.** (A) climbs
(B) is climbing
(C) climbed
(D) will climb

**144.** (A) promotion
(B) result
(C) requirement
(D) condition

**145.** (A) Local companies have requested several additional large conference facilities.
(B) It is important to ensure that all safety and environmental regulations have been followed.
(C) Surveys will be conducted regularly to ensure that local business owners are satisfied.
(D) The necessary permits have already been acquired to begin construction.

**146.** (A) preliminary
(B) temporary
(C) further
(D) disposable

## PART 7

**Directions:** In this part you will read a selection of texts, such as magazine and newspaper articles, e-mails, and instant messages. Each text or set of texts is followed by several questions. Select the best answer for each question and mark the letter (A), (B), (C) or (D) on your answer sheet.

**Questions 147-148** refer to the following letter.

September 30

Dear Mr. Moser,

Congratulations! Your Travel Rewards account has accumulated enough points for a free plane ticket. Instructions on how to use these points along with a special code to use during booking are included with this letter. Also included is a schedule of flights on participating airlines. This offer is valid until December 31.

Account holders get a free flight for every 3,000 points earned. Whenever you make a purchase at a Travel Rewards agency, you accumulate points.

Keep track of your points by logging on to your account at www.travelrewards.co.nz.

Regards,

Travel Rewards
Enclosures

**147.** What did Mr. Moser receive?

(A) A list of flight times
(B) A rewards card
(C) A meal ticket
(D) A voucher for travel accessories

**148.** What can Mr. Moser do online?

(A) Renew an account subscription
(B) Submit feedback on a Web site
(C) Find a Travel Rewards location near his neighborhood
(D) Check the number of points he has accumulated

GO ON TO THE NEXT PAGE

**Questions 149-150** refer to the following text message chain.

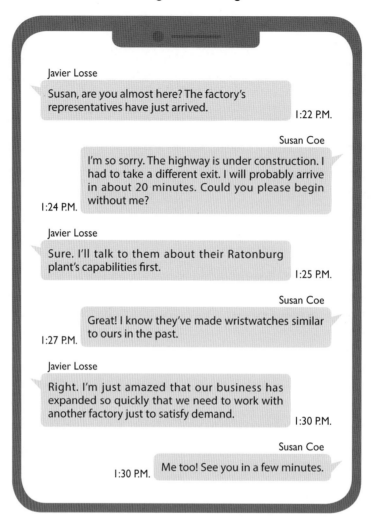

Javier Losse

Susan, are you almost here? The factory's representatives have just arrived.

1:22 P.M.

Susan Coe

I'm so sorry. The highway is under construction. I had to take a different exit. I will probably arrive in about 20 minutes. Could you please begin without me?

1:24 P.M.

Javier Losse

Sure. I'll talk to them about their Ratonburg plant's capabilities first.

1:25 P.M.

Susan Coe

Great! I know they've made wristwatches similar to ours in the past.

1:27 P.M.

Javier Losse

Right. I'm just amazed that our business has expanded so quickly that we need to work with another factory just to satisfy demand.

1:30 P.M.

Susan Coe

Me too! See you in a few minutes.

1:30 P.M.

**149.** What does Ms. Coe want Mr. Losse to do?

(A) Distribute product samples
(B) Meet some company representatives
(C) Finalize a manufacturing contract
(D) Postpone an appointment

**150.** At 1:30 P.M., what does Ms. Coe mean when she writes, "Me too"?

(A) She has traveled to Ratonburg before.
(B) She is also impressed by the expansion of the business.
(C) She thinks a factory should be renovated.
(D) She believes a highway exit will reopen in 20 minutes.

Questions 151-152 refer to the following invitation.

---

## Tess University Hospital

204 Burlington Road
Dublin 4C6 9FD

13 July

Dr. Yoshino Fujioka
403 Orchard Street
Dublin 22G 6NM

Dear Dr. Fujioka,

I would like to cordially invite you to join us in celebrating Dr. Wayne Bradley's 30 years of service at the Tess University Hospital. On top of the quality care he has provided for his patients, Dr. Bradley has put in a significant amount of effort to raise funds for Improved Living, a local charity foundation that promotes health awareness.

As the founder of the charity, Dr. Bradley will be a member of the board after his retirement. We hope that you can attend the banquet we will be holding in his honor at the Beauford Hotel. The banquet is scheduled to take place on 10 September at 6:00 P.M.in the hotel's Grand Ballroom. Please email my assistant Jessica Steele at jsteele@tessunihospital.ie by 30 August to confirm your attendance.

All the best,

*Katie Hawkins*

Katie Hawkins
Director, Tess University Hospital

---

**151.** What type of event is being held?

(A) A corporate anniversary
(B) A retirement dinner
(C) A hospital opening
(D) A charity event

**152.** What are recipients of the invitation recommended to do?

(A) Reply by a specific date
(B) Arrive 30 minutes early
(C) Book a room at a hotel
(D) Make a financial donation

GO ON TO THE NEXT PAGE ━━━━▶

**Questions 153-154** refer to the following e-mail.

**From:** Karl Boucheron
**To:** Susie Bao
**Date:** 29 October
**Subject:** Request

Hello Susie,

My teaching schedule has a few changes that I'd like you to make to the online class listings. Not enough students signed up for my Monday afternoon class, so it has been closed. However, I'm busy this week teaching four other classes, so let's reserve that time for office hours.

Also, Laura Howard had to cancel her presentation at the Omaha Education Conference next month (November 18 – 20), and I agreed to take her place. I will need a flight to Omaha on November 17, ideally leaving after 8:00 P.M., and a return ticket in the afternoon of November 20. If you have questions, just call me.

Karl

**153.** Why did Mr. Boucheron send the e-mail?

(A) To request information about a class
(B) To organize a faculty party
(C) To arrange a pick-up service
(D) To update a Web site

**154.** What is Ms. Bao asked to do?

(A) Reserve a conference room
(B) Arrange a trip
(C) Make an office appointment
(D) Email Ms. Howard

**Questions 155-157** refer to the following information.

Thank you for your purchase of the Speedspin, the most powerful portable air purifier on the market. In order to ensure lasting performance, clean the filter daily with a damp cloth and warm water. Once a week, disassemble the machine and wipe all surfaces with sanitizing fluid, as shown in the owner's guide. Also, note that the filter should be replaced every year.

The Speedspin is powered by a nickel-cadmium battery, which will last for several years. The battery will automatically charge when the machine is plugged in; it is not necessary to turn the machine off to recharge the battery. Please only use the connector cable that came with this product. Use of other cables can damage the machine. Check our Web site at http://www.speedspin.co.uk to learn more.

Speedspin: Fresh air follows!

**155.** Where most likely is this information located?

(A) In a product box
(B) In an appliance catalog
(C) In a newspaper advertisement
(D) In a community newsletter

**156.** What is stated about the Speedspin?

(A) It should be cleaned yearly.
(B) It includes a warranty
(C) It is made of eco-friendly materials.
(D) It can be taken apart.

**157.** What is indicated about the battery?

(A) It is heavy.
(B) It is durable.
(C) It is compact.
(D) It is affordable.

TEST 6

GO ON TO THE NEXT PAGE

| From: | Cecilia Johnson <c.johnson@caicorp.co.uk> |
|---|---|
| To: | Hannah Wall <h.wall@caicorp.co.uk> |
| Date: | December 9 |
| Subject: | Notification |
| Attachment: | Logistics info |

Dear Ms. Wall,

From all of us at Caicorp, I am pleased to congratulate you on your promotion to Senior Manager. The London branch is the main hub for all IT-related support, making it one of the most important facilities in the Caicorp international network.

On January 3, at 8 A.M., you will start your training with Mitch Lee from the Personnel Department. At that time, Mr. Lee will provide information about department policies, future development plans, and the specifics of your position. Also, as we are currently updating our security system, you'll have to check in at the facilities office. Therefore, please aim to get here by at least 7:50 A.M.

Attached is a document containing details about relocating from Dublin. It explains how to order supplies and get your company laptop and phone set up. If I can provide any additional assistance before January 3, please call or send me an e-mail.

Sincerely,

Cecilia Johnson
Human Resources
Caicorp Head Office

**158.** Why did Ms. Johnson contact Ms. Wall?

(A) To confirm some travel arrangements
(B) To discuss information related to a new role
(C) To ask about a lost ID card
(D) To announce an upcoming business merger

**159.** What is suggested about Caicorp?

(A) It will hire more IT employees.
(B) It has recently updated its network.
(C) It will move its headquarters to London.
(D) It has more than one office.

**160.** What is Ms. Wall instructed to do?

(A) Sign an apartment lease
(B) Meet Mr. Lee at a security gate
(C) Purchase supplies for a department
(D) Arrive early for a training session

**Questions 161-164** refer to the newspaper article.

## \<UPSTATE NEW YORK SUCCESS STORY\>

February 16 - Thanks to the success of his first restaurant, The Greek Tower, restaurateur George Pappas will expand his operation into different parts of the state. "I've been to many other cities in the state," Pappas explains, "and I have found some wonderful locations for my restaurant. —[1]—. It also helps when people already have a good opinion of my menu."

—[2]—. His first store opened 15 years ago and has been serving the Utica area successfully ever since. With two restaurants planned for the Albany and Genesee areas, Mr. Pappas will have his hands full. "I want our new restaurants to have the same atmosphere of the original one. Many of my customers are like family, and that is what I want to establish at my new restaurants. Family and good Greek food."

Mr. Pappas started off doing all the cooking himself. —[3]—. These days, he spends most of his time promoting and managing his restaurant to ensure the quality is consistent and his customers feel at home. "You know my mother would always tell me, 'If you feed a person well, he will be your friend for a lifetime.' I instill that same attitude into all of our cooking staff. We want to feed people well and have many lifetime friends who come back to enjoy the food and hospitality."

The Greek Tower was voted Utica's best restaurant, and Mr. Pappas hopes to earn the same title in Albany and Genesee. —[4]—. He plans on spending most of his time at the Albany and Genesee locations until they are strong enough to stand on their own. He will have his younger brother manage the Albany restaurant while his cousin will do the same at the Genesee location.

Both restaurants are scheduled to open in six months. The new locations will offer the same menu as the original location and will also feature a few new dishes. "I think the new places will give me a chance to experiment with recipes while still providing the favorites that have made The Greek Tower so popular."

Sabrina Lowenstein

**161.** What is the purpose of the article?

(A) To describe an entrepreneur's new businesses
(B) To discuss a planned merger between companies
(C) To provide information about a new culinary school
(D) To summarize the performance of a new business

**162.** The word "earn" in paragraph 4, line 2, is closest in meaning to

(A) lose
(B) increase
(C) praise
(D) acquire

**163.** What is indicated about Mr. Pappas' brother?

(A) He took cooking lessons 15 years ago.
(B) He will manage one of the restaurants.
(C) He will help renovate the restaurants.
(D) He borrowed money from a bank.

**164.** In which of the positions marked [1], [2], [3], and [4] does the following sentence best belong?

"He was never formally taught but learned how to cook from his mother and grandmother."

(A) [1]
(B) [2]
(C) [3]
(D) [4]

*GO ON TO THE NEXT PAGE*

# Dashy Corporate Providers

**1881 N. 17th Avenue • Las Vegas 89101**

**www.dashycorproviders.com 702-555-6374**

We are here to help get your company settled into its new space, hassle-free. We do this through specialized planning that takes into account your specific requirements. These are just a few of the services we provide.

- Office relocation: packing, shipping, and unpacking services
- Short- and long-term storage options
- Special handling of fragile items: custom packing and climate-controlled storage
- Secure disposal of unwanted company property
- Cleanup of old and new office spaces

Complimentary evaluation: A specialist will come to your workplace to survey your business' space and logistics needs, and provide you with an estimate for the services you require within 24 hours. After that, we can begin as soon as you're ready. This first visit is free of charge, and there is no further obligation should you choose not to proceed. To make an appointment, send an e-mail to info@dashycorproviders.com.

Trend-setting business practices: Dashy Corporate Providers combines outstanding service with responsible practices. From our reusable packing materials to electric transport systems, we are committed to having minimal environmental impact while offering the same competitive rates as our rivals.

To learn more about our company and its services, call 702-555-6374 or visit www.dashycorproviders.com.

**165.** What type of business is Dashy?

(A) A cleaning company
(B) A packaging factory
(C) An office supply store
(D) A moving service

**166.** How can potential customers receive a cost estimate?

(A) By contacting Customer Support
(B) By visiting Dashy's Web site
(C) By filling out a form
(D) By scheduling a visit from Dashy

**167.** How do Dashy's services differ from those of its rivals?

(A) They are more affordable.
(B) They are specialized for small businesses.
(C) They are backed by a security guarantee.
(D) They are better for the environment.

**Questions 168-171** refer to the following online chat discussion.

---

**Ella Iverson [10:03 A.M.]**
Hello. I'd like to hear any concerns your department members have about the office relocation to Overland Corporate Park that was announced at June's meeting.

**Jirou Mazuka [10:04 A.M.]**
It came as a surprise to everyone. But my staff seems excited about the move.

**Mishka Petrov [10:05 A.M.]**
A couple of employees are wondering how much of the current equipment will be brought over. When will more information be available?

**Hannah Lim [10:07 A.M.]**
Most of the employees here are asking me how this will affect their schedules. But at this point, I have no idea what to tell them.

**Ella Iverson [10:10 A.M.]**
Everything is still being worked out. The executive team will have more to share within the month. I'll give you the complete details during our management conference in July.

**Mishka Petrov [10:11 A.M.]**
I heard a rumor that the new place is going to have open-plan seating, with no individual offices. Is that true?

**Ella Iverson [10:13 A.M.]**
I suppose it's possible. At the start of August, the logistics team will plan where each department will be located and how to position the work stations to make the best use of the new space.

---

**168.** Why did Ms. Iverson write to the department heads?

(A) To explain a new procedure
(B) To receive staff input
(C) To provide policy details
(D) To give a finalized moving date

**169.** At 10:10 A.M., what does Ms. Iverson most likely mean when she writes, "Everything is still being worked out"?

(A) Decisions will soon be made.
(B) A floor plan needs to be revised.
(C) The building's construction is ongoing.
(D) Projects are being reassigned.

**170.** When will the department heads receive an update?

(A) In June
(B) In July
(C) In August
(D) In September

**171.** What is the logistics team expected to do?

(A) Manage employee schedules
(B) Order new equipment
(C) Maintain incoming deliveries
(D) Design an office layout

GO ON TO THE NEXT PAGE

# Custom Carrots?

[January 22] — Carrots have been a key cooking ingredient for many years. —[1]—. Geographically widespread locations including Turkey, South Africa, the U.S., and Russia export millions of pounds of the vegetable. Recent agricultural innovations have allowed farmers to increase the harvesting season to 11 months while also making carrots larger, crunchier, and more colorful.

—[2]—. The way they taste, however, is a quality that has not really been given sufficient attention. That bothers American researcher Sebastian Kang, who thinks that today's larger, more uniformly-shaped carrots would have disappointed consumers just a few decades ago. "When I was a kid, we all ate carrots that tasted much better than anything available in markets these days," he said.

—[3]—. Every modification that produced a new carrot variety resulted in slightly less-flavorful vegetables, Mr. Kang explained, which is why consumers failed to notice much of a difference from year to year. The result is that many simply do not remember the mild, sweet flavor that originally made us like carrots so much.

Getting that lost taste back into carrots, while maintaining enhanced qualities such as texture and appearance, is Mr. Kang's primary goal. —[4]—. "But I think most consumers are fine with smaller vegetables, if the flavor is superior," he adds. Mr. Kang and his colleagues are confident that the desired qualities can be brought out through standard breeding methods, and their initial results have been promising.

**172.** What aspect of the carrots is the focus of the article?

(A) Their weight
(B) Their flavor
(C) Their color
(D) Their texture

**173.** How has the production of carrots changed?

(A) Carrots are all harvested the same way.
(B) Carrots can be harvested year-round.
(C) Carrots are now grown using less water.
(D) Carrots can now be grown in laboratories.

**174.** What is suggested about Mr. Kang?

(A) He has been doing plant-breeding experiments.
(B) He was recognized for his innovative vegetarian dishes.
(C) He was raised in a farming community.
(D) He has done research in several countries.

**175.** In which of the positions marked [1], [2], [3], and [4] does the following sentence best belong?

"The change didn't happen all at once."

(A) [1]
(B) [2]
(C) [3]
(D) [4]

*GO ON TO THE NEXT PAGE*

## Australia Vacation Homes

| |
|---|

**• Property 6735: Greenfield**

- Cozy 2-bedroom condo

- Minimum stay 2 nights

Click here more details

**• Property 2500: Kanwal**

- Stay 4 nights straight
and get a complimentary 5th night stay

- Perfect for those who need to get away
and enjoy a relaxing vacation

- Lake view

Click here more details

**• Property 3038: Melbourne**

- 3-bedroom apartment

- Close to downtown and great for those
who enjoy the bustling city life

Click here more details

**• Property 8220: Hamilton Island**

- A private beach $1,000 per week179

Click here more details

| To | Lorraine Caluso <lcaluso@auvacationrentals.co.au> |
|---|---|
| From | Whitney Johnson <wjohnson@bermaninc.co.au> |
| Date | June 25 |
| Subject | Re: Vacation Plans |

Hello Lorraine,

You helped arrange my family's accommodation for our summer vacation in Melbourne last year, and I was pleased with the rental home and your level of customer service. That being said, I was not fond of the surrounding area. The hectic city life was too much for me. This time, I want to stay in a place that's more relaxing, which has at least three bedrooms with lake or beach access. I cannot afford to spend more than $750-800 for one week. The one that seems most appealing to me is Property 2500. Could you let me know what the dates of availability are for this? It seems to be the most suitable for my needs.

I hope to hear from you soon.

Sincerely,

Whitney Johnson

**176.** What property offers a free night's stay?

    (A) Property 6735
    (B) Property 2500
    (C) Property 3038
    (D) Property 8220

**177.** Why did Ms. Johnson send the e-mail?

    (A) To confirm a payment
    (B) To ask for instructions
    (C) To change a reservation
    (D) To request information

**178.** What aspect of her previous vacation did Ms. Johnson find unsatisfactory?

    (A) The pace of life in the region nearby
    (B) The distance between the rental property and her home
    (C) The customer service provided by a worker
    (D) The condition of the place where she stayed

**179.** Why is Property 8220 probably unsuitable for Ms. Johnson?

    (A) She would prefer to rent a condo.
    (B) She does not enjoy the beach.
    (C) She is looking for something less expensive.
    (D) She does not need more than two bedrooms.

**180.** What location is Ms. Johnson interested in?

    (A) Greenfield
    (B) Kanwal
    (C) Melbourne
    (D) Hamilton Island

*GO ON TO THE NEXT PAGE*

**Questions 181-185** refer to the following schedule and e-mail.

# Council on International Relief Aid (CIRA)

### "The Role of Social Media in Aid Work"
### Sienna College of Bern, June 5-8

◆ **Proposed Itinerary for June 5, Monday**

| | |
|---|---|
| 7:00 A.M. to 8:30 A.M. | Convention Participants Sign in |
| 8:45 A.M. to 9:00 A.M. | **Welcoming Address:**<br><br>Ella Paula, Convention President |
| 9:00 A.M. to 9:30 A.M. | **Keynote Speech:**<br><br>Luca Borer, CIRA Director |
| 9:45 A.M. to 11:00 A.M. | **Get the Audience You Need:**<br><br>Martin Caspari, e-Hoy Marketing Research Institute, Spain |
| 11:10 A.M. to 12:05 P.M. | **A Look at Online Fundraising by Charities:**<br><br>speaker: to be announced, European Fundraising Association, France |
| 12:05 P.M. to 1:30 P.M. | **Lunch:** Laurel Dining Hall |
| 1:40 P.M. to 2:45 P.M. | **Securing Visibility with Sponsorships:**<br><br>Marko Litija, Virusno Studios, Slovenia |
| 3:00 P.M. to 4:15 P.M. | **Presentation title pending:**<br><br>speaker: to be announced, Brighton Association of Emergency Care Professionals, UK |
| 4:20 P.M. to 5:30 P.M. | **Likes: Boost Your Page Views:**<br><br>Miraile Wasson, NetMetrix, Inc., USA |

| To | Ella Paula <epaula@aidfirst.org> |
|---|---|
| From | Luca Borer <lborer@cira.or.it> |
| Date | April 11 |
| Subject | RE: Proposed Monday Itinerary |

Good morning Ella,

Based on your feedback from last Thursday's online discussion, I filled the spaces that were still available on Monday's proposed itinerary. Anja Lehner in France is preparing her talk about online fundraising as they are organized by charities in her country. I also called a contact in Brighton who told me that Dr. Michael Robinson would be delighted to represent his local medical community.

I'm sorry to report that Marko Litija has withdrawn from the convention. His colleague, Sara Kos, will take his place and send us her presentation topic soon.

By the way, my train from Vienna arrives at 5:40 A.M. on Monday. I bought that ticket so that I would have plenty of time to get ready for that morning's speech.

Sincerely,
Luca Borer

**181.** What is indicated about Mr. Borer?

(A) He will work at the information booth.
(B) He will deliver a speech after lunch.
(C) He recently took over CIRA.
(D) He will present on the first day of the convention.

**182.** When will an expert on marketing research be presenting?

(A) At 9:00 A.M.
(B) At 9:45 A.M.
(C) At 1:40 P.M.
(D) At 4:20 P.M.

**183.** In the e-mail, in paragraph 1, line 1, the word "spaces" is closest in meaning to

(A) openings
(B) locations
(C) distances
(D) capacities

**184.** Which session will have to be canceled?

(A) Get the Audience You Need
(B) A Look at Online Fundraising by Charities
(C) Securing Visibility with Sponsorships
(D) Likes: Boost Your Page Views

**185.** According to the e-mail, what information is Mr. Borer waiting to receive?

(A) The biography of a speaker
(B) The topic of a talk
(C) The convention schedule for Tuesday
(D) The telephone number of Mr. Robinson

GO ON TO THE NEXT PAGE

**Norfolk Convention Center Rental Contract**

262 Maplestone Ave.
Norfolk, VA 23504

**Conditions**

This contract is valid for one week, from June 4 to June 11, at the rate of $3,500 per day, to be fully paid on the final day. A penalty of $700 per day will be charged for late payment. Early termination of the lease will result in a $350 penalty. Electricity, water, and concessions are provided free of charge. Meals are not provided and must be negotiated with area businesses. Optional insurance is available for $500 per day. The convention center can accommodate up to 800 vehicles. Additional parking is available in the Norfolk Baseball Stadium's parking area right down the street.

**Obligations**

On April 12, a security deposit of $2,000 was received and will be returned within 15 days of completion of payment. Norfolk Convention Center staff will inspect the facilities both before and after the event is held. Maintenance required before the event will be addressed by the Facility Management. The security deposit will provide for any damage done to the property after the term of the lease.

---

**Norfolk Convention Center Facilities Inspection Form**

**Inspector:** Alan Flint
**Date:** May 31

**Inspector Notes:**
The loading docks, convention hall, and concessions area are in excellent condition. In need of some repairs is the carpet in the front lobby. In addition, the East Wing heating unit needs to be fixed. Norfolk Convention Center maintenance staff will complete this work by June 2.

| | |
|---|---|
| Andrea Lamont | Nasef Ahmed |
| Norfolk Facilities Management | Company Representative, Nexo, Inc. |

| From: | alamont@nccenter.com |
|---|---|
| To: | nasefa@nexo.com |
| Date: | June 10 |
| Subject: | Deposit |
| Attachment: | inspection_form |

Dear Ms. Lamont,

My company, Nexo, Inc., held an event at the Norfolk Convention Center this week and received a part of the security deposit back. I am writing in regard to the $900 deduction made. While we expected to pay a $350 fine, the $550 charge is unacceptable. The invoice lists the charge as carpeting replacement, however the carpet was damaged before our event was held (please refer to the attached document). You stated that the carpet would be replaced by your maintenance staff, however there was not enough time to do the work before our event began. Please refund the $550 charge, accordingly.

Sincerely,

Nasef Ahmed

**186.** What is indicated in the rental contract?

(A) The convention center offers a free shuttle service.
(B) The renter must arrange for meals separately.
(C) The convention center is undergoing electrical repairs.
(D) The renter is allowed to revise the contract terms at any time.

**187.** What is true about the Norfolk Convention Center?

(A) It has a private dining area.
(B) It offers technical support for presenters.
(C) It is building an additional exhibition hall.
(D) It is close to a sports venue.

**188.** In the rental contract, the phrase "provide for" in paragraph 2, line 4, is closest in meaning to

(A) contribute
(B) offer
(C) cover
(D) arrange

**189.** Why must Nexo pay a $350 fine?

(A) It did not decide to purchase insurance.
(B) It used a different parking area.
(C) It canceled its lease early.
(D) It made a payment late.

**190.** What argument does Mr. Ahmed make?

(A) The carpet was delivered late.
(B) The venue was not heated properly.
(C) The damage in the lobby was not Nexo's fault.
(D) The heating unit did not have to be fixed.

GO ON TO THE NEXT PAGE

**Questions 191-195** refer to the following Web page, list, and article.

http://www.localpages.org

**COMING UP THIS MONTH**

Summer Craze Surf Contest
Location: Capi Beach, Fiji
Dates: July 20-21
Amateurs and professionals welcome!
Contact: Laura van Dijk <lvd@wavesurfer.com>

The yearly Summer Craze Surf Contest draws top surfers, their sponsors, and talented amateurs from all over the world. They hope to make a name for themselves, as well as win cash prizes. Every year, attendance has reached nearly 8,000 visitors, making it the single biggest visitor event on any of Fiji's islands. Capi Beach, one of the most renowned surf spots in the world, frequently gets 8-meter waves. In addition to the surfing contest, sponsors have booths with games and activities for all ages set up along the beach. There is no admission fee, but be sure to bring $7 for parking.

## The Winners of the Summer Craze Surf Contest

**International Category**

| Place | Country | Name | Sponsor |
|-------|---------|------|---------|
| 1st | Brazil | Silvio De Souza | Cambera |
| 2nd | Japan | Kanoa Arai | Zelus |
| 3rd | USA | Simon Cole | Nika |
| 4th | Australia | Guy Jacobs | Alala |
| 5th | France | Mathieu Defay | Phonoi |

## Surf's Up at Capi!
By Frank Ganilau

This year's Summer Craze Surf Contest marked a great start to the tourist season. In part due to the unusually good weather, the event attracted easily twice as many spectators as usual.

Globally recognized surfers and amateurs alike faced the challenge of Capi's famously rough surfing conditions throughout the two-day competition. Riding on waves that approached 10 meters, they made surfing through the water look fun and easy. Several truly enormous waves worried lifeguards, but competitors conquered the mountains of water with no injuries reported.

Silvio De Souza took first place, beating fan-favorite Kanoa Arai, who had won the last three Summer Craze Surf Contests. Although it was a close call right to the end, Arai fell during the last wave of the evening. While there were a number of spectacular performances, I was particularly amazed by that of Australia's representative this year. I have watched surfers all over North and South America, but I have never seen moves quite like those.

Visitors had a great time, too. In addition to meeting famous surfers, there was plenty of food, shopping, and activities. As the sun set, everyone left knowing a good summer lay ahead.

**191.** What is mentioned about the surfers?

(A) All of them are professional surfers.
(B) They have met Ms. van Dijk previously.
(C) They come from different countries.
(D) Some of them will bring their own equipment.

**192.** In the article, the word "faced" in paragraph 2, line 2, is closest in meaning to

(A) confronted
(B) looked
(C) crossed
(D) risked

**193.** What is indicated about this year's event?

(A) It took place on Capi Beach for the first time.
(B) It had more than 8,000 spectators.
(C) It charged a $7 admission fee.
(D) It was shorter than last years' event.

**194.** What is indicated about Mr. Arai?

(A) He lives in Australia.
(B) He almost fell during the competition.
(C) He taught surfing lessons.
(D) He has competed in the contest before.

**195.** Which athlete impressed Mr. Ganilau the most?

(A) Silvio De Souza
(B) Kanoa Arai
(C) Simon Cole
(D) Guy Jacobs

GO ON TO THE NEXT PAGE

**Questions 196-200** refer to the following e-mails and text message.

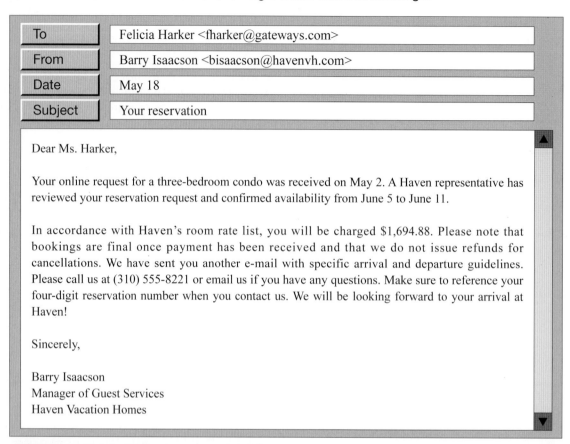

| To | Felicia Harker <fharker@gateways.com> |
|---|---|
| From | Barry Isaacson <bisaacson@havenvh.com> |
| Date | May 18 |
| Subject | Your reservation |

Dear Ms. Harker,

Your online request for a three-bedroom condo was received on May 2. A Haven representative has reviewed your reservation request and confirmed availability from June 5 to June 11.

In accordance with Haven's room rate list, you will be charged $1,694.88. Please note that bookings are final once payment has been received and that we do not issue refunds for cancellations. We have sent you another e-mail with specific arrival and departure guidelines. Please call us at (310) 555-8221 or email us if you have any questions. Make sure to reference your four-digit reservation number when you contact us. We will be looking forward to your arrival at Haven!

Sincerely,

Barry Isaacson
Manager of Guest Services
Haven Vacation Homes

| To | Barry Isaacson <bisaacson@havenvh.com> |
|---|---|
| From | Felicia Harker <fharker@gateways.com> |
| Date | June 2 |
| Subject | RE: Your reservation |

Dear Mr. Isaacson,

I am writing in regard to my reservation (#4502) at Haven Vacation Homes from June 5 to June 11. You mentioned in your e-mail that you would send additional information to me by the end of May. However, I have not received another e-mail from you yet. As I would like to receive this information before leaving for my vacation, please email it to me as soon as possible. I have tried calling you on several occasions, but the line was busy. If you are not able to contact me, I will visit your office when I arrive at the property.

I hope to hear from you soon.

Sincerely,

Felicia Harker

(562) 555-4839

To: Felicia Harker, 562-555-4839

Sent: June 5, 3:00 P.M.

Hello Felicia,

It's Zack Issacson from Haven Vacation Homes. I'm sending you this message because you aren't picking up your phone. It's one hour past your check-in time, so I wanted to know if you were on your way. Please give me a call back once you get this message. Thank you.

**196.** What is Ms. Harker told to provide when contacting Haven Vacation Homes?

(A) Her room number
(B) Her contact information
(C) Her reservation number
(D) Her credit card information

**197.** In the second e-mail, the word "property" in paragraph 1, line 6, is closest in meaning to

(A) location
(B) communication
(C) possession
(D) characteristic

**198.** What information is NOT included in Mr. Issacson's e-mail?

(A) The policy for cancellations
(B) The directions to a place
(C) The accommodation cost
(D) The reservation dates

**199.** What does Ms. Harker request from Mr. Issacson?

(A) Details about check-in and check-out
(B) Rates for room services
(C) A guide for the local area
(D) A statement of credit card charges

**200.** According to the text message, what is suggested about Ms. Harker?

(A) She was supposed to arrive at 2 P.M.
(B) She wants to upgrade her room.
(C) She has not made a payment.
(D) She will depart on June 12.

GO ON TO THE NEXT PAGE →

TES

# READING TEST

In the Reading test, you will read a variety of texts and answer several different types of reading comprehension questions. The entire Reading test will last 75 minutes. There are three parts, and directions are given for each part. You are encouraged to answer as many questions as possible within the time allowed.

You must mark your answers on the separate answer sheet. Do not write your answers in the test book.

# PART 5

**Directions:** A word or phrase is missing in each of the sentences below. Four answer choices are given below each sentence. Select the best answer to complete the sentence. Then mark the letter (A), (B), (C), or (D) on your answer sheet.

**101.** Pathfinder Vacations is looking for qualified individuals with ------- working overseas.

(A) have experienced
(B) experienced
(C) experience
(D) experiencing

**102.** Having culinary certification ------- a candidate's chances of gaining employment at the New Caledonian Resort.

(A) improves
(B) functions
(C) achieves
(D) finalizes

**103.** Mr. Rader's innovative renovation of Vaduz Fine Arts Museum is -------.

(A) commends
(B) commendable
(C) commend
(D) commending

**104.** Ms. Vanleuven asked to have the sign that was broken ------- the flood fixed.

(A) as well as
(B) much like
(C) containing
(D) during

**105.** Due to security concerns, access to the server room is ------- limited.

(A) strictly
(B) barely
(C) slightly
(D) casually

**106.** All staff members are expected to maintain an appropriate level of ------- when interacting with clients.

(A) professionally
(B) professionalism
(C) professional
(D) profession

**107.** The Director of Human Resources, Ms. Conty, will ------- the applicants into two categories.

(A) offer
(B) separate
(C) consider
(D) advise

**108.** Because dairy products are ------- perishable, they must be kept refrigerated as much as possible while they are in transit.

(A) higher
(B) highest
(C) highly
(D) high

**109.** According to the Accounting Department, ------- profits increase in the next quarter, the company will be forced to close some locations.

(A) unless
(B) instead
(C) but
(D) that

**110.** Over the ------- nine months, the Trent Corporation has focused its resources on constructing additional factories.

(A) lasting
(B) lasted
(C) last
(D) lastly

**111.** The market test results indicate that the Cooler X100 does not ------- regulate the temperature of commercial refrigeration systems.

(A) preciseness
(B) precisely
(C) precision
(D) precise

**112.** Emilia Caporetto accepted a management position from a firm offering a benefits package that ------- her expectations.

(A) took
(B) lost
(C) met
(D) gave

**113.** Vertical Interior was picked to renovate the main lobby given that it can complete the job at a ------- price.

(A) severe
(B) promoted
(C) condensed
(D) reasonable

**114.** Maler Surfacing was late with its estimate ------- many due date postponements.

(A) actually
(B) despite
(C) although
(D) still

**115.** The airport's shuttle service is provided to ------- all of the hotels and resorts on the island.

(A) inside
(B) farther
(C) almost
(D) properly

**116.** The latest consumer survey results show that the ------- of RW's new automobile outweigh its benefits.

(A) compliments
(B) disturbances
(C) accomplishments
(D) shortcomings

**117.** During the annual event, Dr. Connor ------- an award for her contribution in the field of applied science.

(A) praised
(B) accepted
(C) wished
(D) nominated

**118.** During her three decades working at the Shimmer Auto Plant, Ms. O'Driscoll ------- various kinds of machinery on the factory floor.

(A) operate
(B) operating
(C) operated
(D) operation

**119.** Alterations to the reservation cannot be made less than 48 hours ------- arrival time.

(A) rather
(B) prior to
(C) owing to
(D) apart from

**120.** Since offline customers are our main source of income, sales training is ------- for all store employees.

(A) exceptional
(B) liable
(C) mandatory
(D) vague

GO ON TO THE NEXT PAGE

**121.** The IT Department was pleased that Jin Ho Park, ------- experience was quite outstanding, was selected as manager.

(A) where
(B) whose
(C) what
(D) why

**122.** Since Ms. Phan will transfer to the Tokyo branch in April, Mr. Sirivithan has already begun the process of ------- her.

(A) interacting
(B) identifying
(C) advancing
(D) replacing

**123.** By cooperating with companies in various sectors and locations, P.L. Howard Ltd. ------- its market share in Central Asia.

(A) was expanded
(B) to be expanding
(C) has been expanded
(D) will be expanding

**124.** Primer Fashion designed an ------- clothing line that has helped increase product sales.

(A) attentive
(B) assorted
(C) innovative
(D) urgent

**125.** As soon as the Marketing Department received authorization, the director ------- assigning interns.

(A) began
(B) were beginning
(C) begin
(D) has begun

**126.** Please make sure your seminar allows ------- time at the end to take questions from the audience.

(A) sufficient
(B) difficult
(C) accurate
(D) dependable

**127.** Mr. Kimble ------- tried to contact Murata, Inc.'s PR team but was unable to receive a response.

(A) repeating
(B) repeatedly
(C) repeated
(D) repetition

**128.** Ms. Edgerton will receive an award for lifetime ------- in medical research.

(A) achieving
(B) achieves
(C) achievable
(D) achievement

**129.** If market trends persist, Portos Programming may ------- recover fully but may become a leading competitor in the software industry.

(A) in addition
(B) as well
(C) as such
(D) not only

**130.** The cheaper cleanser proved to be an effective ------- to the popular brand.

(A) possibility
(B) alternative
(C) choice
(D) option

# PART 6

**Directions:** Read the texts that follow. A word, phrase, or sentence is missing in parts of each text. Four answer choices for each question are given below the text. Select the best answer to complete the text. Then mark the letter (A), (B), (C), or (D) on your answer sheet.

**Questions 131-134** refer to the following information.

**Quarterly Performance Reviews**

The oral and written review is the last ------- of the employee appraisal process. It is an
            **131.**
official evaluation of work performance over a three-month period. An overall grade is

given based on the criteria decided by the department head. -------. This also helps
                                                              **132.**
------- goals for the following quarter. The quarterly review is never a replacement for
**133.**
regular discussions concerning job performance, which are considered ------- for a
                                                                        **134.**
productive work day.

**131.** (A) version
    (B) condition
    (C) edit
    (D) step

**132.** (A) Lately, a lot of firms have been
    implementing monthly reviews.
    (B) The main reason for the review is to
    provide employees with meaningful
    feedback.
    (C) As per company policy, we will
    always keep employee evaluations
    on file.
    (D) Supervisors are allowed to set their
    department's work hours.

**133.** (A) launch
    (B) attempt
    (C) determine
    (D) appreciate

**134.** (A) necessary
    (B) necessity
    (C) necessarily
    (D) necessitating

*GO ON TO THE NEXT PAGE*

**Questions 135-138** refer to the following letter.

---

February 22

Erica Marsh
Regency Court
1423 E. California Rd.
Fort Wayne, IN 46805

Dear Ms. Marsh,

This letter is regarding my lease agreement for 1822 Clinton Avenue, ------- due to end
                                                               **135.**
on February 28. I wish to ------- a renewal of the contract. ------- new house will not be
                         **136.**                                    **137.**
available by March. For this reason, I hope to stay in my current apartment through
March 31. -------.
        **138.**

If you are free, let's plan on speaking by phone some time tomorrow morning. I'm also
open to meet face-to-face if you prefer.

Best regards,

Derek Lagerman

---

**135.** (A) what will
(B) that being
(C) which is
(D) one of

**136.** (A) request
(B) deny
(C) purchase
(D) invest

**137.** (A) Their
(B) Any
(C) My
(D) Its

**138.** (A) I have nearly finished moving out.
(B) Please advise on what can be
arranged.
(C) I would like to see apartments that
match these requirements.
(D) I am currently living in Fort Wayne.

**Questions 139-142** refer to the following e-mail.

From: renaldpark87@mycos.net
To: info@sleekformalwear.com
Date: April 24
Subject: Invoice number 89827

Hello,

Two months ago, I bought a jacket on Sleek Formal Wear's Web site. To make sure it fit properly, I tried it on as soon as I received my order. -------, when I wore it for the first
                                                                                      **139.**
time this morning, I realized there was a small tear in the inside of the jacket. I am aware that all ------- products should be exchanged or returned within one week and
                    **140.**
that my item does not fall within this stated time frame.

-------. If it ------- out, I do not mind selecting another garment of similar value.
**141.**      **142.**

Please advise me on what to do.

Thank you,

Renald Park

**139.** (A) Otherwise
(B) However
(C) Thus
(D) Furthermore

**140.** (A) defective
(B) false
(C) ill-fitting
(D) confirmed

**141.** (A) I returned the item three weeks after it was delivered.
(B) Please wire the money to the bank account I provided.
(C) Nonetheless, I am hoping that you can make an exception this time.
(D) Fortunately, the application period was extended until next month.

**142.** (A) be selling
(B) has sold
(C) having been sold
(D) will sell

*GO ON TO THE NEXT PAGE*

To: Jan Long <jlong@pwc.co.jp>
From: Robert Ferguson <ferg@gspec.co.jp>
Date: 5 March
Subject: Product issue

Dear Ms. Long,

We are grateful for your recent ------- of a G-spec Slim-X laptop. We are informing all
              **143.**
customers who have recently bought this device from us that a limited number of

models require repair.

In some of our laptops, the touchpad, which acts as a pointing device, occasionally

malfunctions. -------. Please ------- whether yours is one of the affected models by
         **144.**          **145.**
checking the product's serial number, which is located on the bottom of your laptop. If

this code starts with the letters "SXRE," a repair must be performed. We will cover all

expenses related to sending back your Slim-X. Additionally, G-spec will fix ------- free
                                          **146.**
of charge.

143. (A) testimonial
    (B) purchase
    (C) test
    (D) donation

144. (A) This defect will continually interfere
        with the navigation of your computer.
    (B) We are confident that you will enjoy
        the laptop.
    (C) This model is considered one of the
        most reliable of its kind.
    (D) For more information, refer to our
        Frequently Asked Questions page.

145. (A) confirm
    (B) confirmed
    (C) confirmation
    (D) confirms

146. (A) theirs
    (B) mine
    (C) these
    (D) it

# PART 7

**Directions:** In this part you will read a selection of texts, such as magazine and newspaper articles, e-mails, and instant messages. Each text or set of texts is followed by several questions. Select the best answer for each question and mark the letter (A), (B), (C) or (D) on your answer sheet.

**Questions 147-148** refer to the following text message.

Frank Ricci [1:45 P.M.]

Hello, Carol. My conference call with the city council members just ended, and they liked our design proposal for the town garden. Councilmember Jason Hicks requested additional client references, but I don't have those files with me. I am on my way to a worksite, so could you call a delivery service to send a copy of the Sawvale Square portfolio to him? Please include one of our brochures, too. Thank you.

**147.** Where does Mr. Ricci most likely work?

(A) At a government agency
(B) At a post office
(C) At an insurance firm
(D) At a landscaping company

**148.** What is Frank asked to do?

(A) Send some client references
(B) Respond to a message
(C) Create an e-mail list
(D) Schedule an appointment

*GO ON TO THE NEXT PAGE*

**Questions 149-150** refer to the following e-mail.

**From:** Pat Merrick
**To:** Carter Hotel staff
**Date:** 21 February
**Subject:** Notice

Effective March 1, Carter Hotel will only provide full refunds for room cancellations when the request is made at least one week in advance.

We will post this information on our Web site and at the front desk before the end of the week. An e-mail explaining the new rule will also be sent to all currently registered guests. If a guest needs to cancel their stay with less than a week's notice, please ask the appropriate manager for help. We appreciate your cooperation.

Pat Merrick
Carter Hotel General Manager

**149.** What is the purpose of the e-mail?

(A) To announce some staff training
(B) To describe an updated hotel facility
(C) To introduce a new policy
(D) To report on recent sales figures

**150.** According to the e-mail, what will managers do?

(A) Select which workers can make schedule changes
(B) Teach guests how to make online reservations
(C) Decide how to arrange new furniture
(D) Assist guests with specific requests

**Questions 151-152** refer to the following text message chain.

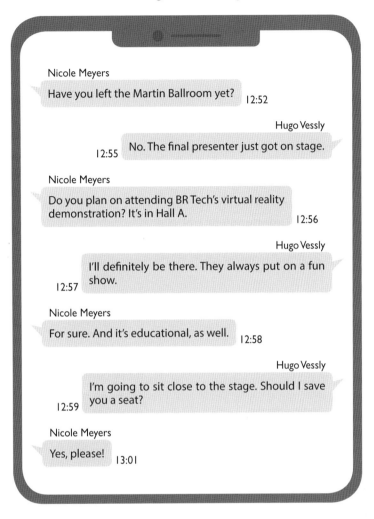

Nicole Meyers

Have you left the Martin Ballroom yet? 12:52

Hugo Vessly

12:55 No. The final presenter just got on stage.

Nicole Meyers

Do you plan on attending BR Tech's virtual reality demonstration? It's in Hall A. 12:56

Hugo Vessly

I'll definitely be there. They always put on a fun show. 12:57

Nicole Meyers

For sure. And it's educational, as well. 12:58

Hugo Vessly

I'm going to sit close to the stage. Should I save you a seat? 12:59

Nicole Meyers

Yes, please! 13:01

TEST 7

**151.** At 12:58, what does Ms. Meyers most likely mean when she writes, "For sure"?

(A) The lecturers in the Martin Ballroom were entertaining.
(B) She agrees with Mr. Vessly's view on BR Tech's demonstrators.
(C) She knows that Mr. Vessly will go to a demonstration.
(D) She plans to have an interview with BR Tech.

**152.** What is most likely true about Mr. Vessly?

(A) He wants Ms. Meyers to give a demonstration.
(B) He is a developer of virtual reality software.
(C) He will be the last speaker in the Martin Ballroom.
(D) He will get to Hall A before Ms. Meyers.

*GO ON TO THE NEXT PAGE*

**Questions 153-154** refer to the following memo.

From: Mark Glover
To: Chuck's Restaurant Employees
Date: July 21
Subject: Requirements

Recently, we have had a high number of requests to work different shifts. Chuck's Restaurant management would like to remind everyone that requests should be made as early as possible and that 12 employees are required for each shift.

Submit a request through the company system at least two weeks in advance to ensure you get your desired shift. Unfortunately, not everyone can be accommodated. In order to maintain our citywide reputation for outstanding service, we need to keep the business fully staffed, and this requires all of your cooperation.

Should you have any questions, please bring them up with your manager.

**153.** What is the purpose of the memo?

(A) To request feedback on new menu options
(B) To highlight an issue with an ordering system
(C) To describe a new process
(D) To remind employees about scheduling work hours

**154.** What should employees do if they have a concern?

(A) Speak to their manager
(B) Email Mr. Glover
(C) Review a handbook
(D) Complete a questionnaire

## Economics Monthly
## Business Bulletin

Soleridge, 20 November – Developer Kenny Ritter has started work on what is going to become the Falcon Central Complex. The building, at 7863 Sears Avenue, used to be the location of the Soleridge Furniture Company. Mr. Ritter's company, the Falcon Investment Corporation, purchased it in June. Construction of the former factory will result in 400 apartments and approximately 8,000 square meters of commercial space.

There will be two stages in the development of the €200 million project. Stage one is estimated to take one and a half years and will have 300 apartments completed. The remaining apartments along with a three-story department store will be constructed during stage two, which will take about seven months. The Falcon Investment Corporation has also recently bought the Leno Building on Lakeview Street. Although development plans for it have not yet been announced, a Falcon Investment spokesperson stated that more information would be released sometime next month.

**155.** What is the main purpose of the article?

(A) To announce the completion of an apartment building
(B) To profile a renowned building developer
(C) To advertise a recently renovated store
(D) To discuss details of a construction project

**156.** What is indicated about the Falcon Central Complex buildings?

(A) It will contain both apartments and retail stores.
(B) It will be completed in seven months.
(C) It is located near a lake.
(D) It is the first building that Mr. Ritter developed.

**157.** What is mentioned about Mr. Ritter's company?

(A) It will relocate next month.
(B) It has purchased more than one property.
(C) Its offices are close to the Soleridge Furniture Company.
(D) It specializes in remodeling old buildings.

GO ON TO THE NEXT PAGE

**Questions 158-161** refer to the following e-mail.

| From | Sabrina San Luciano |
|------|---------------------|
| To | Department supervisors |
| Date | July 5 |
| Subject | Boosting employee productivity |

Greetings supervisors,

—[1]—. In the coming weeks, the personnel team will be holding a series of meetings with the heads of each department to discuss employee work habits and productivity.

Open office workspaces, where employee desks are positioned next to each other, without walls in between, is a design that an increasing number of companies use because it makes it easier for employees to communicate and collaborate with each other on assignments. —[2]—. As the office reconfiguration is set for late December, we are considering whether an open office workspace design would be a better fit for our business. We will make a decision regarding this proposal after reviewing the advantages and disadvantages.

I have written this e-mail to request your input. —[3]—. At this stage, the Personnel Department is still collecting data. Please fill out the open office workspace questionnaire, located on the company's internal Web page. —[4]—. The link is on the right side of your login page.

I appreciate your help. If you have any questions, please send me an e-mail.

Sabrina San Luciano
Personnel Director
Audio Sonic Technologies

**158.** Why was the e-mail written?

(A) To announce a conference schedule
(B) To promote an annual company gathering
(C) To provide notice of a policy change
(D) To request completion of a questionnaire

**159.** What is mentioned as a benefit of open office workspaces?

(A) They allow the company to hire more employees.
(B) They help staff work well together on projects.
(C) They reduce business costs.
(D) They improve air quality in the office.

**160.** What is the company planning to do at the end of the year?

(A) Organize a managers' retreat
(B) Change the design of an office
(C) Launch a Web site
(D) Find a new Personnel Director

**161.** In which of the positions marked [1], [2], [3], and [4] does the following sentence best belong?

"Please keep in mind that we have not yet decided if an open office workspace is right for us."

(A) [1]
(B) [2]
(C) [3]
(D) [4]

**Questions 162-164** refer to the following instructions.

Congratulations on your purchase of the new Estefan Deep Sleep mattress.

To make the best use of your mattress, please follow these simple guidelines.

- In order to keep the mattress clean, always use a mattress cover. Most covers can be washed by machine.

- Never fold the mattress for transport or storage.

- To remove stains, use a water-free upholstery cleaner. If water must be used on the mattress, use it sparingly, as too much water can cause mold to grow. Make sure the mattress is completely dry before using it.

- To avoid wearing out your mattress unevenly, flip the mattress several times a year (so that the topside is facing down and vice versa).

- Replace your mattress every seven to nine years or if it becomes uncomfortable.

- Do not remove the information tag from the mattress. It will serve as identification if you need to make a warranty claim.

**162.** In the instructions, what is suggested as possibly damaging to the mattress?

(A) A non-machine washable cover
(B) Excessive moisture
(C) Using cleaning products
(D) Transporting outdoors

**163.** What are mattress owners told to do regularly?

(A) Iron the mattress
(B) Air out the mattress
(C) Replace the mattress cover
(D) Turn the mattress over

**164.** According to the instructions, why should mattress owners retain the tag?

(A) It is required in order to file a warranty claim.
(B) It provides guidelines on using the product safely.
(C) It describes the type of materials in the mattress.
(D) It contains information about store locations.

GO ON TO THE NEXT PAGE

**Questions 165-168** refer to the following online chat discussion.

---

**Roger Zhu [10:27 A.M.]**
This is Roger over in Human Resources. Ms. Kim and Ms. Ikagami, you're both scheduled to go on the executive retreat next month, correct?

**Laura Kim [10:29 A.M.]**
That's right. We've got flights booked for July 24 at 6:35 P.M. Why?

**Roger Zhu [10:30 A.M.]**
It turns out that Arborita Resort's online system lost our reservations. So, we're going to have to move the retreat to the second week of July.

**April Ikagami [10:32 A.M.]**
Really? I've already paid for my kids to attend summer camp that week. I won't be able to attend if my children are around.

**Roger Zhu [10:33 A.M.]**
Well, that's why I wanted to get in touch — to find out about any special needs you might have. We won't be using Arborita again, of course. So the team is going to be looking for alternative places to hold the retreat.

**Laura Kim [10:35 A.M.]**
April, could you come if they choose a resort with a child care center?

**April Ikagami [10:36 A.M.]**
Well... That should be OK. But I want to read about their services before I give a definite answer.

**Roger Zhu [10:37 A.M.]**
What about you, Ms. Kim? Is there anything you need to make this scheduling change easier?

**Laura Kim [10:39 A.M.]**
Nothing on my end. I'll have my assistant work it out.

**April Ikagami [10:40 A.M.]**
Thanks for letting us know, Mr. Zhu. Please send us brochures of the new place once it's been decided.

**Roger Zhu [10:42 A.M.]**
I will, Ms. Ikagami. Thanks.

---

SEND

**165.** What is the purpose of the discussion?

(A) To apologize for a mistake
(B) To explain a change of schedule
(C) To ask for flight information
(D) To promote an upcoming event

**166.** What is suggested about the executive retreat?

(A) It provides child care services.
(B) It is held once a month.
(C) It takes place on the same week as the summer camp.
(D) It always uses Arborita Resort as its location.

**167.** What does Ms. Ikagami ask Mr. Zhu to do?

(A) Provide information about a venue
(B) Send details about an event calendar
(C) Increase the budget of a project
(D) Explain a payment procedure

**168.** At 10:39 A.M., what does Ms. Kim mean when she writes, "Nothing on my end"?

(A) She did not submit a report yet.
(B) She has not received a document.
(C) She does not need further assistance.
(D) She will not be attending the retreat.

GO ON TO THE NEXT PAGE

**Questions 169-171** refer to the following e-mail.

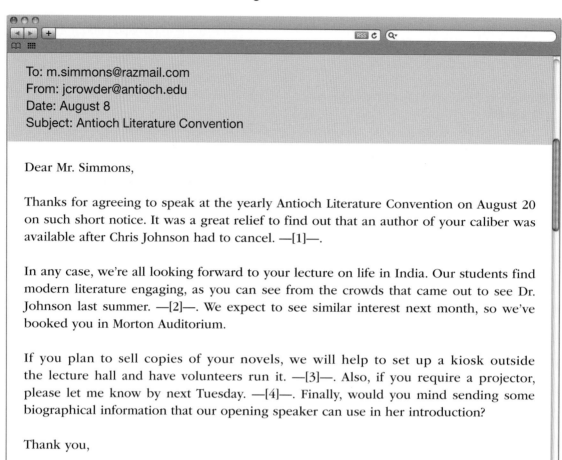

To: m.simmons@razmail.com
From: jcrowder@antioch.edu
Date: August 8
Subject: Antioch Literature Convention

Dear Mr. Simmons,

Thanks for agreeing to speak at the yearly Antioch Literature Convention on August 20 on such short notice. It was a great relief to find out that an author of your caliber was available after Chris Johnson had to cancel. —[1]—.

In any case, we're all looking forward to your lecture on life in India. Our students find modern literature engaging, as you can see from the crowds that came out to see Dr. Johnson last summer. —[2]—. We expect to see similar interest next month, so we've booked you in Morton Auditorium.

If you plan to sell copies of your novels, we will help to set up a kiosk outside the lecture hall and have volunteers run it. —[3]—. Also, if you require a projector, please let me know by next Tuesday. —[4]—. Finally, would you mind sending some biographical information that our opening speaker can use in her introduction?

Thank you,

Jenna Crowder
Event Coordinator

**169.** Why did Ms. Crowder write this e-mail?

(A) To announce the publication of a book
(B) To change the time of a lecture
(C) To confirm Mr. Simmons' participation in an event
(D) To discuss Mr. Simmons' volunteer duties in detail

**170.** What is suggested about Chris Johnson?

(A) He wrote a popular novel about India.
(B) He gave a presentation last year.
(C) He used to work with Mr. Simmons.
(D) He teaches at a university in Antioch.

**171.** In which of the following positions marked [1], [2], [3], and [4] does the following sentence best belong?

"I can have audiovisual equipment set up at your request."

(A) [1]
(B) [2]
(C) [3]
(D) [4]

## Preparing for Your Store's Opening

The first few days of business are a great opportunity to spark interest and gain the attention of potential customers, but you'll need to do considerable planning to make it a success. The following are some important questions to ask yourself before your store's opening:

• What signs or posters will you set up? Decorations are very effective when they showcase a wide range of different products.

• How long will your decorations stay up? If you only put up decorations on the first day, there is a good chance that many customers who work that day won't get to see them.

• What kind of advertising will you use? According to some research, people usually remember what they read better than what they hear. Keep that in mind when debating whether to use print media, TV, or radio advertisements.

• How will you motivate your employees? Your employees play a key role in making customers happy, so consider giving prizes to the best workers.

**172.** For whom is the article intended?

(A) Entrepreneurs who are planning to start a business
(B) Store owners who are planning to expand their operations overseas
(C) Employees who want to take on supervisory roles
(D) Consumers who are looking for new types of products

**173.** The word "gain" in paragraph 1, line 2, is closest in meaning to

(A) build
(B) improve
(C) acquire
(D) grow

**174.** According to the article, what are people less likely to do on days that they work?

(A) Listen to the radio
(B) View job listings
(C) Compare different products
(D) Check out a store

**175.** According to the article, what is a benefit of print media ads?

(A) They are more likely to be read by local residents.
(B) They are cheaper than other forms of advertising.
(C) They are able to provide more information in a single space.
(D) They are forgotten less quickly than other forms of advertising.

GO ON TO THE NEXT PAGE

**Questions 176-180** refer to the following memo and form.

---

## MEMO

Date: May 25
To: Rasta Motors Employees
From: Sarah Clovis, Administrative Department
Subject: GMNS Partnership

As part of the company's employee appreciation program, Rasta Motors has partnered with Global Mobile Network Systems (GMNS) to offer staff members discounted rates on mobile phone service plans. Employees who decide to sign up for a family or individual service plan with GMNS will save 20 percent and 15 percent, respectively, on the first two months of their subscription. In addition, the activation fee will be waived, saving you an extra $25. All subscriptions are for 12 months and will be automatically canceled at the end of this period unless the service is renewed.

Employees who want to take advantage of this deal should call GMNS Customer Support at 914-555-4029. Applications may also be sent electronically at www.gmns.com/promotion. When applying, staff should be ready to provide their employee number and a work email address. Also, a credit card number must be submitted along with a valid form of photo identification such as a driver's license or passport.

---

### GMNS Customer Complaint Form

**Customer Details**

Name: Shay Ryans
Account Number: 85948310
Date: July 30
E-mail Address: sryans@rastamotors.com

**Complaint Details**

In June, I opened a mobile phone account with GMNS after reading about the special deal for Rasta Motors' employees. Based on the promotional material handed out by my company, I do not have to pay an activation fee to begin my service. Also, the GMNS representative that I spoke to on the phone confirmed this when I signed up. Yet, I have been charged an activation fee on my first month's billing statement, dated July 28. Please remove this fee from my bill and mail me an amended version. Just to be sure, the 15 percent discount for the phone charge should still be applied to the updated bill. Thank you.

**176.** Why was the memo issued?

(A) To remind employees not to use company phones for personal calls
(B) To announce a special benefit for employees
(C) To encourage employees to renew their current phone subscription
(D) To notify employees that signing up with GMNS is mandatory

**177.** What is indicated about the activation fee?

(A) It costs $25.
(B) It may be paid in installments.
(C) It will be refunded after one year.
(D) It will be added to the first two bills.

**178.** What is NOT required for the GMNS application?

(A) A promotional code
(B) An employee number
(C) An e-mail address
(D) A credit card number

**179.** What is most likely true about Ms. Ryans?

(A) She applied for an account through Rasta Motor's Web site.
(B) She has used GMNS' services before.
(C) She has subscribed to the individual service plan.
(D) She works in Ms. Clovis' department.

**180.** What does Ms. Ryans request that GMNS do?

(A) Send her a corrected billing statement
(B) Cancel her yearly plan
(C) Provide a discount for two more months
(D) Change the company's renewal policies

*GO ON TO THE NEXT PAGE*

**Questions 181-185 refer** to the following information and form.

## Welcome to the Jeanneret Library of Engineering

The Jeanneret Library of Engineering at Sulgen University is open to students and guests wishing to visit our Public Access areas on the first and second floors, and our Old Archives area, found in the climate-controlled basement. We house texts, films, and photographs, as well as an enormous collection of original building designs and sketches.

**Visitors and students should be aware of the following library rules in place to protect the collections:**

- All guests need to present valid ID and complete the required form to become library members before they are allowed entry.
- Members may freely utilize the contents in the Public Access areas. To ensure that all materials are properly organized, please return items no longer needed to one of the Return areas located throughout the library; members are requested not to shelve items themselves.
- Members found to have caused damage to materials including, but not limited to, markings, scratches, rips, and stains will be fined.
- Two large-format scanners are available on the second floor, by the computer workstations.
- The Jeanneret Library closes at 6:00 P.M. All materials must be returned by 5:45 P.M.

**The Old Archives area requires attention to these extra rules:**

- No personal belongings are permitted in the Old Archives area. Please use the temporary storage service at the library's front desk. Should you need to take notes or make sketches, staff will provide you with pens or pencils.
- Materials must be requested in writing at the Old Archives counter.
- Old Archives' materials may not be taken to other library areas, and only three items may be viewed at one time. Additional items will be held at the counter.
- Old Archives items will be collected at 5:15 P.M. without exception.

Jeanneret Library of Engineering
**Request Form for Old Archives Materials**

Membership Number: 84323-45
Full Name: James Hayes
Date: October 15
Reason for Request: Research

Please enter information into both columns to help our staff locate your materials.

| | Title | Catalog code |
|---|---|---|
| Item 1 | The Comprehensive History of Theo van Thorne's Home Designs | 720.22VF |
| Item 2 | The 1929 Chicago Blueprints of Theo van Thorne | 728JJ |
| Item 3 | The Personal Journal of Theo van Thorne | 720.9AR |
| Item 4 | Urban Engineering Weekly (12/08/1946) | PP325-A |
| Item 5 | | |

**181.** What is mentioned about the Jeanneret Library?

(A) It requires that visitors sign up for a membership.
(B) It provides discounts to local residents.
(C) It has a special section for university students.
(D) It closes early on the weekends.

**182.** According to the rules, what are visitors prohibited from doing?

(A) Reading sensitive documents
(B) Bringing in beverages
(C) Reserving items ahead of time
(D) Reshelving used items

**183.** How can visitors in the Old Archives area record their research?

(A) By having a specialist conduct the recording
(B) By renting a laptop from the library
(C) By asking library staff for writing materials
(D) By using a personal digital camera

**184.** What most likely is the topic of Mr. Hayes' research?

(A) The work of a certain architect
(B) A history of engineering publications
(C) The restoration of old manuscripts
(D) Famous engineering schools in Europe

**185.** What does Mr. Hayes' request for materials suggest?

(A) He will not be able to view all of his requested items at once.
(B) He is an engineering student at Sulgen University.
(C) He will give his items back by 5:45 P.M.
(D) He will need to pay a fee to request additional materials.

TEST 7

GO ON TO THE NEXT PAGE →

**Questions 186-190** refer to the following brochure and e-mails.

## Gerhart Window Frames

Gerhart Window Frames has been supplying building professionals and contractors with all-weather window frames for over 30 years. Listed below are our top-selling products.

**Sunray Super:** Energy saving, long-lasting, and come in over 20 different colors.

**Multiblock Anchor:** Only available in white, rosewood, and black, but most other aspects are similar to that of Sunray Super. However, the frames are thicker, providing extra insulation.

**Sunstopper Plus:** For homes that get a lot of direct sun, these frames are angled to block harsh glare and keep interior temperatures comfortable.

**Cinchfit Extra:** Use for buildings and homes that experience extreme temperatures. Contact a certified professional for installation due to the level of precision required for this product.

For prices and exact specifications, please refer to our catalog. Questions and requests can be emailed to info@gerhartwindowframes.co.uk or call 020-7946-0924.

When choosing window frames, be sure to consider various factors. To find out the dimensions of the frames you need, use our online calculator at www.gerhartwindowframes.co.uk/calc. Just input the height and width of your window.

| | |
|---|---|
| **From:** | m.sheppard@rightbuild.co.uk |
| **To:** | info@gerhartwindowframes.co.uk |
| **Date:** | 7 April |
| **Subject:** | Recent order |

Gerhart Window Frames Customer Service,

I am writing concerning order #55-234A for eggplant purple window frames. My client is concerned that the color of the frames might cause his house to get too hot. I explained that the frames were unlikely to have any effect on the interior temperature, but I would like to hear if this is indeed a problem. The color is a particular favorite of his, and if possible, he would prefer not to change the order.

The last time I ordered from your company, installation videos were available to view on your Web site. I would like to watch those videos again as I have not used this particular product recently. From what I recall, it requires some special care in installation. Could you please send me a link to that page?

Sincerely,
Maria Sheppard

| From | freede@gerhartwindowframes.co.uk |
|------|----------------------------------|
| To | m.sheppard@rightbuild.co.uk |
| Date | 7 April |
| Subject | Re: Recent order |

Dear Ms. Sheppard,

Thank you for contacting Gerhart Window Frames. The frames are made of a material that does not absorb sunlight. Furthermore, based on the address in your order, no other buildings in that area have reported problems with dark colored frames, including ones that are dark blue and charcoal. Should your client wish to revise their order, let me know before the end of the day.

Regarding our Web site, we now refer our customers to the specific manufacturer's home page as they have the latest information about specific frames. We appreciate your business.

Sincerely,
Francis Reede

**186.** According to the brochure, how can customers determine what size frames to purchase?

(A) By consulting a specialist
(B) By using an online service
(C) By ordering product samples
(D) By downloading some graphics

**187.** What aspect of the frames does Ms. Sheppard need more information about?

(A) Their ability to resist humidity
(B) Their tendency to fade quickly
(C) Their thickness compared to similar products
(D) Their likeliness to trap heat

**188.** What type of frames did Ms. Sheppard most likely order for her client?

(A) Sunray Super
(B) Multiblock Anchor
(C) Sunstopper Plus
(D) Cinchfit Extra

**189.** According to Mr. Reede, why would Ms. Sheppard need to contact him again on April 7?

(A) To receive a reimbursement
(B) To request an invoice
(C) To track a delivery
(D) To revise an order

**190.** What is suggested about the installation videos?

(A) Ms. Sheppard accidentally deleted the files.
(B) They are not available on Gerhart Window Frames' Web site.
(C) Gerhart Window Frames will email them to Ms. Sheppard.
(D) They feature local contracting companies.

TEST 7

GO ON TO THE NEXT PAGE

Questions 191-195 refer to the following brochure, review, and e-mail.

## LEARN JOURNALISM IN PARIS

Located in the center of Paris, the Parisian Journalism Institute (PJI) provides a range of courses for students planning to further their academic careers in graduate programs. With field offices of most global media companies nearby, it's a good place to make valuable contacts while studying. Our classes cover audio and video recording, data mining, and of course, writing for features and articles. Our classes also prepare students applying to graduate schools by providing tips on writing personal statements, crafting résumés, and compiling portfolios. Hundreds of our students have gone on to attend prestigious schools worldwide. One way we ensure their success is by employing instructors who are highly respected in the field, like Dylan Andersson, Editor-in-Chief of *International Nightly*, and Bethany Kilpatrick, of *London News Bureau*. To apply, to learn more about our school and courses, or to arrange a consultation with an academic counselor, visit our Web site at www.pji.ed.fr.

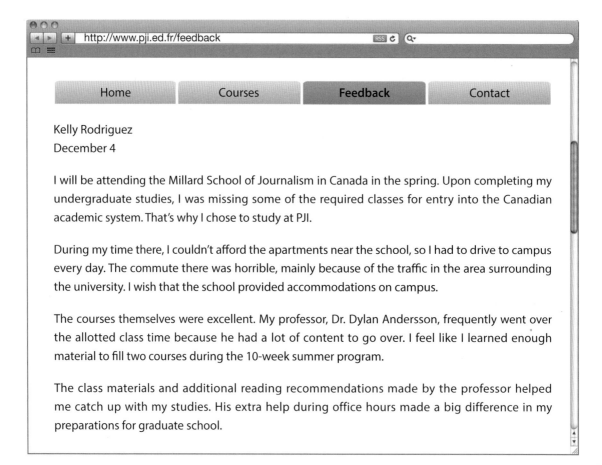

http://www.pji.ed.fr/feedback

| Home | Courses | **Feedback** | Contact |

Kelly Rodriguez
December 4

I will be attending the Millard School of Journalism in Canada in the spring. Upon completing my undergraduate studies, I was missing some of the required classes for entry into the Canadian academic system. That's why I chose to study at PJI.

During my time there, I couldn't afford the apartments near the school, so I had to drive to campus every day. The commute there was horrible, mainly because of the traffic in the area surrounding the university. I wish that the school provided accommodations on campus.

The courses themselves were excellent. My professor, Dr. Dylan Andersson, frequently went over the allotted class time because he had a lot of content to go over. I feel like I learned enough material to fill two courses during the 10-week summer program.

The class materials and additional reading recommendations made by the professor helped me catch up with my studies. His extra help during office hours made a big difference in my preparations for graduate school.

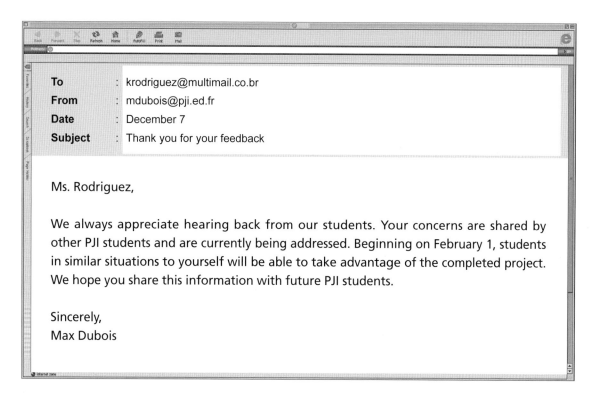

| To | : | krodriguez@multimail.co.br |
|---|---|---|
| From | : | mdubois@pji.ed.fr |
| Date | : | December 7 |
| Subject | : | Thank you for your feedback |

Ms. Rodriguez,

We always appreciate hearing back from our students. Your concerns are shared by other PJI students and are currently being addressed. Beginning on February 1, students in similar situations to yourself will be able to take advantage of the completed project. We hope you share this information with future PJI students.

Sincerely,
Max Dubois

**191.** Who is the brochure intended for?

(A) Potential graduate students
(B) Television producers
(C) Professors looking for a job
(D) Business journalists

**192.** What is indicated about PJI?

(A) It provides university scholarships.
(B) It helps students find employment.
(C) It has a program for interns.
(D) It is in a crowded location.

**193.** What does Ms. Rodriguez mention about her professor?

(A) He required students to engage in many interactive activities.
(B) He was rarely available for office visits.
(C) He took extra time to cover class materials.
(D) He assigned projects on a weekly basis.

**194.** Where does Ms. Rodriguez's instructor work when he is not teaching?

(A) At PJI
(B) At *International Nightly*
(C) At *London News Bureau*
(D) At a Parisian news agency

**195.** How will PJI be addressing Ms. Rodriguez's complaint?

(A) By expanding classroom space
(B) By offering student housing
(C) By increasing public transportation choices
(D) By shortening the lengths of courses

TEST 7

GO ON TO THE NEXT PAGE

**Questions 196-200** refer to the following list of features and Web pages.

SWIRLER 12kg Jet-Stream Washing Machine Model JS-4425

**FEATURES**

- Super-sized basin can take larger loads than standard washing machines, which saves time.
- Stainless steel interior prevents odor and rust buildup.
- A signal lets you know if you have left an item in the machine after the end of a cycle. LED display lights also show the status of your wash cycle.
- New Blue Shift Technology assesses the amount of laundry and sets the proper amount of motion, reducing electricity use.
- A wide range of options for water, temperature, wash cycles, and different kinds of fabric.
- Anti-vibration Technology enables your machine to operate more quietly than the average washing machine, allowing you to wash your clothes at any time.

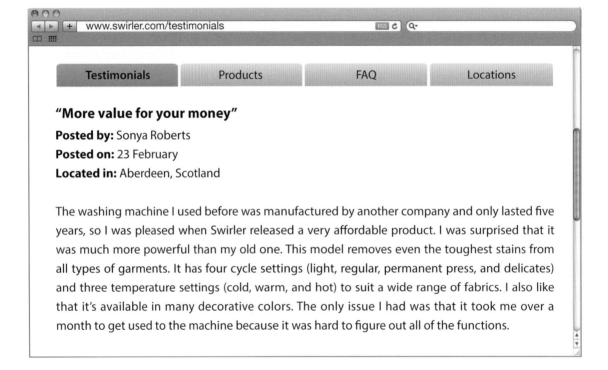

www.swirler.com/testimonials

| Testimonials | Products | FAQ | Locations |

**"More value for your money"**
**Posted by:** Sonya Roberts
**Posted on:** 23 February
**Located in:** Aberdeen, Scotland

The washing machine I used before was manufactured by another company and only lasted five years, so I was pleased when Swirler released a very affordable product. I was surprised that it was much more powerful than my old one. This model removes even the toughest stains from all types of garments. It has four cycle settings (light, regular, permanent press, and delicates) and three temperature settings (cold, warm, and hot) to suit a wide range of fabrics. I also like that it's available in many decorative colors. The only issue I had was that it took me over a month to get used to the machine because it was hard to figure out all of the functions.

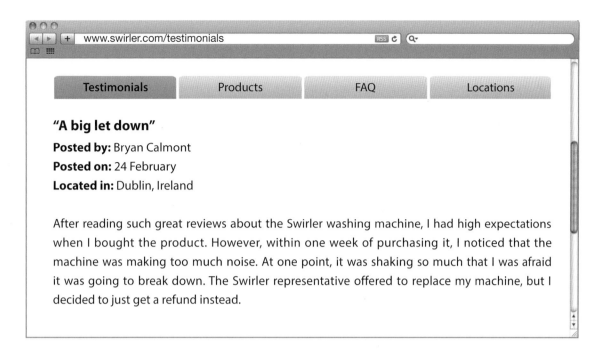

www.swirler.com/testimonials

| Testimonials | Products | FAQ | Locations |

**"A big let down"**

**Posted by:** Bryan Calmont
**Posted on:** 24 February
**Located in:** Dublin, Ireland

After reading such great reviews about the Swirler washing machine, I had high expectations when I bought the product. However, within one week of purchasing it, I noticed that the machine was making too much noise. At one point, it was shaking so much that I was afraid it was going to break down. The Swirler representative offered to replace my machine, but I decided to just get a refund instead.

**196.** Where would the list of features most likely be found?

(A) Printed in a clothing catalog
(B) Shown on the box of a product
(C) Included with an order of fabric
(D) Posted inside a repair shop

**197.** In the first Web page, the word "suit" in paragraph 1, line 5, is closest in meaning to

(A) appeal to
(B) qualify
(C) dress up
(D) accommodate

**198.** What criticism does Ms. Roberts make about the product?

(A) It is complicated.
(B) It is loud.
(C) It is heavy.
(D) It is pricey.

**199.** What feature does Ms. Roberts like that is NOT mentioned in the product description?

(A) Its various settings
(B) Its metal interior
(C) Its large load capacity
(D) Its decorative appearance

**200.** What feature does Mr. Calmont not like about his product?

(A) The Anti-vibration Technology
(B) The Blue Shift Technology
(C) The LED display lights
(D) The alert signal

*GO ON TO THE NEXT PAGE*

TEST 7

# READING TEST

In the Reading test, you will read a variety of texts and answer several different types of reading comprehension questions. The entire Reading test will last 75 minutes. There are three parts, and directions are given for each part. You are encouraged to answer as many questions as possible within the time allowed.

You must mark your answers on the separate answer sheet. Do not write your answers in the test book.

## PART 5

**Directions:** A word or phrase is missing in each of the sentences below. Four answer choices are given below each sentence. Select the best answer to complete the sentence. Then mark the letter (A), (B), (C), or (D) on your answer sheet.

**101.** The customer canceled his order ------- the computer monitor he requested was sold out.

(A) therefore
(B) for instance
(C) despite that
(D) because

**102.** Passengers are advised to keep their luggage tag stubs to prove that claimed suitcases are indeed -------.

(A) them
(B) they
(C) themselves
(D) theirs

**103.** An executive suite has been ------- for the contract negotiations with Cortel Corp next Friday.

(A) notified
(B) reserved
(C) postponed
(D) determined

**104.** The enhanced account management software helps Dewey Financial associates to respond to customer inquiries more -------.

(A) quick
(B) quickly
(C) quicker
(D) quickness

**105.** To ensure ------- with safety standards, random batches of light bulbs are selected for testing before they are packaged.

(A) compliance
(B) cooperation
(C) operation
(D) expiration

**106.** We appreciate you updating us ------- the progress of the landscaping work on our gardens.

(A) without
(B) near
(C) through
(D) regarding

**107.** To attach the insulation to the window frames, ------- small nails spaced about 20 centimeters apart.

(A) use
(B) useful
(C) using
(D) used

**108.** When you are arranging your client meetings, remember to keep your schedule ------- of any conflicts.

(A) freeing
(B) freedom
(C) free
(D) frees

**109.** The Lagos Resort advises booking rooms two months ------- to secure your reservation.

(A) in advance
(B) at last
(C) then
(D) so as

**110.** The yearly corporate picnic is held to give employees an opportunity to meet ------- in other teams.

(A) colleagues
(B) tenants
(C) positions
(D) businesses

**111.** This device allows researchers to get a ------- reading than the previous model.

(A) accurately
(B) more accurate
(C) more accurately
(D) accurate

**112.** All technicians at Gelco Pharmaceuticals ------- to wash their hands before entering the laboratories.

(A) expects
(B) expecting
(C) are expected
(D) to be expecting

**113.** It is just the first week of winter, but the airport ------- had to cancel flights due to a heavy snowstorm.

(A) best
(B) rather
(C) thoroughly
(D) already

**114.** Heber Industries' best-selling crane can lift ------- of up to 10 tons.

(A) loader
(B) loads
(C) load
(D) loaded

**115.** Ms. Kusanagi was ------- retire when she was invited to manage the Security Team at the Asian headquarters.

(A) close to
(B) about to
(C) ahead of
(D) aside from

**116.** Before starting a new project, it is the team manager's ------- to assign work to each project member.

(A) precision
(B) functioning
(C) condition
(D) responsibility

**117.** While the information gathered in this survey will enable us to improve our customer service, your participation is completely -------.

(A) volunteers
(B) voluntary
(C) volunteering
(D) voluntarily

**118.** Various goods and services are provided by the Healthy Living Society, a non-profit organization that ------- a balanced lifestyle.

(A) dispenses
(B) deserves
(C) encourages
(D) expects

**119.** Members of the Trainlink board of directors argued ------- for a high speed line at the last shareholders meeting.

(A) forcefully
(B) routinely
(C) infrequently
(D) lastingly

**120.** Ceylon Corporation's ------- Customer Service personnel provide callers with any kind of assistance they require.

(A) inevitable
(B) continuous
(C) dedicated
(D) established

*GO ON TO THE NEXT PAGE*

**121.** The goal of this portfolio review is to figure out ------- the allocation of Providential Investment's funds matches client objectives.

(A) although
(B) whether
(C) because
(D) either

**122.** Greenville consistently enjoys a 10 percent annual property value -------.

(A) payment
(B) census
(C) statistic
(D) increase

**123.** Ayoub Publications has ------- of the most devoted readerships in Lebanese news media.

(A) one
(B) still
(C) those
(D) instead

**124.** Babylon Real Estate has seen ------- sales over the last three quarters.

(A) complete
(B) refillable
(C) steady
(D) specific

**125.** The Web site created by Ceylon Tech Solutions has been ------- to meet your customers' needs.

(A) customize
(B) customized
(C) customizes
(D) customizing

**126.** Programming on the Educational Broadcasting Network is made ------- thanks to financial support from companies like Broadmoor Investing.

(A) recognized
(B) clear
(C) thoughtful
(D) possible

**127.** Since its first international contract was signed last quarter, the Yutani Corporation has received record-high -------.

(A) earnings
(B) earns
(C) earn
(D) earner

**128.** The popular documentary series, *The Blue World*, ------- a well-known narrator.

(A) realizes
(B) marks
(C) features
(D) applies

**129.** We expect to receive many more online orders next month, so it is crucial that our server be functioning -------.

(A) relying
(B) reliable
(C) relies
(D) reliably

**130.** Dessous la Table's steadfast devotion to quality is consistent ------- its entire menu of authentic French wines and cheeses.

(A) near
(B) between
(C) into
(D) across

# PART 6

**Directions:** Read the texts that follow. A word, phrase, or sentence is missing in parts of each text. Four answer choices for each question are given below the text. Select the best answer to complete the text. Then mark the letter (A), (B), (C), or (D) on your answer sheet.

**Questions 131-134** refer to the following article.

## Airport Forecast

January 22

According to figures from the National Airport Authority, cargo shipments through Ontario Airport have once again increased. -------, this marks the fifth straight year of
**131.**
significant growth. Ontario is a point of transit for a wide array of merchandise, with
------- like clothing, medicine, and construction equipment topping the list. -------.
**132.** **133.**
Because of this, hiring at the airport has also continued. Analysts ------- the increase in
**134.**
cargo as a sign that economic activity will continue to grow in this area.

---

**131.** (A) Even though
(B) However
(C) Still
(D) In fact

**132.** (A) goods
(B) advantages
(C) facilities
(D) costs

**133.** (A) About half of this cargo will be sent overseas.
(B) Deliveries of other products decreased this year.
(C) The airport recently released updated figures.
(D) More staff is required to handle the shipments.

**134.** (A) seeing
(B) see
(C) were seen
(D) sees

GO ON TO THE NEXT PAGE

**Questions 135-138** refer to the following e-mail.

---

To: Danielle Bandy <dbandy@benmail.com>
From: Eric Calhoun <e.calhoun@terryvalechildrenszoo.org>
Date: June 20
Subject: Your membership

Dear Ms. Bandy,

Thank you for your support over the past year. Please remember that your Terryvale Children's Zoo membership ------- on July 31. If you renew now, you will receive a $50
**135.**
gift certificate to our gift shop. This offer is available only ------- June 30. Just mention
**136.**
the code, TCZFAN3, to one of our Customer Service representatives. We appreciate all of our members, and we hope that you will decide to renew and continue to enjoy all the advantages of membership without -------. Also, keep in mind that zoo members
**137.**
will be receiving guest passes to our new exhibit, *the African Safari Trail*. The exhibit will be available to the public on August 15. -------.
**138.**

Warmest regards,

Eric Calhoun
Director of Member Services

---

**135.** (A) should have expired
(B) to be expiring
(C) will expire
(D) has expired

**136.** (A) through
(B) except
(C) including
(D) among

**137.** (A) interruption
(B) interrupt
(C) interrupting
(D) interrupted

**138.** (A) The construction should be completed by the end of the month.
(B) We apologize in advance for any inconvenience this may cause.
(C) Please let us know what type of exhibit you would like us to create in this area.
(D) Our members, however, will be invited to a special preview of it on August 11.

**Questions 139-142** refer to the following information.

---

**Setting Up Appointments at Istanbul Dissiz Hospital**

We at Istanbul Dissiz Hospital make our best effort to meet with patients at their booked times. ------- is possible due to our efficient reservation system. To help us
     **139.**

------- it, make sure to arrive on time for your appointment. Even though we do all we
**140.**

can to stick to the schedule, sudden delays can occur because of unexpected

situations. -------. In these cases, we ask for your -------.
     **141.**                      **142.**

We encourage you to give us a call on the day of your appointment to confirm the

expected wait time.

---

**139.** (A) Here
    (B) Other
    (C) Some
    (D) This

**140.** (A) enter
    (B) consider
    (C) adjust
    (D) maintain

**141.** (A) There are times when our doctors have to perform urgent surgeries.
    (B) It is important to make a note of this in your file.
    (C) You can reschedule your appointment at any time.
    (D) To ensure this does not happen, you should follow your physician's advice carefully.

**142.** (A) preparation
    (B) cooperation
    (C) participation
    (D) anticipation

**Questions 143-146** refer to the following notice.

---

**UBV Financial: Company Vehicle Policy**

Company vehicles are for the ------- use of the Sales Department staff. Members of
**143.**
other departments should use their own vehicles or public transportation. Sales

Department members can each drive a company car a maximum of 200 kilometers a

week without prior approval. Sales staff should obtain their branch manager's

authorization before driving ------- distances.
**144.**

Remember that company vehicles ------- for business activities only. -------. UBV
**145.** **146.**
Financial automobiles can only be driven by employees with a valid driver's license and

proper insurance coverage.

We appreciate your cooperation in this matter.

---

**143.** (A) unique
(B) delicate
(C) exclusive
(D) traditional

**144.** (A) further
(B) those
(C) any
(D) limited

**145.** (A) provides
(B) providing
(C) should provide
(D) are provided

**146.** (A) Currently, only the economy sized
vehicle is available.
(B) Personal use of the vehicle is not
allowed.
(C) This vehicle has recently been
inspected and repaired.
(D) The company plans on upgrading all
of its vehicles.

# PART 7

**Directions:** In this part you will read a selection of texts, such as magazine and newspaper articles, e-mails, and instant messages. Each text or set of texts is followed by several questions. Select the best answer for each question and mark the letter (A), (B), (C) or (D) on your answer sheet.

**Questions 147-148** refer to the following voucher.

## Hyacinth Bistro

**Hyacinth Thank-you Voucher**

To receive a free medium-sized drink of your choice, present this voucher with the order of any soup, pasta, or steak entrée. This voucher may be used during regular business hours, Tuesdays through Sundays (closed Mondays).

**Let us hear from you!**

Check our events board, next to entrance, to see what's going on at Hyacinth! While you're there, fill out a customer questionnaire and give it to any staff member for a chance to win a free dinner.

**147.** What complimentary item can be obtained by using a voucher?

(A) A beverage
(B) A steak
(C) Some soup
(D) Some pasta

**148.** How can a customer win a prize?

(A) By completing a questionnaire
(B) By participating in an event
(C) By visiting the restaurant on a Sunday
(D) By making a reservation on a Monday

*GO ON TO THE NEXT PAGE*

**Questions 149-150** refer to the following e-mail.

To: sjacobs@sjacobsfashion.co.uk
From: orders@fleurdelis.co.fr
Date: November 7
Subject: Purchase #09345A

Dear Mr. Jacobs,

We regret to inform you that the red and pink sunglasses you purchased from our Web site in November (70 pairs in all) are not currently available. Right now, we have no way to complete and ship your order, and therefore, cannot provide you with an exact arrival date. However, we have similar models that we think you might like. One has red and white striped frames, and another has solid purple frames. To make modifications to your order, just log on to our Web site and click on the shopping cart at the top of your screen. Once again, we'd like to apologize for this situation and look forward to earning your continued business.

Sincerely,
Brenda Chang
Customer Support

**149.** What is the purpose of the e-mail?

(A) To explain an issue with a purchase
(B) To announce a change in prices
(C) To check a shipping date
(D) To describe a refund process

**150.** What is Mr. Jacobs asked to do?

(A) Visit a Web site
(B) Call for more details
(C) Pay an additional fee
(D) Update some billing information

**Questions 151-152** refer to the following text message chain.

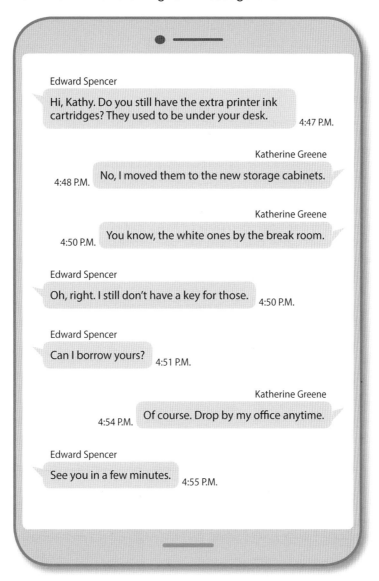

Edward Spencer

Hi, Kathy. Do you still have the extra printer ink cartridges? They used to be under your desk.
4:47 P.M.

Katherine Greene

4:48 P.M.  No, I moved them to the new storage cabinets.

Katherine Greene

4:50 P.M.  You know, the white ones by the break room.

Edward Spencer

Oh, right. I still don't have a key for those.
4:50 P.M.

Edward Spencer

Can I borrow yours?  4:51 P.M.

Katherine Greene

4:54 P.M.  Of course. Drop by my office anytime.

Edward Spencer

See you in a few minutes.  4:55 P.M.

**151.** Why did Mr. Spencer contact Ms. Greene?

(A) To discuss a furniture order
(B) To confirm the location of some supplies
(C) To submit a complaint about a process
(D) To inquire about a meeting room reservation

**152.** At 4:54 P.M., what does Ms. Greene mean when she writes, "Drop by my office anytime"?

(A) She will lend an item to Mr. Spencer.
(B) She encourages Mr. Spencer to use her printer.
(C) She would like Mr. Spencer to bring a document.
(D) She is only available to meet for a limited time.

*GO ON TO THE NEXT PAGE*

February 10
RLA Parts & Supplies

Dear Mr. Estrada,

I am writing to inform you of my interest in the recently posted International Marketing Director position at RLA. I was referred to your company by Haewon Choi, with whom I closely worked with at Kelson Metal Manufacturers. She believes I would be a good fit for RLA and urged me to contact you.

With my 10 years of experience as the Global Advertising Manager for Kelson in Asia and Europe, I have no doubt that I can contribute to RLA's goal of increasing its international sales. My history at Kelson will show that I have not only established a large client base, but also increased revenue each year in my assigned regions. Moreover, I have developed an extensive understanding of all of the metal parts and products sold in the industry.

Please review the enclosed résumé for more detailed information regarding my background and experience. Contact me at 682-555-4352 or abrea@clpemail.com at your convenience. Thank you, and I look forward to hearing from you.

Sincerely,

*Abby Brea*
Abby Brea
Enclosure

**153.** Why did Ms. Brea write the letter?

(A) To follow up on a recent interview
(B) To communicate her desire to work at RLA
(C) To ask about some driving directions
(D) To recommend a colleague for a position at RLA

**154.** What did Ms. Brea do while at Kelson Metal Manufacturers?

(A) She hired new marketing staff members.
(B) She proposed alternative means of revenue.
(C) She created several new designs for metal parts.
(D) She secured many clients from different countries.

**155.** According to Ms. Brea, what has she been able to develop?

(A) Effective management abilities
(B) Innovative advertising campaigns
(C) Relevant industry knowledge
(D) Sophisticated metal making skills

---

### Workplace Solutions – Monthly Tips
## Inspire your team!
#### Cornelia Hulbert

Although increasing salaries and offering more benefits are probably the best ways to recognize employees with outstanding performance records, managers usually are not in a position to give out these kinds of rewards. However, there are other effective, low-cost ways of showing appreciation to raise morale and encourage even better performance. Here are a few tips to do that.

- Make use of the company's newsletter to announce any awards received or goals that staff members have achieved. Employees can also be acknowledged for doing volunteer work in the community.
- Allow workers to have a flexible work schedule when possible.
- Bring in treats such as cakes and donuts to celebrate the end of a project.
- Organize luncheons to celebrate employees' birthdays; each person can bring food to share.
- Offer staff members further development opportunities through additional training.

Cornelia Hulbert is the CEO of Hulbert Management Consultations.

---

**156.** Why was the article written?

(A) To describe the benefits of working as a management consultant
(B) To outline methods for hiring volunteers to help out with projects
(C) To explain the best ways to evaluate employee performance
(D) To give supervisors ideas for motivating staff members

**157.** What activity is NOT mentioned in the article?

(A) Mentioning employees' achievements in a newsletter
(B) Providing learning opportunities
(C) Giving free tickets to a community event
(D) Recognizing special occasions

**Questions 158-160** refer to the following business profile.

## Gonzalez Glass Makers

Gonzalez Glass Makers is a medium-sized glass producer based in Barcelona, Spain. The company manufactures high-quality, heavy-duty glass for use in skyscrapers and other high-rise commercial buildings. The company's products are mainly distributed in Southwestern Europe–approximately 50 percent of the products are used in buildings in Spain. Currently, the company has almost 900 employees throughout the world (600 of whom work in Barcelona), a 25 percent increase from the year before. In addition to its headquarters and manufacturing facilities in Spain, the company has shipping centers in Lisbon, Rome, Athens, and Sofia. CEO Lauren Torres joined Gonzalez Glass last year, and under Ms. Torres' direction, the company has greatly expanded its Research Department with the aim of developing products that are more environmentally-friendly and energy-efficient. To facilitate this effort, earlier this year, Gonzalez acquired Leon Systems, a small research company located in Sevilla.

**158.** Who most likely are customers of Gonzalez Glass Makers?

(A) Research centers
(B) Construction companies
(C) Pharmaceutical firms
(D) Eyeglasses manufacturers

**159.** What did Gonzalez Glass Makers do last year?

(A) It purchased another company.
(B) It hired a new CEO.
(C) It built a shipping center.
(D) It moved its headquarters.

**160.** What is mentioned about Gonzalez Glass Makers?

(A) It increased the size of its research division.
(B) It was featured in a magazine article.
(C) It reduced its energy use by 25 percent.
(D) It participated in a conference in Sevilla.

**Questions 161-163** refer to the following e-mail.

---

To: Tech Support team
From: HR team
Date: November 12
Subject: Arabic courses

Hello all,

Due to our firm's upcoming expansion to Lebanon, there will be more projects that require familiarity with Arabic to work with our regional partners and clients. In preparation for this move, Arabic courses will be offered to all tech support employees who will be interacting with Arabic speakers online. There is no obligation to take the courses, but we believe that this chance to improve your language abilities is a valuable one.

We will be bringing in the Polyglobe Language Academy, a leader in the field of language learning here in Busan. The courses will be held in the downstairs conference rooms, to save on travel time, and free drinks will be offered. Three levels of Arabic will be offered (intermediate, advanced, and high-advanced). Participating employees will be given a test to place them in the appropriate class. The courses will be offered Mondays and Fridays at 7:00 P.M.

Please consider signing up for this valuable professional development opportunity. Reply to this e-mail by Friday to be put on a list for next week's test.

Sincerely,

Mina Shin
HR team
Arcturus Software, Inc.

---

**161.** Why is the firm offering Arabic courses?

(A) It will be doing business in Lebanon.
(B) It is planning to hire more Arabic speakers.
(C) Some staff members will move to Lebanon.
(D) A language academy is offering free courses.

**162.** What is implied about some tech support team members?

(A) They travel frequently to meet partner companies.
(B) They have moved to a new office in Busan.
(C) They are currently attending courses at Polyglobe Academy.
(D) They already know how to speak some Arabic.

**163.** What is NOT suggested about the courses?

(A) Beverages will be provided.
(B) They will be held twice a week.
(C) There is a one-time fee.
(D) There are three available levels.

GO ON TO THE NEXT PAGE

**Questions 164-167** refer to the following e-mail.

To: Addy Lukin <a.lukin@emorymedical.org>
From: Mark Hinton <hinton@arwn.org>
Date: October 3
Subject: Conference

Dear Ms. Lukin,

The Appalachian Rural Wellness Network (ARWN) is hosting a conference on the subject of "Digitizing Medical Records to Boost Patient Care" on Friday, November 10, and Saturday, November 11, in Washington D.C. —[1]—. Medical professionals who, like you, have devoted their lives to serving rural areas will discuss the challenges they have faced over the years. These speakers will also share ways to raise money to invest in technology that can drastically reduce your paperwork and improve the overall quality of the patient experience. —[2]—.

Featured presenters will be Dr. Miranda Tam, Director of Charlottesville Regional Clinics; Dr. Jun-seo Park, CEO of Appalachian Insurance Cooperative; and Allison Bryce, MD, President of the Organization of Clinical Medical Education. —[3]—. All are knowledgeable experts whose work has appeared in a variety of publications.

To register, visit www.arwnconference.org/register by Friday, November 3. To watch the presentations on that day, you must have a media player installed on your Internet-enabled device. —[4]—. The entire conference will be recorded and uploaded to our Web site on November 20.

Regards,

Mark Hinton
ARWN Members Coordinator

**164.** What is the subject of the conference?

(A) Improving healthcare in rural communities with technology
(B) Promoting medical education in rural communities
(C) New medical treatments for patients in rural communities
(D) Research findings of insurance options in rural communities

**165.** Who most likely is Ms. Lukin?

(A) A rural real estate agent
(B) A rural healthcare professional
(C) An insurance salesperson
(D) A medical journalist

**166.** What will happen on November 20?

(A) Presentation slides will be emailed.
(B) An article on rural health will be published.
(C) A professional gathering will begin.
(D) A video will become available.

**167.** In which of the positions marked [1], [2], [3], and [4] does the following sentence best belong?

"As an alternative, you can tune into the event via radio."

(A) [1]
(B) [2]
(C) [3]
(D) [4]

**Questions 168-171** refer to the following online chat discussion.

---

**Andy Palas [7:43 A.M.]**
Good morning, Kim and Ari. Can anyone help me out? I'm heading to Gavin Industries to go over their R&D supply requirements, but I forgot the glassware samples for their laboratory experiments.

**Kimberly Lee [7:45 A.M.]**
Our product catalog is available online. Can't you just use your laptop?

**Andy Palas [7:46 A.M.]**
Those images won't do. It is impossible to emphasize the clarity and strength of our glass on a computer screen.

**Kimberly Lee [7:48 A.M.]**
You'll probably have to drive back and get them from the office then.

**Arianna Noskov [7:51 A.M.]**
Well, I might be able to help. I still have a kit containing our glassware with me from a meeting yesterday. I'm stopped at 3rd Avenue right now.

**Andy Palas [7:55 A.M.]**
That's great news! I'm parked on 10th Avenue and Laurel Street. Could we meet nearby?

**Arianna Noskov [7:56 A.M.]**
OK. Let's meet at the coffee shop on 5th Avenue.

**Kimberly Lee [7:57 A.M.]**
Ari, you could just make the exchange at the client's office.

**Arianna Noskov [7:58 A.M.]**
I have to get into the office early to prepare for a 9:30 A.M. conference call.

**Andy Palas [7:59 A.M.]**
The coffee shop sounds good. It'll take me about 10 minutes to get there. Can you be there by then?

**Arianna Noskov [8:02 A.M.]**
Sure. I'll see you soon.

SEND

---

**168.** Who most likely is Mr. Palas?

(A) A sales associate
(B) A computer technician
(C) A Gavin Industries staff member
(D) A client of Ms. Lee

**169.** At 7:46 A.M., what does Mr. Palas most likely mean when he writes, "Those images won't do"?

(A) He will provide a Web site address.
(B) He plans to offer the client a catalog subscription.
(C) He prefers to show a client some product samples.
(D) He will purchase some glassware for a lab.

**170.** Where is Mr. Palas?

(A) In a conference room
(B) In a laboratory
(C) In a vehicle
(D) In a coffee shop

**171.** What does Ms. Noskov offer to do?

(A) Prepare a presentation for a client
(B) Purchase coffee for her colleagues
(C) Arrive at a meeting early
(D) Deliver some merchandise to Mr. Palas

*GO ON TO THE NEXT PAGE*

| From | Calleigh Stokes <callstokes@evergreenmail.com> |
|------|------------------------------------------------|
| To | Jonathon Bauer <jonbauer@tenymail.com> |
| Date | November 13, 3:47 P.M. |
| Subject | Evergreen TFP |
| Attach | TFP |

Dear Mr. Bauer,

Thank you for expressing interest in Evergreen Solutions' Tailored Fertilizing Program (TFP). We are sorry that you were unable to access this information directly via our Web site, but the page featuring the program is currently undergoing routine maintenance. Attached to this message you will find a thorough and detailed explanation of the program, but I would like to take the time to give you a basic outline here.

Fertilizing is an integral part of agriculture and has been for thousands of years. —[1]— Methods and materials have changed over time, but the advent of inorganic fertilizers in the 19th century has arguably had the greatest effect on the farming industry. Their use dramatically raised crop yields and supported population growth. —[2]—

When properly managed, organic fertilizers have far less environmental impact and can be just as effective, if not more so. Our trained experts examine the soil properties of individual fields and develop fertilizer blends that will provide the desired crop with its ideal nutrition. Our ingredients are 100 percent natural, and they all have Environmental Security Agency approval for use. —[3]—

However, the benefits of our products are not limited to environmental concerns and sustainability. —[4]— In a survey we conducted with the customers we have had since our founding 20 years ago, all of them reported savings when they used chemical fertilizers; some as much as 30 percent. We currently have contracts with some of the largest agricultural collectives in the country, as well as hundreds of smaller family-owned farms. These clients include a wide variety of farming types from rice paddies to corn fields to apple orchards. Therefore, we are confident that we can help you produce more, with less impact on the environment and on your wallet.

Sincerely,

Calleigh Stokes
Customer Service Director
Evergreen Solutions

**172.** What is indicated about Evergreen Solutions?

(A) It is a division of the Environmental Security Agency.
(B) It is currently updating a part of its Web site.
(C) It was established by a single individual.
(D) It owns several large farm collectives.

**173.** The word "integral" in paragraph 2, line 1, is the closest in meaning to

(A) collected
(B) critical
(C) regulated
(D) productive

**174.** What is NOT mentioned about TFP?

(A) It was developed 20 years ago.
(B) It reduces a farm's pollution output.
(C) It was designed for smaller farms.
(D) It uses only organic ingredients.

**175.** In which of the positions marked [1], [2], [3], and [4] does the following sentence best belong?

"Unfortunately, their use has also led to incredible amounts of pollution and soil toxicity."

(A) [1]
(B) [2]
(C) [3]
(D) [4]

GO ON TO THE NEXT PAGE

**Questions 176-180** refer to the following article and e-mail.

## The Sweet Life

How would you like to get paid to eat ice cream all day? If this sounds too good to be true, then you should know that there are people who work as ice cream tasters.

Marianna Duncan works as an ice cream taster for Tommen Frozen Delights, a New Zealand-based company that produces handmade ice cream and sorbet. Contrary to popular belief, many years of study and training are required for this position. After studying for five years and receiving her food science degree at Purnett University, she interned at Huggins Ice Cream Factory in Canada for one year. Ms. Duncan then returned to New Zealand and was recruited by Tommen, where she has been tasting ice cream for the last decade.

One of the perks of her job is that she gets to travel around the world in search of rare and exotic ingredients for the company's new ice cream varieties. One year, she spent a summer tasting curry in India and the next season savoring basil in Thailand. She explains, "I bring the ingredients to our lab in New Zealand, where our production staff and food chemists use them to create amazing tasting ice cream."

As for the actual tasting, she carefully inspects the ice cream with her eyes before sampling it. "I look at the product as if a consumer would. If the ice cream doesn't look appealing, they're not going to buy it." Even though she tastes up to 30 different flavors of ice cream daily, she never gets tired of her work. She enthusiastically claims, "No life could be sweeter."

Hector Mendoza
Staff Writer, *Gourmet Flavors Magazine*

| From | Kazuki Hachiro <k.hachiro@huggins.com> |
|---|---|
| To | Marianna Duncan <m.duncan@tommendelights.co.nz> |
| Date | 10 November |
| Subject | *Gourmet Flavors Magazine* Article |

Dear Marianna,

I saw the article about you in *Gourmet Flavors Magazine* and got your e-mail address from your company's Web site. We used to work together at an ice cream company as interns. I'm sure you remember me. Anyway, I'm going to be visiting Auckland in three weeks for the Food Science Symposium, and I thought it would be great to see each other again! If you have time, maybe we could have lunch and catch up. I'll look forward to your reply.

Best regards,

Kazuki

**176.** What is the purpose of the article?

(A) To explain a manufacturing process at a factory
(B) To compare different brands of ice cream
(C) To preview a company's products
(D) To describe a professional's career

**177.** What is suggested about Tommen Frozen Delights?

(A) It creates ice cream with unusual flavors.
(B) It is the most successful company in its industry.
(C) It was founded five years ago.
(D) It has laboratories in several countries.

**178.** What is suggested about Ms. Duncan?

(A) She has limited work experience.
(B) She enjoys her job.
(C) She trains interns at Tommen Frozen Delights.
(D) She is business partners with Mr. Hachiro.

**179.** Why did Mr. Hachiro send the e-mail to Ms. Duncan?

(A) To inquire about a job position
(B) To share information for a presentation
(C) To arrange a meeting
(D) To request feedback on an article

**180.** Where did Mr. Hachiro and Ms. Duncan first meet?

(A) At Huggins Ice Cream Factory
(B) At *Gourmet Flavors Magazine*
(C) At the Food Science Symposium
(D) At Purnett University

TEST 8

GO ON TO THE NEXT PAGE

## Rascat Jazz Trio
### For Immediate Release

Topeka, Kansas, April 5 – The Rascat Jazz Trio, the country's leading jazz group, has just announced the dates of their June tour. This six-day tour includes a performance at the popular Toro Theater, where the trio first made their concert appearance 10 years ago. Scheduled performances are listed below.

| DATE | LOCATION | VENUE |
|------|----------|-------|
| JUNE 5 | Topeka | Blaine Concert Hall |
| JUNE 8 | Wichita | Versa Theater |
| JUNE 11 | Lawrence | Toro Theater |
| JUNE 14 | Derby | Rolla Performing Arts Center |
| JUNE 17 | Overland Park | Dirkwood Stadium |
| JUNE 20 | Pittsburg | Kurtis Stadium |

Tickets range from $30 for balcony level seats to $100 for front-row seats in the center section at all tour stops, and they can be purchased at participating venue box offices and Blimp Music Stores. Members of the newly formed Rascat Jazz Trio Fan Club can order tickets at 20 percent off by logging in to the Member's Only section at www.rascatjazz.com. A complete list of fan club benefits and a detailed explanation of annual dues are available at www.rascatjazz.com/membership_fanclub.

Contact: Hershel Delotte, 785-555-4936, hdelotte@rascatjazz.com

**Dirkwood Stadium**

**Immediate Release**

Canceled and Postponed Performances

Overland Park, Kansas, May 20 – Nearly all performances scheduled for June at Dirkwood Stadium have been postponed due to emergency repairs being made to the building. Concert goers are asked to keep their tickets as all performances, with the exception of the Rascat Jazz Trio concert, will be held at a later date, and tickets for the June performances will be honored.

For the most up-to-date information on the rescheduled performances, please visit the Dirkwood Stadium Web site, www.dirkwoodstadium.com. If you wish to receive a refund for the canceled Rascat Jazz Trio concert, call 913-555-3042.

Contact: Janice Riker, 913-555-3020, jriker@dirkwoodstadium.com

**181.** Where did the Rascat Jazz Trio play its first concert a decade ago?

(A) In Topeka
(B) In Lawrence
(C) In Overland Park
(D) In Pittsburg

**182.** What is stated about the tickets for the Rascat Jazz Trio's concert?

(A) Their costs have increased from last year's tour.
(B) They are cheaper for students who present their school identification card.
(C) Their prices are the same for balcony seating at each concert venue.
(D) They are sold only through online ticketing vendors.

**183.** What is suggested about the Rascat Jazz Trio Fan Club?

(A) Its members have to pay a fee every year.
(B) It meets annually in the month of June.
(C) Its members receive discounts through Blimp Music Stores.
(D) It was founded over 10 years ago.

**184.** When will the Rascat Jazz Trio be unable to play a scheduled performance?

(A) On June 5
(B) On June 8
(C) On June 17
(D) On June 20

**185.** According to the second press release, what will be posted on Dirkwood Stadium's Web site?

(A) New venue locations
(B) A revised list of dates
(C) Details about building repairs
(D) A refund request form

*GO ON TO THE NEXT PAGE*

**Questions 186-190** refer to the following notice, advertisement, and e-mail.

To: Aster Valley Ski & Resort Staff
From: Lisa Rose
Date: October 7
Subject: Seasonal Offerings

Greetings Sales Representatives,

As most of you are aware, a lot of Aster University students remain in town over their winter break. As usual, our annual 40 percent student holiday discount applies to anyone signing up during the last two weeks of November. Management is also debating two other potential deals that we could offer to all resort members for the upcoming winter season (December 1-February 1).

We are soliciting your feedback to help choose between the two potential promotions. One option is a discount extended to the families of existing Aster Valley Ski & Resort members. Members would be able to put any member (at least 17 years old) of their immediate family under their current membership plan for 20 percent off the regular rate.

The other option is that Blue-level members would receive a complimentary one-day pass for a friend that is good between Mondays and Fridays. This would provide access to all resort areas, including the ski slopes. However, the spa would be excluded from this offer as our members already wait quite a long time to use it.

We ask that you respond to this e-mail with what you believe would best please our members.

We appreciate your help in this matter.

Sincerely,
Lisa Rose
Vice President, Marketing Department
Aster Valley Ski & Resort

## Winter Promotions

Aster University Students Welcome!
Register between November 15 and December 15 and get 40% off a resort membership—and your first ski or snowboard rental will be on us!

Ski with a friend for a day!
Starting December 1, all Blue- and Black-level resort members are eligible to bring a friend for a day of skiing fun, at no additional charge. Members' friends must present a photo ID upon arrival to receive a guest pass.

Aster Valley Ski & Resort

To: Sam Hermann
From: Seong-hee Lim
Date: February 2
Subject: Re: Results are in

Hi Sam,

Thank you for emailing the charts from the latest report. I'm really excited by the 18 percent increase in sales of Blue-level memberships due to the winter promotions.

The boost in our numbers mostly came from Aster University, with the majority of students registering for our Blue-level membership. I think we should offer the same promotion again next winter. Also, the university's athletic facilities will be remodeled next year, which means that students will need somewhere else to engage in physical activities. As we're the closest location to the university that offers extensive recreational facilities, we should look into partnering with the school to provide transportation services to their students. This would certainly increase our membership numbers.

I'll keep you updated.

Seong-hee Lim
Manager, Marketing Department
Aster Valley Ski & Resort

**186.** What is the purpose of the notice?

(A) To congratulate some workers on a completed project
(B) To announce a scheduled closure
(C) To inform resort members of a new service
(D) To request comments from staff

**187.** What is implied about the spa?

(A) It will have new equipment soon.
(B) It will charge an extra fee.
(C) It is closed for repairs.
(D) It is a popular facility.

**188.** How did the special for the students change since October?

(A) The sign-up period was extended.
(B) The discount rate was reduced.
(C) Students can make monthly payments.
(D) Students can visit the resort only once a week.

**189.** What is indicated about Aster Valley Sky & Resort?

(A) Many students brought their friends during the winter season.
(B) It opens earlier between Monday and Friday.
(C) All relatives of current members can receive a discount.
(D) Black-level members receive free ski accessories.

**190.** What will happen at Aster University?

(A) The school year will start in the winter.
(B) Sales courses will be added.
(C) Its athletic facilities will undergo renovations.
(D) Skiing lessons will be offered to its faculty.

TEST 8

*GO ON TO THE NEXT PAGE*

**Questions 191-195** refer to following product description, e-mail, and online review.

https://www.kitchendesignco.com/catalog

| Home | **Catalog** | Feedback | Contact |

### Item: Kotka 90 island cart

The Kitchen Design Company proudly announces the Kotka 90, our first kitchen storage product. We've merged our attractive modern designs with the futuristic functionality we apply to all of our electronic kitchen utensils to bring the Kitchen Design Company's signature style to your culinary workspace. This island cart is built with light, durable materials, and features a stainless steel countertop and wheels for mobility. The countertop can be pulled out to create a spacious but stable surface for all sorts of kitchen tasks. Its sleek look will also complement any cooking area.

Catalog No.: #8345A
Price: $579.00*
Comes in white, black, or brown.

*Coupon codes are not valid for the purchase of this item. We ship anywhere in the world, but shipping charges vary according to the destination.

| From | Bernard O'Rourke <borourke@infovision.com> |
|---|---|
| To | Customer Support <cs@kitchendesignco.com> |
| Date | June 28 |
| Subject | Kotka 90 |

Hello,

I have several questions about the Kotka 90 island cart, which I am thinking about purchasing. Could I get a granite countertop, rather than a stainless steel one? Additionally, I've heard some reviewers discussing their difficulties in assembling the island cart, which is an issue I would prefer to avoid.

Is it possible to get one that has been put together beforehand? Please let me know how much extra that would cost.

Sincerely,

Bernard O'Rourke

https://www.kitchendesignco.com/catalog/kotka90islandcart

Bernard O'Rourke, July 19

I was worried about putting the island cart together, so I spoke with a company representative. It was definitely time well spent! The Kitchen Design Company did a great job of answering all my questions. They directed me to a Web page where I could look at the instructions before making a purchase. They also gave me a number to call for if I needed further assistance. But I never called that number, as it didn't even take me even 20 minutes to put the island cart together.

The island cart is very sturdy and easy to push around. But I should mention that there are a few things that could be improved. First of all, this product is more expensive than many similar ones. And it's heavy, so depending on where you are, shipping expenses can add quite a bit to the final cost. Second, although the expanded countertop provides an impressive amount of space, it just wouldn't be stable enough if you were doing very detailed work. Lastly, repackaging this product would be challenging, should you need to return it. But that's fine— I have no intention of sending it back.

**191.** What does the product description suggest about the Kitchen Design Company?

(A) It has more than one location.
(B) It mainly sells kitchen equipment.
(C) It plans to manufacture kitchen counters.
(D) It offers reduced prices for first-time customers.

**192.** According to the e-mail, what is probably true about Mr. O'Rourke?

(A) He checks customer feedback when shopping for items.
(B) He regularly purchases from the Kitchen Design Company.
(C) He is ordering an island cart for his restaurant.
(D) He recently learned an item is out of stock.

**193.** What is one reason Mr. O'Rourke wrote the review?

(A) To suggest a step be added to some instructions
(B) To recommend a better kitchen accessory
(C) To compliment a company's customer service
(D) To complain about the lack of delivery options

**194.** What is suggested about the Kotka 90?

(A) It is not sold in certain countries.
(B) It is available in different sizes.
(C) It has a one-year warranty.
(D) It cannot be purchased preassembled.

**195.** According to the review, what aspect of the product description is inaccurate?

(A) The company's shipping costs
(B) The island cart's price
(C) The company's refund policy
(D) The island cart's stability

GO ON TO THE NEXT PAGE

TEST 8

**Questions 196-200** refer to the following job advertisement and e-mails.

The Auckland branch of Superior Distribution is looking for a motivated individual to lead our warehouse team. Superior Distribution is one of the leading companies in the transportation and distribution of high-quality fruits and vegetables in New Zealand.

The warehouse manager must monitor work conditions and processes in the warehouse to ensure the employees' safety. Candidates must have a minimum of five years of relevant experience in the same industry. Evening and weekend hours are occasionally necessary to make sure that shipments are sent out on schedule. Applicants should be knowledgeable in warehousing and shipping. Familiarity with SWP inventory tracking software is required.

Applicants should email their cover letter and résumé to Ms. Tricia Helfor at thelfor@superiordist.co.nz. Three recommendation letters are also required and must be sent directly from the person writing the letter.

| To | Tricia Helfor <thelfor@superiordist.co.nz> |
|---|---|
| From | Mao Lai <mlai@kalexperts.com> |
| Date | 18 September |
| Subject | Owen Recommendation |

Dear Ms. Helfor,

I am writing on behalf of Owen Carter for the warehouse manager position at Superior Distribution. I have been Owen's manager for six of his nine years at KAL Experts, since he was promoted from a part-time position to a full-time employee here. As the current shift manager, he has proven more than capable of handling his tasks.

Owen possesses all the required qualifications, including the necessary work experience and technical background. Our company also uses the SWP program, which Owen has worked with extensively, and he has trained many staff members to use it.

I am confident that Owen will adapt to the demands of any new work setting quickly and successfully. Should you have any questions, feel free to contact me.

Sincerely,

Mao Lai
KAL Experts, Shipping Director

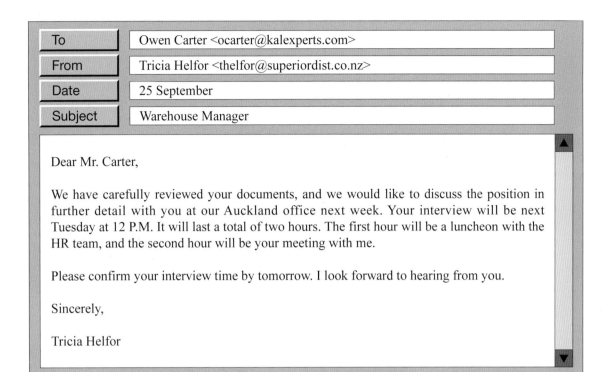

| To | Owen Carter <ocarter@kalexperts.com> |
| From | Tricia Helfor <thelfor@superiordist.co.nz> |
| Date | 25 September |
| Subject | Warehouse Manager |

Dear Mr. Carter,

We have carefully reviewed your documents, and we would like to discuss the position in further detail with you at our Auckland office next week. Your interview will be next Tuesday at 12 P.M. It will last a total of two hours. The first hour will be a luncheon with the HR team, and the second hour will be your meeting with me.

Please confirm your interview time by tomorrow. I look forward to hearing from you.

Sincerely,

Tricia Helfor

**196.** What is suggested about Superior Distribution?

(A) It owns a large chain of supermarkets.
(B) It specializes in handling food items.
(C) It is headquartered in Auckland.
(D) It offers a wide selection of software products.

**197.** According to the job advertisement, what must the warehouse manager be willing to do?

(A) Lift heavy items
(B) Take safety training classes
(C) Sign a three-year contract
(D) Work some weekend hours

**198.** Why does Mr. Lai write the e-mail?

(A) To explain a schedule change
(B) To welcome a new warehouse manager
(C) To express a positive opinion of an employee
(D) To learn more about a job applicant

**199.** What is indicated about Mr. Carter?

(A) He is skilled in the use of inventory tracking software.
(B) He is seeking a part-time position at Superior Distribution.
(C) He has recently moved to New Zealand.
(D) He has experience developing new software programs.

**200.** According to the second e-mail, what is mentioned about the interview?

(A) A meal will be provided.
(B) It will last one hour.
(C) A CEO will make a speech.
(D) It has been moved.

GO ON TO THE NEXT PAGE

# TES

# READING TEST

In the Reading test, you will read a variety of texts and answer several different types of reading comprehension questions. The entire Reading test will last 75 minutes. There are three parts, and directions are given for each part. You are encouraged to answer as many questions as possible within the time allowed.

You must mark your answers on the separate answer sheet. Do not write your answers in the test book.

## PART 5

**Directions:** A word or phrase is missing in each of the sentences below. Four answer choices are given below each sentence. Select the best answer to complete the sentence. Then mark the letter (A), (B), (C), or (D) on your answer sheet.

---

**101.** The causes of the increase in car ownership throughout the area are not ------- clear.

(A) entirely
(B) steadily
(C) firmly
(D) justly

**102.** Laurentine Corporation received many applications for the management position but few were -------.

(A) qualifies
(B) qualify
(C) qualified
(D) qualification

**103.** The company will be making new business cards, ------- contact Mr. Lebeau if you need to change any of your information.

(A) so
(B) than
(C) to
(D) ahead

**104.** Critics of Bradford Seaside Resort ------- the claim that it has attracted more visitors to the city.

(A) depend
(B) suggest
(C) reject
(D) extend

**105.** Takata Solutions helps companies apply innovative management techniques to greatly increase team -------.

(A) productivity
(B) produce
(C) productively
(D) produced

**106.** The Web site is programmed to send a confirmation e-mail within five minutes to customers ------- place an order.

(A) once
(B) theirs
(C) they
(D) who

**107.** Building construction that requires street space can start only ------- a street use permit is obtained from the Public Works Department.

(A) through
(B) from
(C) after
(D) on

**108.** Carrie Mendoza has been acting ------- since her first role at age 10.

(A) professionals
(B) professionalism
(C) profession
(D) professionally

**109.** Readers showed so much ------- for the novels that the publisher asked to turn them into a movie trilogy.

(A) indication
(B) enthusiasm
(C) belief
(D) knowledge

**110.** Overland Hotel has 75 rooms, ------- with a terrace facing the mountains.

(A) most
(B) highly
(C) much
(D) nearly

**111.** Although Albert Lain was going to retire from Meadows Tech, he ------- has a seat on the board of directors.

(A) once
(B) besides
(C) especially
(D) still

**112.** After merging with Ramshead Savings and Loan, Milton Ltd. ------- a broad selection of financial services.

(A) to offer
(B) offered
(C) offer
(D) offering

**113.** Osnabruck University students have to file a renewal ------- for a dormitory room each semester.

(A) application
(B) specification
(C) formation
(D) contribution

**114.** The abandoned Willowcrest textile factory and the ------- properties are being renovated into an upscale apartment complex.

(A) surrounds
(B) surround
(C) surroundings
(D) surrounding

**115.** The Costa Rojo Resort and Hotel is always searching for methods to ------- the visitor experience.

(A) gain
(B) notify
(C) cure
(D) enhance

**116.** Reliant Electric's new Web site lets company representatives contact repair specialists who are ------- service calls.

(A) here
(B) going
(C) within
(D) on

**117.** Lancer Sporting Goods signed contracts with several famous athletes, and ------- it will begin advertising its products more widely.

(A) for that reason
(B) since
(C) once
(D) on account of

**118.** The winter clothes collection was featured on Outdoor Wear's Web site, leading to a ------- increase in sales.

(A) considerably
(B) considerable
(C) consider
(D) considering

**119.** Dr. Engstrom's gentle ------- to explaining diagnoses has aided him in putting many patients at ease.

(A) example
(B) approach
(C) meeting
(D) appearance

**120.** When visiting Smarter Kitchen's booth at the convention, remember to help ------- to a free sample.

(A) yourself
(B) you
(C) yours
(D) your

TEST 9

*GO ON TO THE NEXT PAGE*

**121.** You must enter a ------- of passwords every time you access your personal account on the company database.

(A) comprehension
(B) specification
(C) series
(D) proof

**122.** ------- Friday is a factory inspection day, shipments this week will be sent out a day later than usual.

(A) Yet
(B) When
(C) But
(D) As

**123.** Passengers should have their ticket and passport ------- to present to the Immigration Control officer at the counter.

(A) whether
(B) openly
(C) ready
(D) since

**124.** The IT team was able to find out exactly ------- made the company's Web site go offline this morning.

(A) this
(B) these
(C) whose
(D) what

**125.** Lowering prices on products made of recyclable materials ------- consumers to purchase them more and reduce waste.

(A) encourage
(B) encouraging
(C) is encouraged
(D) would encourage

**126.** Many businesses ------- overprice their products so that their sale discounts seem like bargains.

(A) strategize
(B) strategy
(C) strategically
(D) strategic

**127.** Since the complete financial report would take too much time to explain, Machiko will present a ------- version at the meeting.

(A) duplicate
(B) condensed
(C) steady
(D) fulfilled

**128.** A competent supervisor usually ------- authority to other personnel in order to improve employee morale and performance.

(A) delegates
(B) organizes
(C) introduces
(D) initiates

**129.** ------- low first quarter sales, the Marketing team remains positive about the product line's potential.

(A) In spite of
(B) Relying on
(C) According to
(D) Because of

**130.** If a staff member ------- to transfer to another branch, the employee must first speak to his or her supervisor.

(A) wish
(B) wishes
(C) will wish
(D) was wishing

## PART 6

**Directions:** Read the texts that follow. A word, phrase, or sentence is missing in parts of each text. Four answer choices for each question are given below the text. Select the best answer to complete the text. Then mark the letter (A), (B), (C), or (D) on your answer sheet.

**Questions 131-134** refer to the following notice.

**Richard Boyce Web Marketing Lecture**

Richard Boyce is a nationally recognized ------- in online advertising and promotion. Mr.
                                              **131.**
Boyce ------- as Creative Director for Media Zero for 17 years. With the experience from
        **132.**
his time spent at Media Zero, Mr. Boyce now gives lectures that use real world

techniques. -------. As a result, Mr. Boyce's audiences receive invaluable practice
            **133.**
applying theory to actual marketing endeavors. Please be aware that the lectures on

January 24 and 27 are now full. -------, a small number of seats remain for the February
                                **134.**
12 and 15 sessions.

**131.** (A) authorization
(B) authorized
(C) authority
(D) authorizing

**132.** (A) is working
(B) will work
(C) had been working
(D) has worked

**133.** (A) One is to involve the audience in a social networking campaign.
(B) During his time at Media Zero, he conducted several employee events.
(C) Audience members are requested to provide workplace recommendations.
(D) He received a degree from the Seattle School of Journalism.

**134.** (A) However
(B) Therefore
(C) Particularly
(D) Lastly

*GO ON TO THE NEXT PAGE*

Questions 135-138 refer to the following information.

---

**Safety Regulations: Emergency Fire Doors**

Emergency fire doors are located on every floor of the building and must be kept ------- **135.** of any obstacles. Every door must be checked annually by the local Fire Department. -------. **136.** However, staff should also examine the doors on a weekly basis. ------- **137.** for any electronic malfunctions, damage, or obstructions. Make sure that the signs above the doors are ------- **138.** lit and visible from all angles.

---

135. (A) obvious
   (B) broken
   (C) clear
   (D) distinct

136. (A) Management plans on revising these procedures within the coming weeks.
   (B) You should see an up-to-date inspection sticker in the upper left-hand corner of each exit.
   (C) At this time, we are not sure who will take over the responsibilities.
   (D) We hope to extend this period by one month.

137. (A) Look
   (B) Arrange
   (C) Take
   (D) Sign

138. (A) full
   (B) fuller
   (C) fully
   (D) fullness

**Questions 139-142** refer to the following e-mail.

To: Natherman employees
From: Personnel Department
Date: November 20
Subject: Corporate party

The end-of-the-year corporate party will take place on Thursday, December 9, from 1 P.M. to 5 P.M. at the Shamforth Banquet Hall. All staff are invited to join and have a great time with their coworkers in this wonderful -------. All of our branches will close at
**139.**
1 P.M. on that day so that employees -------.
**140.**

To obtain tickets to the party, please drop by the personnel office. Staff will still be paid for their time (a total of four hours) at the event. Alternatively, staff can opt to go home early instead of participating. -------, these employees will need to use half a day from
**141.**
their remaining vacation days.

-------.
**142.**

---

**139.** (A) demonstration
(B) town
(C) exhibition
(D) setting

**140.** (A) can attend
(B) attendance
(C) who attended
(D) attending

**141.** (A) Moreover
(B) Nevertheless
(C) However
(D) Consequently

**142.** (A) Most employees agreed that they had a good time at the party.
(B) Please direct any questions you might have to your manager.
(C) The banquet hall now features a much larger dining area.
(D) We anticipate that sales for the fourth quarter will be high.

GO ON TO THE NEXT PAGE

**Questions 143-146** refer to the following e-mail.

To: All Staff
From: richard.haber@locatrans.com
Date: 15 October
Subject: Payment Procedure
Attachment: paymentform.rtf

Dear Translators,

We ------- our procedure for paying our freelance translators for their work. Instead of
   **143.**

sending a payment for each assignment, we will make just one payment on the 10th of

every month. I realize this could be a -------. But, it has become a big hassle to process
   **144.**

an invoice for each completed assignment. From now on, there is no need to fill out an

online invoice every time you finish a project. -------, just send one invoice at the end of
   **145.**

the month for all work completed in that month. Please print out the document

attached to this e-mail and return a signed copy to me by next Monday. -------.
   **146.**

Thank you in advance for your understanding on this matter.

Sincerely,

Richard Haber
Manager, Accounting and Payroll
Locatrans Translation

**143.** (A) should revise
(B) would have revised
(C) are revising
(D) may be revising

**144.** (A) burden
(B) chance
(C) cancelation
(D) priority

**145.** (A) Depending on that
(B) Similarly
(C) In light of this
(D) Instead

**146.** (A) Translations must meet the
previously detailed standards.
(B) This will serve as confirmation that
you have read and agreed to the
new system.
(C) Contact us immediately if your
payment appears incorrect.
(D) Some sections of the document
require changes.

# PART 7

**Directions:** In this part you will read a selection of texts, such as magazine and newspaper articles, e-mails, and instant messages. Each text or set of texts is followed by several questions. Select the best answer for each question and mark the letter (A), (B), (C) or (D) on your answer sheet.

**Questions 147-148** refer to the following text message.

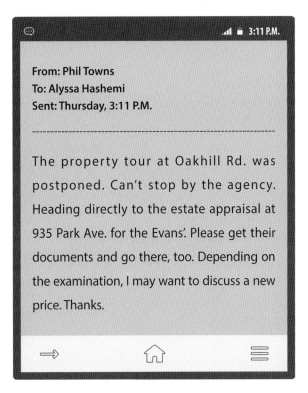

From: Phil Towns
To: Alyssa Hashemi
Sent: Thursday, 3:11 P.M.

---

The property tour at Oakhill Rd. was postponed. Can't stop by the agency. Heading directly to the estate appraisal at 935 Park Ave. for the Evans'. Please get their documents and go there, too. Depending on the examination, I may want to discuss a new price. Thanks.

**147.** In what industry does Mr. Towns most likely work?

(A) Insurance
(B) Housing
(C) Transportation
(D) Banking

**148.** What does Mr. Towns ask Ms. Hashemi to do?

(A) Discuss an agreement
(B) Bring some paperwork
(C) Analyze some examination results
(D) Arrange a conference

*GO ON TO THE NEXT PAGE*

**Questions 149-150** refer to the following text message chain.

Bernard Gallagher

Do you have time to meet with me about the Pickens' wedding? The groom's family is asking for some major changes to the menu.

11:34 A.M.

Valerie Timmermans

11:40 A.M.

I have a lunch meeting with a client, but I'll be back in my office after 1 o'clock. Why don't you stop by then?

Bernard Gallagher

Wonderful. I'll bring their request, along with my plans for handling it.

11:43 A.M.

Valerie Timmermans

11:46 A.M.

And try to relax. I know this is the first wedding you're arranging catering for, but it will be fine.

Bernard Gallagher

Thank you. I'm grateful that you're guiding me through the process.

11:48 A.M.

Valerie Timmermans

11:52 A.M.

It's my pleasure. OK, I am taking off. I'll see you in the afternoon.

**149.** What is most likely true about Mr. Gallagher?

(A) He is learning from Ms. Timmermans.
(B) He is going to purchase a gift for Ms. Timmermans.
(C) He has a job interview at 1 P.M.
(D) He recently attended a relative's wedding celebration.

**150.** At 11:52 A.M., what does Ms. Timmermans mean when she writes, "I am taking off "?

(A) She must leave to attend a meeting.
(B) She removed some items from a list.
(C) She will schedule a vacation day.
(D) She agreed to handle another task.

Questions 151-153 refer to the following e-mail.

**From:** Joel Admunsen
**To:** Madison Lee, Sam O'Caroll
**Date:** July 14
**Subject:** Plans for the restaurant

Good afternoon Madison and Sam,

I've got great news. I went to City Hall this morning and received the business license for our bistro. Now the hard work begins. To be ready by our grand opening date of November 10, I've planned out our monthly tasks.

August: Plan the interior and contract with a renovation company. Contact suppliers and choose dinnerware. Set up a Web site and print business cards.

September: Schedule building safety inspections. Supply the kitchen with cookware and utensils. Advertise job openings online and in local newspapers.

October: Finalize the hiring decisions and begin training. Print ads and contact food critics.

If this plan doesn't seem realistic, please let me know what changes you think are needed. But don't forget that our doors open in less than four months, so everything needs to get done within that time frame.

Joel

**151.** What is indicated about Mr. Admunsen?

(A) He is looking for business investors.
(B) He will sell his restaurant to Ms. Lee.
(C) He is attending a convention with colleagues in November.
(D) He recently registered a business.

**152.** What goal is proposed for September?

(A) Printing promotional materials
(B) Arranging necessary inspections
(C) Training new staff
(D) Ordering kitchen supplies

**153.** Why does Mr. Admunsen ask for feedback?

(A) He is concerned a timeline may not be feasible.
(B) He would like suggestions for a recruiting program.
(C) He would like input on some design options.
(D) He is revising a newspaper advertisement.

GO ON TO THE NEXT PAGE

**Questions 154-157** refer to the following e-mail.

| | |
|---|---|
| **To:** | sponsor_list@weststart.org |
| **From:** | aweiser@weststart.org |
| **Date:** | Wednesday, September 16 |
| **Subject:** | Charity Race on Saturday |

Dear Sponsors,

It is with regret that I must write to tell you that this Saturday's charity race in Westfall State Park has been canceled. Due to unfinished renovation work, in addition to the weekend's forecast of unseasonable heavy snowfall, we must postpone the event.

Westfall State Park representatives alerted me on Monday that the covered picnic area where we planned to set up is still being renovated and will not be done by the end of the week. Instead, it was suggested that we use the parking area for the start and finish lines and set up booths. However, the parking area is not paved, making it impossible to access in this type of weather.

While the event was going to be held even if the weather was cold, the safety of all participants must come first. I apologize for this situation, but please understand that it is not up to the Planning Committee. This move was ultimately made by Westfall State Park management.

We hope to hold the event in late October and ask that you offer your support then. For the time being, please note that your sponsor fees will be refunded to you via wire transfer by the end of the business day on Friday. If you would prefer to have the fee returned by check, reply to this e-mail with your current address and a contact number where we can reach you.

Regretfully,

Andrew Weiser

**154.** Who most likely is Mr. Weiser?

(A) A government official
(B) A professional athlete
(C) A local reporter
(D) An event planner

**155.** What is suggested about the unpaved parking area at Westfall State Park?

(A) It is frequently full on weekends.
(B) It is currently under construction.
(C) It can be used only by Westfall residents.
(D) It cannot be accessed during snowy weather.

**156.** The word "move" in paragraph 3, line 3, is the closest in meaning to

(A) relocation
(B) shift
(C) decision
(D) transfer

**157.** What will the charity race sponsors receive?

(A) An updated contract
(B) A gift certificate
(C) A reimbursement
(D) A brochure

**Questions 158-160** refer to the following Web page.

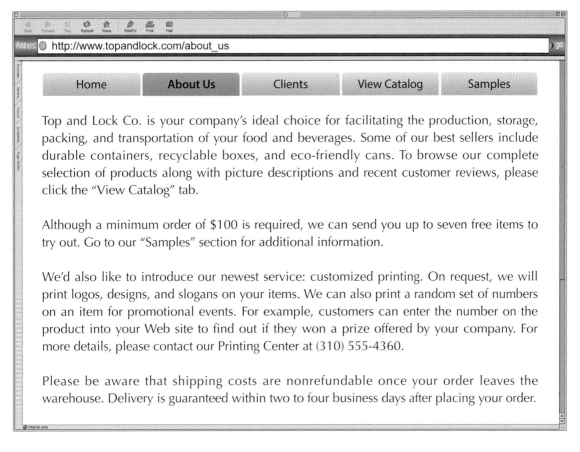

Address: http://www.topandlock.com/about_us

| Home | **About Us** | Clients | View Catalog | Samples |

Top and Lock Co. is your company's ideal choice for facilitating the production, storage, packing, and transportation of your food and beverages. Some of our best sellers include durable containers, recyclable boxes, and eco-friendly cans. To browse our complete selection of products along with picture descriptions and recent customer reviews, please click the "View Catalog" tab.

Although a minimum order of $100 is required, we can send you up to seven free items to try out. Go to our "Samples" section for additional information.

We'd also like to introduce our newest service: customized printing. On request, we will print logos, designs, and slogans on your items. We can also print a random set of numbers on an item for promotional events. For example, customers can enter the number on the product into your Web site to find out if they won a prize offered by your company. For more details, please contact our Printing Center at (310) 555-4360.

Please be aware that shipping costs are nonrefundable once your order leaves the warehouse. Delivery is guaranteed within two to four business days after placing your order.

**158.** For whom is the Web page most likely intended?

(A) Transportation services
(B) Local recycling centers
(C) Publishing firms
(D) Food preparation companies

**159.** What is NOT stated as a service offered by Top and Lock Co.?

(A) Giving a discount to first-time customers
(B) Providing a limited number of sample items
(C) Writing messages on products at the customer's request
(D) Displaying the latest opinions of customers

**160.** What is indicated about orders placed through Top and Lock Co.?

(A) They can be shipped at no cost with a minimum purchase of $100.
(B) They can be delivered within four working days.
(C) They can be paid for in installments.
(D) They can be exchanged within one month of the purchase date.

GO ON TO THE NEXT PAGE

TEST 9

Questions 161-164 refer to the following information.

## Special Thanks

I owe a great deal to all those who aided me in the creation of this book, which took a total of 10 years to complete. A *Geological Study of Wyoming* would not exist without your support and encouragement.

A lot of people were involved in the development of this work. In particular, I would like to thank Dr. Patrick Flynn for going over my drafts, in spite of his full-time teaching schedule, and providing ideas that simplified several concepts discussed in sections regarding crystals and gemstones. Also, I would like to extend my heartfelt gratitude to Ms. Ha Yang, whose elaborate illustrations introduce each chapter.

Above all, I would especially like to express my appreciation for Ms. Evelyn Ionesco. Ms. Ionesco showed me around important rock layers located far off the main Wyoming highways, drawing upon her extensive knowledge of regional geologic formations. A long-time resident of the state, she knew exactly the right places to go to see the best samples of rocks from different geological eras. Without her expertise, this project would have been nearly impossible to complete.

Anna Kilday

**161.** What is NOT indicated about *A Geological Study of Wyoming*?

(A) It contains detailed drawings.
(B) It took 10 years to finish.
(C) It includes maps of different states.
(D) It was written by Ms. Kilday.

**162.** What is mentioned about Dr. Flynn?

(A) He often traveled to Wyoming.
(B) He helped revise some content.
(C) He recently changed occupations.
(D) He recommended an artist.

**163.** The word "formations" in paragraph 3, line 3, is closest in meaning to

(A) establishments
(B) compilations
(C) structures
(D) layouts

**164.** For what is Ms. Ionesco acknowledged?

(A) Doing research
(B) Being a guide
(C) Teaching classes
(D) Reviewing a draft

---

**Xiwei Wong [2:34 P.M.]**
Good afternoon, all. I hope everyone is getting ready for our upcoming marketing meeting on Wednesday. We didn't see an increase in sales at all last quarter. We should think about a new course of action.

**Kylie Losse [2:35 P.M.]**
What would you like us to do?

**Xiwei Wong [2:37 P.M.]**
The demand for leather wallets and purses is dropping, so we should look into increasing Galloway's product offerings.

**Angela Kim [2:38 P.M.]**
We could try mobile phone cases. It seems like everyone has one these days.

**Caleb Steuter [2:40 P.M.]**
That's a pretty good idea. Or we could consider making special cases for tablets and laptops.

**Kylie Losse [2:41 P.M.]**
Right. We might even try airplane carry-on luggage for business travelers who have all of those devices.

**Xiwei Wong [2:44 P.M.]**
Excellent ideas, everyone. For the meeting, please look up some suppliers online and find out price quotes to include in your presentation to the team. With that information, I will then make a budget estimate for our department head to go along with the proposals.

**Caleb Steuter [2:45 P.M.]**
Got it.

**Xiwei Wong [2:44 P.M.]**
If you run into any problems, send me an e-mail, and we'll talk them over.

SEND

---

**165.** What kind of product does Galloway currently sell?

(A) Leather accessories
(B) Metal luggage
(C) Fitness watches
(D) Mobile phones

**166.** At 2:34 P.M., what does Mr. Wong mean when he writes, "We should think about a new course of action"?

(A) Each presentation should focus on a different topic.
(B) The company should provide more training workshops.
(C) Each presentation should last for at least 10 minutes.
(D) The company should expand its line of merchandise.

**167.** What will Mr. Steuter most likely do next?

(A) Draft a proposal
(B) Email a supervisor
(C) Conduct some research
(D) Book a conference room

**168.** What will Mr. Wong submit to the department head?

(A) Data on product vendors
(B) A monthly sales report
(C) Results of a customer survey
(D) An event calendar

TEST 9

GO ON TO THE NEXT PAGE

**Questions 169-171** refer to the following Web page.

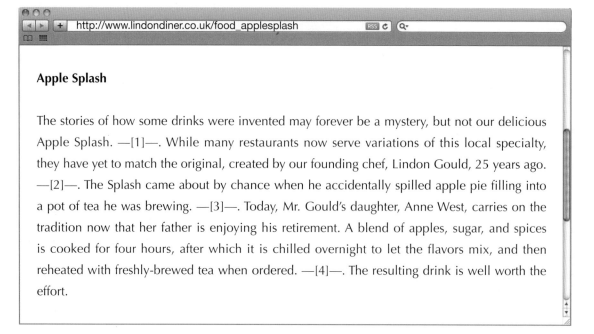

http://www.lindondiner.co.uk/food_applesplash

**Apple Splash**

The stories of how some drinks were invented may forever be a mystery, but not our delicious Apple Splash. —[1]—. While many restaurants now serve variations of this local specialty, they have yet to match the original, created by our founding chef, Lindon Gould, 25 years ago. —[2]—. The Splash came about by chance when he accidentally spilled apple pie filling into a pot of tea he was brewing. —[3]—. Today, Mr. Gould's daughter, Anne West, carries on the tradition now that her father is enjoying his retirement. A blend of apples, sugar, and spices is cooked for four hours, after which it is chilled overnight to let the flavors mix, and then reheated with freshly-brewed tea when ordered. —[4]—. The resulting drink is well worth the effort.

**169.** What is suggested about the beverage?

(A) It does not contain artificial ingredients.
(B) It is only served in the winter.
(C) It comes with a side of dessert.
(D) It is always served hot.

**170.** What is implied about Chef Gould?

(A) His mentor was Ms. West.
(B) He enjoys reading mystery novels.
(C) His diner has relocated several times.
(D) He no longer works in a restaurant.

**171.** In which of the positions marked [1], [2], [3], and [4] does the following sentence best belong?

"This mishap resulted in Lindon Diner's signature beverage."

(A) [1]
(B) [2]
(C) [3]
(D) [4]

May 15

Erin Sanders
1022 W. Wesleyan Dr.
Santa Cruz, CA 95060

Dear Ms. Sanders,

Thank you for your support of *Iden Global Journal* over the years. This letter is to inform you of some changes to our annual subscription package. —[1]—. Starting June 1, annual subscription prices are going up from $114 to $138. The new rate ($11.50 per month) is still much cheaper (40 percent less) than purchasing it at the regular store price of $18.40 for one issue. —[2]—.

Be sure to take advantage of your special access to the *Iden Global Journal* Web site. Not only does it provide everything contained in the print journal, but as a subscriber, you can go online and access the Members-only section for additional content, including member-submitted reviews of recipes and comment forums on a variety of culinary topics, such as ingredient substitutions, special kitchen equipment, and tips for artful meal presentation. —[3]—.

Take advantage of the feedback section of the Web site to send a letter to our knowledgeable editorial staff. Selected letters will get published in the Journal Correspondence section.

Your subscription ends with next month's issue. Take advantage of this short window to re-subscribe at the lower rate before prices go up either by filling out the included subscription order form and mailing it back or by contacting our subscription hotline. —[4]—.

We look forward to hearing from you!

*Caley Bowen*
Caley Bowen
Subscription Services Representative

Subscription Hotline: (831) 555-2941

Enclosure

---

**172.** What is implied about Ms. Sanders?

(A) She has long been interested in cooking.
(B) She is relocating to Santa Cruz in June.
(C) She wrote a letter that was published in *Iden Global Journal*.
(D) She is a frequent commenter on Iden Global Journal's forums.

**173.** How much will an issue of *Iden Global Journal* cost next month if purchased through a subscription?

(A) $11.50
(B) $18.40
(C) $22.50
(D) $25.00

**174.** In which of the positions marked [1], [2], [3], and [4] does the following sentence best belong?

"Our staff is standing by for your call from 9 A.M. to 6 P.M. every day."

(A) [1]
(B) [2]
(C) [3]
(D) [4]

**175.** According to Ms. Bowen, what is available only on the journal's Web site?

(A) Advertising for business subscribers
(B) Recipe submissions by members
(C) Restaurant reviews
(D) Special discounts

GO ON TO THE NEXT PAGE

| From: | Cian Rousseau <c.rousseau@eurofox.fr> |
|---|---|
| To: | Milla Grzesik <milla.g@maplage.fr> |
| Date: | December 6 |
| Subject: | Bus 749 |

The holiday season is always a busy one for travelers, and your scheduled bus trip (EFX 749) from Marseille to Vienna is certainly an example. Due to the large number of bookings, EuroFox Express will be putting additional vehicles into service for those who are willing to switch to a different bus. In exchange, we will provide a travel coupon good for future savings on any EuroFox Express route in France and throughout Europe, valued at €120.00, good for six months from the date of issuance.

Below are two alternative routes that might interest you. The first leaves on the same day, but stops in Milan along the way.

| EFX 430 | Marseille | Dec 20 7:20 P.M. | Milan | Dec 21 3:40 A.M. |
|---|---|---|---|---|
| EFX 430 | Milan | Dec 21 4:50 A.M. | Vienna | Dec 21 2:10 P.M. |

The second, a direct route, leaves early in the morning the day after you were originally scheduled to depart.

| EFX 789 | Marseille | Dec 21 6:25 A.M. | Vienna | Dec 21 11:50 P.M. |
|---|---|---|---|---|

To volunteer your seat, please call the EuroFox Express ticketing office at 0800 4 91 01 39 21. Because of high passenger volume, we suggest arriving at least an hour before your scheduled departure. For general information, please visit our Web site at www.eurofox.fr.

On behalf of EuroFox Express, we hope you have a wonderful holiday season.

Sincerely,

Cian Rousseau
Ticketing
EuroFox Express

---

**Passenger Name: Milla Grzesik**

| Route | Date | Boarding | Departing |
|---|---|---|---|
| EFX 789 | Dec 21 | 6:10 A.M. | 6:25 A.M. |
| **To** | **From** | **Gate** | **Seat** |
| Vienna | Marseille | 5 | 10B |

Please board with GROUP 3 passengers. Be aware that all wheeled baggage must be stored underneath the carriage to comply with European safety regulations.

**176.** Why was the e-mail written?

(A) To promote a new destination for holiday vacations
(B) To warn passengers about long wait times
(C) To update a traveler on new routes to Vienna
(D) To encourage a traveler to change buses

**177.** What is indicated about the coupon?

(A) It must be used within a certain period.
(B) It is valid for multiple bus companies.
(C) It was given to Ms. Grzesik as a gift.
(D) It can only be used in France.

**178.** What did Ms. Grzesik most likely do after receiving the e-mail?

(A) Downloaded a booking application
(B) Contacted a ticketing office
(C) Sent an e-mail response
(D) Left for the bus station

**179.** What does the bus ticket indicate about Ms. Grzesik's new bus route?

(A) Passengers must not use wheeled suitcases.
(B) It passes through Milan.
(C) It departs in the evening.
(D) Passengers must board according to their group number.

**180.** When is Ms. Grzesik scheduled to arrive at her final destination?

(A) At 4:50 A.M.
(B) At 6:25 A.M.
(C) At 2:10 P.M.
(D) At 11:50 P.M.

GO ON TO THE NEXT PAGE

**Questions 181-185** refer to the following announcement and e-mail.

---

### Global Corporation Philanthropy Association (GCPA)
Business Education

The GCPA welcomes you to take part in a live, online lecture titled "How to Receive Corporate Grants." The lecture focuses on important information to be included in a grant proposal which will increase your organization's chances of receiving financial or other types of support from various local and international companies.

Dimitri Rio, Director of Development at the Baltar Foundation, will present this event. The lecture, which will be on 23 March from 4:15 P.M. to 6:15 P.M. EST, will be hosted by Janice Lacherman from the television news program, *International Business Relations*. Registration must be completed by 28 February; please visit www.gcpa.org/1512_lecture for more information on fees and other details. While filling out the registration form, you will have the option of including a question for Mr. Rio. During the lecture, he will answer as many as he can. In addition, all answers to questions submitted by those participating will be posted online by 1 April.

---

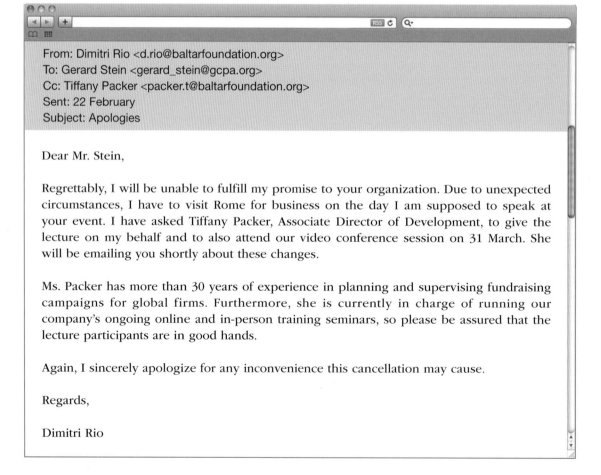

From: Dimitri Rio <d.rio@baltarfoundation.org>
To: Gerard Stein <gerard_stein@gcpa.org>
Cc: Tiffany Packer <packer.t@baltarfoundation.org>
Sent: 22 February
Subject: Apologies

Dear Mr. Stein,

Regrettably, I will be unable to fulfill my promise to your organization. Due to unexpected circumstances, I have to visit Rome for business on the day I am supposed to speak at your event. I have asked Tiffany Packer, Associate Director of Development, to give the lecture on my behalf and to also attend our video conference session on 31 March. She will be emailing you shortly about these changes.

Ms. Packer has more than 30 years of experience in planning and supervising fundraising campaigns for global firms. Furthermore, she is currently in charge of running our company's ongoing online and in-person training seminars, so please be assured that the lecture participants are in good hands.

Again, I sincerely apologize for any inconvenience this cancellation may cause.

Regards,

Dimitri Rio

**181.** What is suggested about the lecture?

(A) It has been paid for by corporate grants.
(B) It is intended for news reporters.
(C) It will be broadcasted live on a television network.
(D) It will provide fundraising advice.

**182.** What is indicated about lecture participants?

(A) They will receive a professional certificate.
(B) They should send any questions to Ms. Lacherman.
(C) They must sign up for the event in advance.
(D) They must be GCPA members.

**183.** When will Mr. Rio go on a business trip?

(A) On February 22
(B) On March 23
(C) On March 31
(D) On April 1

**184.** What has Mr. Rio has arranged?

(A) To send a financial contribution to the GCPA
(B) To meet with Mr. Stein in Rome
(C) To have a colleague take his place at an event
(D) To have his presentation made available on a Web site

**185.** What is suggested about the Baltar Foundation?

(A) It is looking for a new Director of Development.
(B) It offers online training opportunities.
(C) It has been in business for 30 years.
(D) It is regularly featured on *International Business Relations*.

*GO ON TO THE NEXT PAGE*

**Questions 186-190** refer to the following Web page, article, and review.

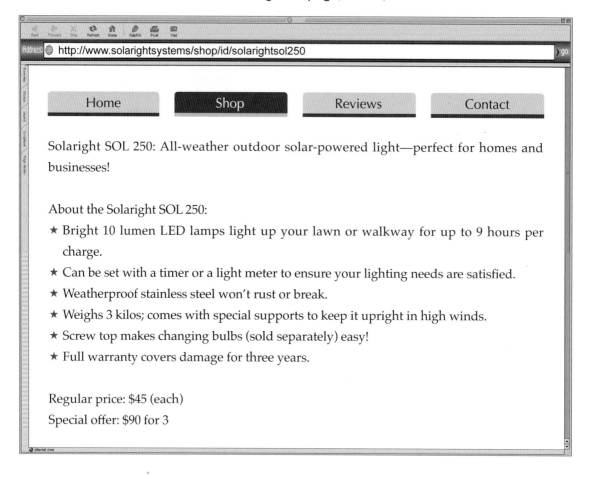

Solaright SOL 250: All-weather outdoor solar-powered light—perfect for homes and businesses!

About the Solaright SOL 250:

★ Bright 10 lumen LED lamps light up your lawn or walkway for up to 9 hours per charge.
★ Can be set with a timer or a light meter to ensure your lighting needs are satisfied.
★ Weatherproof stainless steel won't rust or break.
★ Weighs 3 kilos; comes with special supports to keep it upright in high winds.
★ Screw top makes changing bulbs (sold separately) easy!
★ Full warranty covers damage for three years.

Regular price: $45 (each)
Special offer: $90 for 3

---

## Notice to Solaright Owners

OAKDALE (Jan 23) – The popular Solaright SOL 250, an outdoor light that charges during the daytime, has a problem.

A public relations coordinator for Solaright Systems issued a notice earlier today stating that, "Some SOL 250 units have been found to have an issue with the charging panel. Solaright Systems guarantees customer satisfaction. Businesses with large installations can request a service technician to come and repair faulty units. Residential owners can return any faulty units and get a replacement, free of charge."

Questions about any of Solaright's products can be directed to their 24-hour helpdesk at info@solarightsystems.com.

---

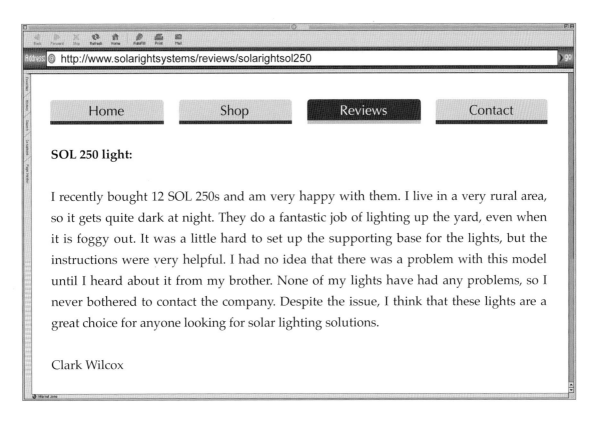

SOL 250 light:

I recently bought 12 SOL 250s and am very happy with them. I live in a very rural area, so it gets quite dark at night. They do a fantastic job of lighting up the yard, even when it is foggy out. It was a little hard to set up the supporting base for the lights, but the instructions were very helpful. I had no idea that there was a problem with this model until I heard about it from my brother. None of my lights have had any problems, so I never bothered to contact the company. Despite the issue, I think that these lights are a great choice for anyone looking for solar lighting solutions.

Clark Wilcox

**186.** What is included in the price of the SOL 250?

(A) A three-year warranty
(B) Free delivery
(C) Replacement components
(D) Protective covers

**187.** Why was the article written?

(A) To announce a new home appliance
(B) To correct inaccurate pricing information
(C) To compare several products
(D) To alert readers to a product defect

**188.** In the article, the word "issued" in paragraph 2, line 1, is the closest in meaning to

(A) made public
(B) brought out
(C) assigned
(D) appeared

**189.** What does Mr. Wilcox confirm about the SOL 250's product description?

(A) The light is difficult to charge.
(B) The light is easy to clean.
(C) The light is very bright.
(D) The light is simple to set up.

**190.** What does Mr. Wilcox suggest about his lights?

(A) Their warranty was unable to cover everything.
(B) Their maintenance costs are much more expensive than expected.
(C) Their materials are not very strong.
(D) Their charging panels work well.

*GO ON TO THE NEXT PAGE*

**Questions 191-195** refer to the following form, e-mail, and text message.

---

### VISITOR ACCESS CODE (VAC) APPLICATION FORM

Send this form to Ms. Jacqueline Yakazuki, fax number 410-555-6953.

**VAC recipient's information:**
**Name:** Sally Paige      **Department:** IT
**Staff/Company ID number:** 8027
   **Basic access:** Monday to Friday, 8:00 A.M. – 8:00 P.M.
_X_ **Extended access:** Monday to Friday, 8:00 A.M. – 10:30 P.M.
_X_ **Special access** (Fill in relevant days and times): Saturdays, 10:30 A.M. – 5:30 P.M.
**Building(s):**   Benford  X  Pine
**Start date:** February 8      **End date:** March 5

**Requestor's information** (Requestor must be either a manager or director of the recipient's department)
**Name:** Donnie Shaw
**E-mail:** dshaw@epsen.gov
**Signature and date:** *Donnie Shaw* January 28

**Note:**
After we receive your VAC request, it will take a minimum of four working days to process. Once access has been granted, an e-mail containing a 5-digit VAC will be sent to the recipient.

---

| | |
|---|---|
| **To** | Sally Paige <s_paige@epsen.gov> |
| **From** | Jacqueline Yakazuki <j_yakazuki@epsen.gov> |
| **Date** | February 3 |
| **Subject** | VAC |

Dear Ms. Paige,

Your request for special and extended access to the Pine Building has been approved. To gain entry, you must use the provided visitor access code (VAC) along with your employee card. Your VAC is 27795. To enter the building after normal business hours, please follow these steps:

• Place your card to the card reader. An orange light on the reader will begin to flash.
• Next, enter your VAC using the touch screen.
• The flashing orange light will then turn green, allowing you to enter the building.

If you input your VAC incorrectly, the light will turn red, and you will hear a loud beep for five seconds. You will then have three more chances to input the correct code before you are completely locked out. Should you have any issues accessing the building, or once you are inside, please contact me at 410-555-4033.

Sincerely,

Jacqueline Yakazuki, Security Management

From: Sally Paige, 351-555-7240

Received: Monday, February 8, 8:02 A.M.

Hello Ms. Yakazuki,

I tried calling, but I couldn't reach you. I entered the VAC (27795) you emailed me, but the light keeps flashing red. Could you please contact me as soon as you receive this message? I have been shut out of the building.

**191.** What is suggested about Mr. Shaw?

(A) He has a leadership role in the IT Department.
(B) He submitted the application in February.
(C) He works in a different office than Ms. Paige.
(D) He will have a meeting with Ms. Paige regarding her project.

**192.** What is indicated about the VAC application form?

(A) It must be emailed to the security management office.
(B) It must provide a reason for the access request.
(C) It must include a copy of the employee's card.
(D) It must be filed at least four days in advance of the code being used.

**193.** How will Ms. Paige know that the VAC she enters is valid?

(A) The color of a light will change.
(B) A sound will ring for five seconds.
(C) A light will repeatedly flash.
(D) The volume of a sound will increase.

**194.** What is NOT indicated about the Security Management Office?

(A) It has a fax machine.
(B) It provides after-hours access.
(C) It issues access codes to employees.
(D) It has introduced new security policies.

**195.** What is suggested about Ms. Paige?

(A) She interviewed with Ms. Yakazuki.
(B) She will be promoted to a manager.
(C) She entered her VAC more than three times.
(D) She would like an extension to her access period.

GO ON TO THE NEXT PAGE

## QiTech Electronics

32 Westpark Road, Charleston, WV 25302

(304) 555-0722

Seven Days a Week, 10 A.M. to 7 P.M.

### Get Great Deals at Our Weeklong New Year's Sale!

Saturday, January 1, to Sunday, January 9

Desktop and laptop computers, monitors, and accessories - 30% Off

Cameras, A/V equipment, and portable storage - 10% Off

Mobile phones and tablets - 20% Off

Software - 25% Off

**Note:** To get ready for the sale, QiTech will close its doors at 5 P.M. on December 31. Refunds for products sold during the sale will be made in in-store credit only.

QiClub members will receive an additional 5% discount and extended warranties on all products. Sign up today on our Web site! Questions? Ask any of our helpful staff members at any time.

---

| **To:** | All Staff |
|---|---|
| **From:** | Michael Chan <m.chan@qitech.com> |
| **Date:** | November 26 |
| **Subject:** | Availability |

Hello all,

In order to move stock to the shelves and clean the store, a crew will be needed to work through the night of December 31. I have organized a late-night meal from Icarus so that everyone who works that day will be able to enjoy dinner as well as receive overtime pay. Contact Rebekah Johnson by December 20 if you are able to work that shift.

Sincerely,

Michael Chan, General Manager

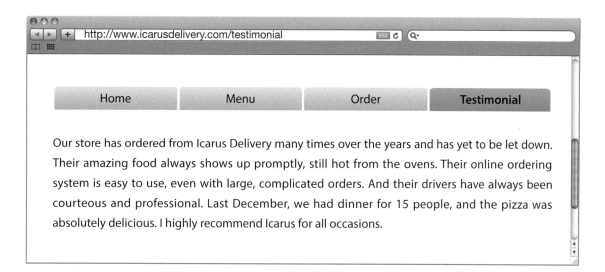

Our store has ordered from Icarus Delivery many times over the years and has yet to be let down. Their amazing food always shows up promptly, still hot from the ovens. Their online ordering system is easy to use, even with large, complicated orders. And their drivers have always been courteous and professional. Last December, we had dinner for 15 people, and the pizza was absolutely delicious. I highly recommend Icarus for all occasions.

**196.** According to the advertisement, what will happen on December 31?

(A) An electronics sale will begin.
(B) A Web site will be updated.
(C) A business will close early.
(D) A delivery of merchandise will arrive.

**197.** What does Mr. Chan ask employees to do?

(A) Join a quarterly meeting
(B) Prepare for a weeklong event
(C) Explain a scheduling process
(D) Add additional staff to help customers

**198.** In the e-mail, the word "organized" in paragraph 1, line 2 is closest in meaning to

(A) classified
(B) arranged
(C) adjusted
(D) straightened

**199.** How many employees responded to Mr. Chan's request?

(A) 10
(B) 15
(C) 25
(D) 30

**200.** What is NOT mentioned in Icarus's online testimonial?

(A) The performance of its employees
(B) The simplicity of its Web site
(C) The low prices of its dishes
(D) The speed of its service

GO ON TO THE NEXT PAGE

TEST 9

# READING TEST

In the Reading test, you will read a variety of texts and answer several different types of reading comprehension questions. The entire Reading test will last 75 minutes. There are three parts, and directions are given for each part. You are encouraged to answer as many questions as possible within the time allowed.

You must mark your answers on the separate answer sheet. Do not write your answers in the test book.

# PART 5

**Directions:** A word or phrase is missing in each of the sentences below. Four answer choices are given below each sentence. Select the best answer to complete the sentence. Then mark the letter (A), (B), (C), or (D) on your answer sheet.

**101.** Mr. Kang asked some coworkers to help ------- with the staff training workshop.

(A) he
(B) him
(C) his
(D) himself

**102.** Prager Engineering's staff members have thorough ------- of the latest drafting software.

(A) known
(B) knowledgeable
(C) know
(D) knowledge

**103.** ------- 50,000 people are anticipated to visit the amusement park over the holiday weekend.

(A) Considerably
(B) Fairly
(C) Roughly
(D) Heavily

**104.** Masie Stark's newest article is a ------- and revealing analysis of stock market trends.

(A) wisest
(B) wisdom
(C) wise
(D) wisely

**105.** ------- the end of the convention, company representatives are requested to fill out an exhibitor opinion survey.

(A) When
(B) While
(C) Toward
(D) Since

**106.** Before opening the access panel, make sure that the power cord has not been ------- connected.

(A) accident
(B) accidental
(C) accidents
(D) accidentally

**107.** Dartmoor Clinical College is committed to keeping costs ------- for its medical students.

(A) necessary
(B) trimming
(C) affordable
(D) allowed

**108.** Ms. Hatcher ------- posts in many parts of the organization before she retired.

(A) occupied
(B) occupation
(C) occupational
(D) occupying

**109.** To publish the book on time, designers must send all ------- to the illustrations to the editor by Monday.

(A) articles
(B) proposals
(C) suggestions
(D) revisions

**110.** Full-scale production of the selected design will not be ------- before the new year.

(A) checked in
(B) carried out
(C) turned away
(D) packed up

**111.** Refurbishing the Merseyside Assembly Plant is the ------- of the four relocation proposals.

(A) costly
(B) costing
(C) cost
(D) costliest

**112.** Luigi Produce provides the freshest fruits and vegetables to stores thanks to advanced ------- and delivery methods.

(A) preservation
(B) preserve
(C) preserved
(D) preserves

**113.** ------- the demand for the PFS-2x model smart phone, production will be tripled next quarter.

(A) Even if
(B) Just as
(C) As a result of
(D) Moreover

**114.** Depending on the results of your interview, we ------- you to take a written test.

(A) are asking
(B) must be asking
(C) have been asked
(D) may ask

**115.** A red tag means that a shipment must be inspected, ------- a green tag means that it can be sent out.

(A) almost
(B) whereas
(C) both
(D) whether

**116.** Always mention the reference number of your transaction in any ------- with our client service associates.

(A) correspondence
(B) corresponds
(C) correspondent
(D) correspondingly

**117.** The editorial team at the *Calumet Gazette* ------- prefers articles with short headlines.

(A) generally
(B) finally
(C) originally
(D) annually

**118.** Lerner Associates focuses on ------- promotional campaigns to help businesses market their services.

(A) personally
(B) personality
(C) personalizes
(D) personalized

**119.** ------- the subscription fee is less than 150 dollars, Kwak Financial Services will continue to receive the publication.

(A) Otherwise
(B) In addition
(C) As long as
(D) Together with

**120.** Tipton Freight's union leaders meet monthly with staff to make sure that labor laws ------- properly.

(A) would have followed
(B) are being followed
(C) to be followed
(D) had been followed

*GO ON TO THE NEXT PAGE*

**121.** Inquiries about our new products should be directed to the ------- sales representative.

(A) appropriate
(B) subsequent
(C) traceable
(D) critical

**122.** Dr. Akihara normally ------- only with patients who made appointments, but she decided to make an exception today.

(A) appears
(B) suits
(C) meets
(D) comments

**123.** Company stakeholders are carefully examining the monthly budget ------- proposed to them by the contracting firm.

(A) attributes
(B) planners
(C) requirements
(D) transmissions

**124.** The designer admitted that the popularity of his new line of clothing was ------- the result of opportune timing.

(A) parting
(B) partly
(C) parted
(D) parts

**125.** Ms. Patel kept records of ------- the employee training program covered in the last quarter.

(A) several
(B) everything
(C) other
(D) any

**126.** Initially manufacturing only computer software, Dyno Tech ------- produces wireless audio devices as well.

(A) thereby
(B) soon
(C) much
(D) now

**127.** The research shows that television commercials have a more ------- impact than either internet or radio advertisements.

(A) lasted
(B) last
(C) lasting
(D) lastly

**128.** Mr. Chen finished his ------- of his client's accounts this Tuesday.

(A) submission
(B) renovation
(C) audit
(D) comment

**129.** ------- events in the fourth quarter of last year caused Wisdan Publishing's production schedule to be delayed.

(A) Characteristic
(B) Unforeseen
(C) Entire
(D) Marginal

**130.** Ms. Koike accessed the online database ------- the progress reports from the last two quarters.

(A) to analyze
(B) will analyze
(C) analyzed
(D) analyzes

**Directions:** Read the texts that follow. A word, phrase, or sentence is missing in parts of each text. Four answer choices for each question are given below the text. Select the best answer to complete the text. Then mark the letter (A), (B), (C), or (D) on your answer sheet.

**Questions 131-134** refer to the following letter.

Pamela Stone
8920 Alderman Drive
San Jose, CA 94088

Dear Ms. Stone,

This letter is to confirm your reservation for the Executive Suite at the Gaze Sky Hotel from October 12 to October 14. You can check in ------- at 1 P.M. on Thursday. -------.
        **131.**                  **132.**
You will be charged extra if you check out later.

We are confident that you and your husband will like the ------- designed facilities. The
        **133.**
hotel has both an indoor and outdoor pool. We also have a state-of-the-art fitness center for your exercise needs. If you need to print something, stop by our advanced media room. Information on other ------- can be found on our Web site.
        **134.**

We look forward to welcoming you to the Gaze Sky Hotel.

Sincerely,

*Bernard Witson*

Bernard Witson
Head of Guest Services

---

**131.** (A) starts
(B) started
(C) start
(D) starting

**132.** (A) You must leave your room before 12 P.M. on the last day.
(B) We have applied the family discount to your invoice.
(C) Fortunately, our hotel is conveniently located in the downtown area.
(D) Thank you for filling out the guest satisfaction survey.

**133.** (A) possibly
(B) tastefully
(C) initially
(D) nearly

**134.** (A) utilities
(B) amenities
(C) costs
(D) visits

GO ON TO THE NEXT PAGE

Kensoi Transport operates the biggest public parking lot in Jeffmont. Commuters who wish to reserve a parking spot can do so by registering online or in person. A range of contract ------- are offered to interested individuals. There are occasions when all 3,000
**135.**
spots in the parking lot are -------. In this case, commuters without a designated spot
**136.**
may park their vehicles in the overflow garage ------- the street. Those with a reserved
**137.**
spot can rent a spot for three months at a time. -------. Please review the agreement
**138.**
and submit it to Kensoi's main office. To receive more details, send an e-mail to info@kensoitp.com.

**135.** (A) typing
(B) types
(C) type
(D) typed

**136.** (A) constructed
(B) filled
(C) tight
(D) accessible

**137.** (A) through
(B) within
(C) beyond
(D) across

**138.** (A) The terms and conditions of use can be found online.
(B) Kensoi operates another lot in a neighboring city.
(C) Jeffmont has recently increased its public parking fees.
(D) Commuters should download a mobile traffic application.

**Questions 139-142** refer to the following letter.

November 30

*Tasteful Eats Magazine*
8000 Duferford Road
Pittsburgh, PA 15106

Dear *Tasteful Eats Magazine* readers,

We are sending you this letter to inform you that starting January 1, the annual subscription price for *Tasteful Eats Magazine* will be -------. The usual fee of $35.99 will
**139.**
increase to $37.85. Rest assured that this ------- does come with advantages. Seven
**140.**
new sections ------- in the magazine, including a coupon page and a restaurant review
**141.**
column. To terminate your subscription, please call our customer service center. -------.
**142.**

**139.** (A) refunded
(B) raised
(C) exchanged
(D) stopped

**140.** (A) obstacle
(B) association
(C) team
(D) adjustment

**141.** (A) features
(B) will be featured
(C) a feature
(D) have featured

**142.** (A) Several local restaurants will be participating in the program.
(B) A discount coupon will be sent to you as a sign of appreciation.
(C) *Tasteful Eats Magazine* is celebrating its 50 year anniversary in December.
(D) If we don't hear anything from you, your contract will be automatically renewed.

**Questions 143-146** refer to the following review.

---

**Theater Performance Wows Spectators**

By Ashraf Iftikhar

Karachi (May 22) – The critically-acclaimed new production, *Zindabad!*, had its opening night last Saturday at the Sindh Theater.

Presented by members of Karachi's Acting Wheel Drama Club, this play ------- the
                                                                        **143.**
cultural and spiritual traditions that have deeply influenced the values of modern
Pakistan.

------- are seen from the perspective of Ali Bhagat, who finds a new home in Karachi
**144.**
after leaving behind his home in India.

This play is powerful and moving, and the acting is amazing, especially knowing that it
is an amateur production. -------. The performance takes just an hour to cover the story
                          **145.**
of a lifetime. A story like this requires more time to fully develop, and that is my only
complaint about ------- was otherwise a superb performance.
                **146.**

---

**143.** (A) will examine
(B) had examined
(C) examines
(D) to examine

**144.** (A) Attendees
(B) Stages
(C) Events
(D) Directions

**145.** (A) The actors really bring their characters to life.
(B) However, there will be no opportunity to rehearse for a while.
(C) Theater management will have to be careful about expenses.
(D) It is clear that professional assistance is necessary.

**146.** (A) what
(B) which
(C) one
(D) some

# PART 7

**Directions:** In this part you will read a selection of texts, such as magazine and newspaper articles, e-mails, and instant messages. Each text or set of texts is followed by several questions. Select the best answer for each question and mark the letter (A), (B), (C) or (D) on your answer sheet.

**Questions 147-148** refer to the following e-mail.

| | |
|---|---|
| **From:** | Wishsong Ceramics <cs@wishsongceramics.com> |
| **To:** | Da-eun Kang <dkang@bindlestiffscafe.com> |
| **Date:** | March 19 |
| **Subject:** | Order 335401 |

Dear Ms. Kang,

This is to verify that your order has been canceled. Please keep the following order summary for your records:

Order 335401:
120 white 20oz coffee mugs (payment processed on March 18)
Current status: canceled

The amount billed to your credit card will be refunded within three business days.

Thank you for your interest in Wishsong Ceramics.

Affordable, attractive dishware for every culinary need!

**147.** Why was the e-mail sent?

(A) To confirm an original order quantity
(B) To provide notice of a changed order
(C) To update a customer about a shipping delay
(D) To offer details about a store policy

**148.** What information does Ms. Kang receive about a payment?

(A) She will be sent a receipt in three days.
(B) She will receive a discount on her next purchase.
(C) She will not get a full refund.
(D) She will not pay for the items.

GO ON TO THE NEXT PAGE

**Questions 149-150** refer to the following e-mail.

To: staff_list@theomarketing.com
From: ctheobald@theomarketing.com
Date: March 8
Subject: Personnel Update

Good afternoon everyone,

I'm pleased to introduce our latest addition to the Marketing Department, Andrew Hendriksson. He will be taking over many of Blake Hirano's responsibilities, including creating online advertising and promotions. Ian Young and Kasim Aksoy are also going to take care of some of Blake's daily tasks. Ian will now be in charge of writing press releases, and Kasim will manage our social media accounts, including our own Web site. On behalf of everyone in the department, I would like to wish Blake a happy retirement and also congratulate Andrew on joining our team!

Regards,
Cory Theobald

**149.** What is one purpose of the e-mail?

(A) To discuss a recent press release
(B) To announce a job vacancy
(C) To welcome a new employee
(D) To request staff feedback

**150.** Who used to create online promotions?

(A) Blake Hirano
(B) Ian Young
(C) Kasim Aksoy
(D) Cory Theobald

**Questions 151-152** refer to the following text message chain.

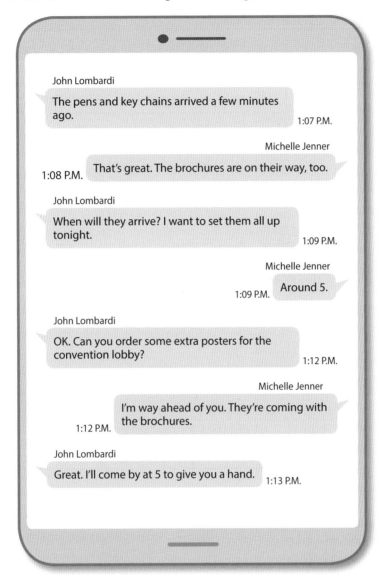

John Lombardi
The pens and key chains arrived a few minutes ago.
1:07 P.M.

Michelle Jenner
1:08 P.M. That's great. The brochures are on their way, too.

John Lombardi
When will they arrive? I want to set them all up tonight.
1:09 P.M.

Michelle Jenner
1:09 P.M. Around 5.

John Lombardi
OK. Can you order some extra posters for the convention lobby?
1:12 P.M.

Michelle Jenner
I'm way ahead of you. They're coming with the brochures.
1:12 P.M.

John Lombardi
Great. I'll come by at 5 to give you a hand.
1:13 P.M.

**151.** What does Mr. Lombardi plan to do?

(A) Redesign a convention poster
(B) Organize some promotional materials
(C) Pick up more brochures for the booth
(D) Leave the office at five o'clock

**152.** At 1:12 P.M., what does Ms. Jenner mean when she writes, "I'm way ahead of you"?

(A) She has arrived at an event early.
(B) She made a payment in advance.
(C) She has already requested additional supplies.
(D) She would like directions to a venue.

*GO ON TO THE NEXT PAGE*

TEST 10

**Questions 153-155** refer to the following information on a Web page.

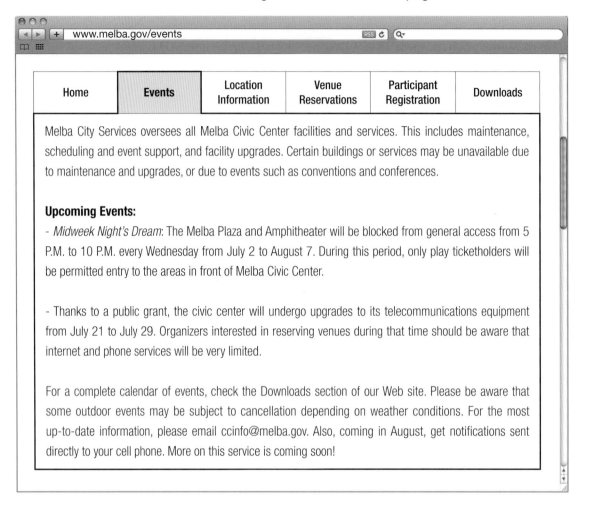

| Home | Events | Location Information | Venue Reservations | Participant Registration | Downloads |
|------|--------|---------------------|-------------------|-------------------------|-----------|

Melba City Services oversees all Melba Civic Center facilities and services. This includes maintenance, scheduling and event support, and facility upgrades. Certain buildings or services may be unavailable due to maintenance and upgrades, or due to events such as conventions and conferences.

**Upcoming Events:**

- *Midweek Night's Dream*: The Melba Plaza and Amphitheater will be blocked from general access from 5 P.M. to 10 P.M. every Wednesday from July 2 to August 7. During this period, only play ticketholders will be permitted entry to the areas in front of Melba Civic Center.

- Thanks to a public grant, the civic center will undergo upgrades to its telecommunications equipment from July 21 to July 29. Organizers interested in reserving venues during that time should be aware that internet and phone services will be very limited.

For a complete calendar of events, check the Downloads section of our Web site. Please be aware that some outdoor events may be subject to cancellation depending on weather conditions. For the most up-to-date information, please email ccinfo@melba.gov. Also, coming in August, get notifications sent directly to your cell phone. More on this service is coming soon!

**153.** What is the purpose of the Web page?

(A) To describe some services
(B) To advertise a conference
(C) To announce some Melba City projects
(D) To highlight cultural attractions in Melba City

**154.** Why will some areas of the Melba Civic Center be closed to the public on Wednesdays?

(A) They will be undergoing renovation work.
(B) They will host a performance.
(C) They were affected by inclement weather.
(D) They will be part of a local race route.

**155.** According to the Web page, how can people get the most current event schedule?

(A) By reviewing a calendar
(B) By visiting a Web site
(C) By sending an e-mail
(D) By signing up for text message alerts

## Metro Business Update

MAPLE CITY (Aug. 12) – DGC Industries will be acquired by Peyton Automation, according to an announcement yesterday. That's good news for city residents as Peyton affirmed that it would resume the expansion of DGC's manufacturing plant.

DGC's local plant handles the bulk of its manufacturing needs, providing work for thousands in Maple City. However, due to decreasing sales over the past five years, the expansion on the facility was put on hold. Peyton spokesperson Jesse Jarvi confirmed plans to begin hiring after the work on the plant is completed.

"Final job interviews will be conducted in November, and the new fabrication areas are expected to come online in December," said Jarvi.

The plant will continue to make DGC's main line of industrial products, as well as become the main production site for Peyton's new, six-axis assembly robots.

Peyton Automation has been the leader in the automation equipment market for three years in a row, according to industry experts. It is based in Singapore.

---

**156.** What is the purpose of the article?

(A) To report on the relocation of a business
(B) To confirm the opening of a new store
(C) To give an update on a halted project
(D) To review changing trends in manufacturing.

**157.** According to Mr. Jarvi, what will happen in November?

(A) A business will hire more staff.
(B) A new product line will be announced.
(C) A plant will undergo repairs.
(D) A building will be demolished.

**158.** What is indicated about Peyton Automation?

(A) It is closing its Singapore office.
(B) It has its headquarters in Maple City.
(C) It manufactures assembly robots.
(D) It has recently lost important clients.

GO ON TO THE NEXT PAGE

**Questions 159-162** refer to the following online chat discussion.

---

**Frank Carver [2:07 P.M.]**
Hello, everyone. Do we have any updates on the Lawson Building bid?

**Kiyoma Aditya [2:08 P.M.]**
I spoke with Ms. Rasan over the phone on Tuesday. She said the executives were still looking over the proposals and that a decision would be made within the week.

**Frank Carver [2:09 P.M.]**
I'm concerned. We need to order the custom lighting we included in our estimate by tomorrow. Otherwise, even if we complete the flooring ahead of schedule, we won't be able to finish on time.

**Anna Kang [2:10 P.M.]**
Oh, I put in that order yesterday afternoon.

**Frank Carver [2:11 P.M.]**
That might be problematic. If we don't win the bid, we'll be stuck with those lighting fixtures. We don't have any other current projects that need them. When do we have to cancel the order by before needing to pay a fee?

**Anna Kang [2:14 P.M.]**
I assumed that we'd be selected again this time as we've done business with them for many years now. I'll look into it.

**Frank Carver [2:15 P.M.]**
Kiyoma, would you please contact Ms. Rasan to see if she has any news for us?

**Anna Kang [2:21 P.M.]**
We're able to back out before 6 P.M. today without incurring a fine.

**Kiyoma Aditya [2:22 P.M.]**
Actually, Frank, I've just spoken with Ms. Rasan, and Lawson has selected Mangrove Co. to do the work.

**Frank Carver [2:24 P.M.]**
That's unfortunate. But this wasn't the only pending contract we have, so let's not get too disappointed.

---

SEND

**159.** What industry do the writers most likely work in?

(A) Gardening
(B) Interior design
(C) Photography
(D) Real estate

**160.** At 2:14 P.M. what does Ms. Kang indicate she will do when she says, "I'll look into it"?

(A) Check the quantity of an item
(B) Inquire about a deadline
(C) Reschedule a shipment
(D) Calculate the price of a service

**161.** What information does Ms. Rasan give?

(A) How to provide a product refund
(B) Who will renovate the Lawson Building
(C) Where to locate affordable flooring
(D) Why Mr. Lawson did not call back

**162.** What will Ms. Kang most likely do next?

(A) Try to persuade Ms. Rasan
(B) Draft a new proposal
(C) Cancel a purchase
(D) Plan a work schedule

**Questions 163-165** refer to the following e-mail.

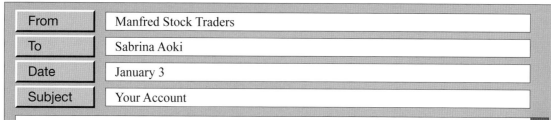

| From | Manfred Stock Traders |
|---|---|
| To | Sabrina Aoki |
| Date | January 3 |
| Subject | Your Account |

Dear Ms. Aoki,

Please note that the password to your account has been successfully updated. If you did not make this change, please contact us at (800) 555-1212 within 48 hours. —[1]—. This is an automated e-mail, so please do not reply or send it to another address. —[2]—.

If you requested to change your information, no further action is required on your part. —[3]—.

This alert has been sent as part of our effort to keep your account safe. —[4]—.

Sincerely,
Daniel Pasqualetti
Manfred Stock Traders

Make strategic stock purchases with our revolutionary trading software, available at www.mstrade.com!

**163.** Why was the e-mail sent to Ms. Aoki?

(A) To announce a promotional event
(B) To ask for a payment
(C) To notify her of some account activity
(D) To inform her of a new security program

**164.** What is Ms. Aoki advised to do?

(A) Call if she did not request a change
(B) Check a monthly billing statement
(C) Download a program
(D) Change her account settings

**165.** In which of the positions marked [1], [2], [3], and [4] does the following sentence best belong?

"An Operations Support representative will help you to resolve the situation."

(A) [1]
(B) [2]
(C) [3]
(D) [4]

GO ON TO THE NEXT PAGE

TEST 10

**Questions 166-168** refer to the following e-mail.

From: info@towercontrolvid.com
To: registered-user list
Date: August 23
Subject: Version 4.5

Hello,

We are happy to announce that Towercontrol 4.5, the latest version of the video editing software you have purchased is available for download.

**Visual and Sound Effects:** An additional 50 effects are included in the updated effects library. All effects feature several options which can be turned on and off. To get them, access your online account and select the "updates" tab. A manual that explains how to use these new effects will be delivered by express shipping soon.

**Introducing Stock Video:** You can now take advantage of free video clips; use them for transitions between your clips whenever you want to add extra content to your project. There are many stock videos to choose from, so be sure to set aside some time to become familiar with them.

**Manage Online Distribution Quickly:** Share quickly, whether with a movie studio or with friends on social media! Download the file sharing manual at www.towercontrolvid.com/sharing to find step-by-step instructions to bridge your various network accounts to your video masterpiece.

Your support is important to us. We welcome the opportunity to help you make your video editing experience a pleasure!

Regards,

Towercontrol Video Customer Support Team

166. What is the purpose of the e-mail?

(A) To offer long-time customers a reward
(B) To promote a new software product
(C) To ask for additional information
(D) To provide details about a computer program

167. What is being mailed to the customers?

(A) A magazine about the latest electronic devices
(B) A tutorial on installing an update
(C) A large gallery of stock videos
(D) A guide on using some new effects

168. In the e-mail, the word "bridge" in paragraph 4, line 3, is closest meaning to

(A) link
(B) extend
(C) reach
(D) cross

**Questions 169-171** refer to the following letter.

---

To the Editor:

This letter is in regard to the hospitality review, "Timeless Vacation Destinations: Hatheh Resort," that was printed in the September issue of *Comfy Traveler*. The pictures of the resort were beautiful, and it was wonderful to see the business get some much-deserved attention. But I noticed something that should be mentioned. —[1]—.

The reviewer says Arthur Taylor originally designed the resort's unique buildings. However, while he was certainly an important contributor, his role was mainly to provide funding. —[2]—. Instead, Kyle Silva was in charge of Hatheh's planning and construction. The reason why I know this is that I was the main person that Hatheh Resort hired to design the gardens and outdoor areas of the facility, so I interacted with Mr. Silva frequently. —[3]—.

The building design only gets a short mention in the review, but I feel that it's important to the history of Hatheh Resort. Thanks to Mr. Silva, tourism to our island has greatly increased and helped local businesses thrive, though he rarely gets credited for it. —[4]—. I feel it is important to set the record straight.

Sincerely,

*Afa Faiz*
Afa Faiz

---

**169.** Why was the letter written?

(A) To highlight a CEO's accomplishments
(B) To describe a vacation
(C) To correct some information
(D) To review some accommodations

**170.** Who most likely is Mr. Faiz?

(A) A facility custodian
(B) A travel writer
(C) A landscape architect
(D) A hotel manager

**171.** In which of the positions marked [1], [2], [3], and [4] does the following sentence best belong?

"He had little to no role in the decision-making process at that stage of the resort's development."

(A) [1]
(B) [2]
(C) [3]
(D) [4]

GO ON TO THE NEXT PAGE

Beach Tree Enterprises
92 E. Chadwell Ct., Pennington, NJ

October 27

Dear Ms. Sirko,

It is my pleasure to inform you that you have been selected for the position of Senior Marketing Manager, starting Tuesday, November 15, at a base salary of $76,000 per year. Per company policy, you will start with a 6-month introductory period. After that time, your performance will be reviewed to determine your eligibility for continued employment.

Please verify your intention to accept this offer no later than Tuesday, November 8. You may do this by either texting or calling (609) 555-0058. If you must start on a date other than the one indicated, be sure to include that information when you contact us. However, due to ongoing projects and the need to actively support our current client accounts, we will not be able to postpone your starting date beyond Thursday, November 24.

On your first day, please visit the Personnel Office before reporting to your department. Please bring this letter, since you will have to sign and date it in front of a Personnel employee (be sure to keep a copy for your own records). Also, during this time, you will need to turn in a copy of your driver's license or passport.

To make your training experience as smooth as possible, we always try to place new hires with a mentor who works in the same role. For this reason, you will work closely with Mr. Kyle Wesleyan, who has held this position for many years. If you have any questions before your first day about our company culture or special requirements, please feel free to get in touch with him by e-mail at kwesleyan@beachtree.com. You are scheduled for the standard staff orientation on Wednesday, November 16, to review company guidelines and procedures, although this can be rescheduled depending on your availability.

We are pleased to welcome you to Beach Tree Enterprises and look forward to working with you.

Sincerely,
Janet Roper
Personnel Director

Acknowledgement of Initial Terms and Conditions
I hereby agree to the terms and conditions as given to me by Beach Tree Enterprises.

Employee signature: *Dasha Sirko*
Employee name: Dasha Sirko
Signed on: November 15

**172.** What is NOT a requirement for new staff?

(A) Submitting the job offer letter
(B) Training under an experienced employee
(C) Providing a form of identification
(D) Showing proof of address

**173.** What is true about Mr. Wesleyan?

(A) He is a client of Beach Tree.
(B) He will lead a staff orientation.
(C) He will evaluate Ms. Sirko in six months.
(D) He is a Senior Marketing Manager.

**174.** When will Ms. Sirko learn more about the company's rules?

(A) On Tuesday
(B) On Wednesday
(C) On Thursday
(D) On Friday

**175.** What is suggested about Ms. Sirko?

(A) She did not reschedule her first working day.
(B) She did not contact anyone about the company culture.
(C) She will not get a pay raise after six months.
(D) She will not work directly with clients during the introductory period.

*GO ON TO THE NEXT PAGE*

## Seaside Escape

Rudy Paula

October 2 – Autumn is officially here, so I set out to check out Maine's countryside. I was anticipating a peaceful, but perhaps somewhat dull, drive along the back roads. Instead, it was gorgeous, with trees bursting with color around every curve. I arrived in Bar Harbor, a quaint seaside town, which can be reached by bus from nearby Portland four times a day. It has a history dating back to 1796 and is bordered by an incredible national park.

I stayed in an inn run by Mr. Bartholomew Dagney called the Critter Lodge. Once I entered, I felt like I was in another era—it was wonderful. Not only is the interior the same as it was more than 100 years ago, some of the food is the same as well! Mr. Dagney specializes in lobster chowder, a dish that the town is famous for. If you happen to be in the area, you should definitely consider visiting this lodge.

Take a look at my Web site for more information:
www.rudygetsout.com
or visit the lodge's site for room availability and bookings:
www.critterlodge.com

| From | Anish Khan <akhan@springertech.com> |
|---|---|
| To | Blaze Larson <blaze.l@takefive.com> |
| Date | October 8 |
| Subject | Convention schedule |

Good morning Mr. Larson,

I appreciate you organizing my trip for the convention I will be attending. However, I just found out that the Critter Lodge, www.critterlodge.com, is just a short way outside of the city hosting the convention. I'd like to be able to end each day with a drive through the beautiful countryside, followed by a relaxing evening by the sea. Would you please find out if they can accommodate my schedule for the same dates? If so, you will also need to cancel the reservations at the Hardport Hotel. According to the confirmation document you emailed to me, they need two days' notice (i.e., by October 13) to avoid a penalty.

Sincerely,

Anish Khan
Vice President, Springertech, Inc.

**176.** What is the purpose of the article?

(A) To recommend accommodations
(B) To describe a new menu
(C) To promote a car rental service
(D) To review an online magazine

**177.** What is stated about the lobster chowder?

(A) It is a regional dish.
(B) It contains many ingredients.
(C) It is affordable.
(D) It is only available in the fall.

**178.** Who most likely is Mr. Larson?

(A) A hotel clerk
(B) A waiter
(C) A programmer
(D) A travel agent

**179.** What is suggested about the convention?

(A) Its lead organizer is Mr. Khan.
(B) Its early registration deadline is October 13.
(C) It offers lunch for participants.
(D) It is taking place in Portland.

**180.** Why does Mr. Khan mention about the Hardport Hotel?

(A) A Web site gave it positive reviews.
(B) It provides transportation to Bar Harbor.
(C) A booking has been made there.
(D) It has no vacancies in October.

GO ON TO THE NEXT PAGE

**Questions 181-185** refer to the following information and form.

# Holderfield Parks

## Event Permits

Any party that wishes to hold an event of 30 people or more at any of the community parks within the Holderfield city limits must obtain an event permit from Holderfield's Parks and Recreation Department.

### Things to Note Before Applying

* All event permits require a $30.00 processing fee, which is nonrefundable. Checks should be made out to the Holderfield Parks and Recreation Department.

* A request for a permit must be submitted to the Holderfield Parks and Recreation Department at least one month prior to the date of the event.

* Applications for event permits must be made in person at the Holderfield Parks and Recreation Department office between 9:00 A.M. and 6:00 P.M., Monday to Friday. Applications will not be accepted online or by postal mail. A completed application form and the application fee must be submitted at the time of processing.

* Applications will be reviewed on a first-come, first-served basis. Please view our event calendar at www.holderfieldparksrecdept.com to see the available dates for each of the parks.

### Other Fees

Most events do not require an additional fee aside from the permit fee. For considerably larger events that involve multiple outside food vendors or live music equipment, other fees will be added. Applicants should include all relevant information on the permit application.

# Holderfield Parks
## Event Permit Application

**Requester:** Carissa Kosko

**Organizations and Number:** Markos Greek Cultural Association, 555-3937

**Event Name:** Flavors of the Mediterranean

**Event Description:** The purpose of the event is to promote different types of Mediterranean foods. Participants can enjoy cooking demonstrations, meet with local chefs, and try authentic Mediterranean cuisine from various food vendors.

**Event Start Time / Date:** 11:00 A.M. / Sunday, August 25

**Event End Time / Date:** 5:00 P.M. / Sunday, August 25

**Location:** Oak Creek Park

**Anticipated Attendance:** 400-700 people

--------------------------------------------------------------------------------

This portion is to be completed by a Holderfield Parks and Recreation Department staff member only: **APPROVED**

---

**181.** For whom is the information sheet intended?

(A) Job candidates
(B) Park employees
(C) Event planners
(D) Travel agents

**182.** What is indicated about the Holderfield Parks and Recreation Department?

(A) It oversees space in several parks.
(B) It accepts online applications.
(C) It issues only 30 permits per year.
(D) It is open seven days a week.

**183.** What is implied about Ms. Kosko?

(A) She gives cooking demonstrations every Sunday.
(B) She recently moved to Holderfield.
(C) She works at a popular local restaurant.
(D) She submitted the application before July 25.

**184.** What is indicated about Flavors of the Mediterranean?

(A) It will feature a music performance.
(B) It is expected to attract over 400 people.
(C) It will require an entrance fee.
(D) It is scheduled to run for two days.

**185.** What will Ms. Kosko probably need to do?

(A) Renew her current permit
(B) Reserve space in another park
(C) Sell tickets at a discount
(D) Pay more than one fee

*GO ON TO THE NEXT PAGE*

TEST 10

**Questions 186-190** refer to the following article, agreement, and information.

---

## K.A. Roth's Archives on Display

The treasured archives of historian and writer K.A. Roth are now open for research at the Wayfield Center, a history research library located at 50 Grove Avenue. "K.A. Roth is one of the most respected writers in the country," said Wayfield Center staff member Clarice Royce. The documents, which contain all of his notable writings as well as a few handwritten copies of his first books, trace Roth's successful career. Also, the archives include interviews, biographies, public speeches, as well as the documentary film based on his life.

The Wayfield Center allows access to rare books, manuscripts, audio materials, and other texts for research purposes only. Patrons must read the Wayfield Center regulations and sign an agreement at the front desk. They also have to go to the third floor, where they must watch a brief video about using the library's materials and facilities. The Wayfield Center is open Monday-Saturday, 10:00 A.M. - 6:00 P.M.

---

## Wayfield Center

### Membership Registration Agreement

Welcome to the Wayfield Center. To ensure that all documents are used for research and to preserve the quality of the collections, patrons must adhere to the regulations regarding the usage of library materials. Please read over the attached document and confirm your understanding of the Wayfield Center's regulations by providing your signature at the bottom. Submit this form at the front desk along with a copy of your photo identification to receive a two-year membership card. Please note that you are not allowed to take any materials from the center.

I have read and accept the terms and conditions of the Wayfield Center.

Date: _February 26_

Name: _Bernard Porter_

Signature: _Bernard Porter_

**186.** In the article, the word "treasured" in paragraph 1, line 1, is closest in meaning to

(A) cherished
(B) hidden
(C) perished
(D) conserved

**187.** Who is Ms. Royce?

(A) A researcher
(B) A novelist
(C) A library employee
(D) A film producer

**188.** What is indicated about the Wayfield Center?

(A) It is available for research only.
(B) It is looking for new materials.
(C) It is revising its policies.
(D) It is adding more storage space.

**189.** What is Mr. Porter required to do?

(A) Return some materials he signed out
(B) Submit a sample of his writing
(C) Pay a fee for membership
(D) Watch an informational video

**190.** What rule in the agreement is NOT mentioned in the information?

(A) Patrons should not bring snacks into the library.
(B) Patrons may not take any library documents.
(C) Patrons may have their bags searched.
(D) Patrons should take care of their personal belongings.

GO ON TO THE NEXT PAGE

TEST 10

**Questions 191-195** refer to the following e-mails and article.

| To | Katherine Ahn |
|---|---|
| From | Jessica Estes |
| Date | 3 July |
| Subject | New space |

Dear Katherine,

I appreciate the time you took to meet with me yesterday. Like I said, I am in search of a new commercial space for my cosmetics shop. My current lease ends in November. I am interested in downtown locations, in or around Aspen Plaza, which cost £3500 or less per month. It's important that the size be close to what we have now, but I'm flexible on the interior design and layout.

In consideration of my employees' financial situations, I need to open at the start of December. So, I am primarily interested in newer spaces that will need less work. The current building we are located in is adequate, but both my workers and I believe moving will help grow the business even further.

Thank you,
Jessica Estes

| To | Jessica Estes |
|---|---|
| From | Katherine Ahn |
| Date | 6 July |
| Subject | RE: New space |

I have found several available locations that I believe may suit your needs. Call me at your convenience, and let me know when you will have time to look at them. I can book visitations around your schedule.

**A. 1029 W. Southern Ave.**
£3430/mo.
Previously occupied by a bakery. Metered street parking available for customers in front. Kitchen area can be converted into a stockroom or office. Limited area for merchandise displays.

**B. 78 Myrtle Pl.**
£3180/mo.
Prime spot opposite First City Bank's headquarters. Underground parking garage located next door. Wheelchair ramp in front of the entrance is damaged. Will need renovations.

**C. 839 S. 10th Dr.**
£3240/mo.
Second floor of Flatpine Mall in the Riverfront neighborhood. Well served by public transportation. Many opportunities for advertising throughout the facility.

Sincerely,
Katherine Ahn

## The Glamour Cat Finds New Spot

By Yvonne Garner

BAYPORT (9 Dec) — The Glamour Cat, a mainstay at 17 Sayer Drive for more than a decade, has been the community's go-to shop for beauty products. Last Saturday, it reopened for business at 78 Myrtle Place, next to the Muon Building.

You can still expect the Glamour Cat to offer you high-quality products and great customer service. If you stop by, I highly recommend treating yourself to a manicure or face massage. Our employees are talented artists in their own right!

Long-time patrons should be aware that the seating area for massages and manicures is slightly smaller than it used to be. It can fill up quickly on weekend afternoons, but the reward for your wait will be great products and the amazing service that has kept the store going all these years.

The new downtown storefront is conveniently located near the Federal Street Commercial Center. The shop itself is wheelchair-friendly. It is open every day, from 10 A.M. to 7 P.M.

---

**191.** Who most likely is Ms. Ahn?

(A) A building owner
(B) A loan officer
(C) A real estate agent
(D) A cosmetics designer

**192.** What is implied about Ms. Estes?

(A) She created a new beauty product line.
(B) She was able to reopen her business on time.
(C) She could not afford higher rent.
(D) She did not want to renovate some displays.

**193.** What is indicated about The Glamour Cat?

(A) It closes early on weekends.
(B) Its services have improved.
(C) It repaired a ramp.
(D) Its stockroom can store more items.

**194.** How is the new cosmetics shop different from the original?

(A) It holds fewer customers.
(B) It is located in a shopping mall.
(C) It provides more manicure services.
(D) It no longer offers face massages.

**195.** In the article, the word "going" in paragraph 3, line 7, is closest in meaning to

(A) operating
(B) passing
(C) departing
(D) traveling

GO ON TO THE NEXT PAGE

**Questions 196-200** refer to the following advertisement and e-mails.

**Intern Needed**

Bluefly, an award-winning marketing firm, is looking for an intern to join our team in its downtown Atlanta office. The successful applicant will have previous experience in office work, preferably with extensive knowledge of social media services. Duties will include responding to online inquiries, tracking subscriber data, posting announcements on social media Web sites, and other administrative tasks. This part-time internship is 15 hours a week and may involve some evening and weekend work to be done at home. Students and recent graduates interested in the position should send their résumés to internship@bluefly.com.

| To | : | internship@bluefly.com |
|---|---|---|
| **From** | : | wrasmussen@esuarts.edu |
| **Date** | : | May 19 |
| **Subject** | : | Internship |
| **Attachments** | : | Rasmussen-résumé; Rasmussen-slides |

Dear Bluefly HR,

I hope that you will consider my interest in applying for the internship at Bluefly. While I am currently in school studying design, I already have two years of experience in positions related to social media. I have maintained Web pages for several university clubs, and I am also very active on my personal social media accounts. In addition, I am familiar with most of the necessary software for creating great online content.

Right now, I am working as a museum guide four mornings a week. I'm looking for an internship that allows me to maintain this schedule. Although I have not worked in marketing before, I am eager to learn and believe that my skills would benefit your agency. Attached to this e-mail are my résumé and a set of slides highlighting my artistic abilities. They show my skill at creating attractive, interesting content, and my meticulous attention to quality.

Thank you for your time, and I hope to hear from you soon.

Sincerely,
Wendy Rasmussen

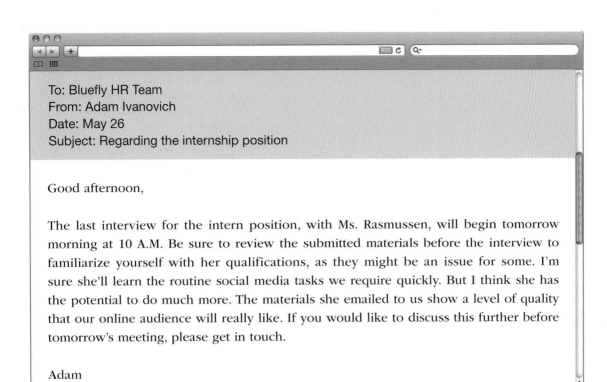

To: Bluefly HR Team
From: Adam Ivanovich
Date: May 26
Subject: Regarding the internship position

Good afternoon,

The last interview for the intern position, with Ms. Rasmussen, will begin tomorrow morning at 10 A.M. Be sure to review the submitted materials before the interview to familiarize yourself with her qualifications, as they might be an issue for some. I'm sure she'll learn the routine social media tasks we require quickly. But I think she has the potential to do much more. The materials she emailed to us show a level of quality that our online audience will really like. If you would like to discuss this further before tomorrow's meeting, please get in touch.

Adam

**196.** According to the advertisement, what is a duty of the internship?

(A) Holding client meetings
(B) Updating Web sites
(C) Contacting new subscribers
(D) Sorting office bills

**197.** What aspect of the position is likely the most appealing to Ms. Rasmussen?

(A) The salary figure
(B) The work schedule
(C) The company's reputation
(D) The company's location

**198.** What is indicated about Ms. Rasmussen?

(A) She plans to move to Atlanta.
(B) She has recently graduated from university.
(C) She regularly showcases her work at a museum.
(D) She has no experience in marketing.

**199.** What is the purpose of the second e-mail?

(A) To request that interviewers review a candidate's documents
(B) To inform employees why an interview has been delayed
(C) To alert employees to a company policy
(D) To ask that interviewers reach a decision soon

**200.** Why does Mr. Ivanovich think Ms. Rasmussen is a good candidate for the position?

(A) Her willingness to travel
(B) Her experience in advertising
(C) Her knowledge of computers
(D) Her skills as an artist

GO ON TO THE NEXT PAGE

# TEST 1

| | | | | | | | | | |
|---|---|---|---|---|---|---|---|---|---|
| 101 (B) | 111 (C) | 121 (D) | 131 (A) | 141 (B) | 151 (C) | 161 (D) | 171 (D) | 181 (D) | 191 (C) |
| 102 (A) | 112 (D) | 122 (B) | 132 (B) | 142 (D) | 152 (A) | 162 (A) | 172 (C) | 182 (A) | 192 (A) |
| 103 (B) | 113 (A) | 123 (B) | 133 (C) | 143 (B) | 153 (D) | 163 (A) | 173 (B) | 183 (D) | 193 (C) |
| 104 (C) | 114 (B) | 124 (B) | 134 (D) | 144 (B) | 154 (B) | 164 (D) | 174 (B) | 184 (B) | 194 (D) |
| 105 (D) | 115 (C) | 125 (C) | 135 (C) | 145 (D) | 155 (A) | 165 (B) | 175 (C) | 185 (D) | 195 (D) |
| 106 (D) | 116 (C) | 126 (C) | 136 (D) | 146 (C) | 156 (C) | 166 (B) | 176 (B) | 186 (C) | 196 (A) |
| 107 (D) | 117 (D) | 127 (B) | 137 (C) | 147 (B) | 157 (B) | 167 (A) | 177 (D) | 187 (D) | 197 (C) |
| 108 (B) | 118 (D) | 128 (B) | 138 (A) | 148 (C) | 158 (A) | 168 (A) | 178 (D) | 188 (A) | 198 (D) |
| 109 (C) | 119 (B) | 129 (D) | 139 (C) | 149 (A) | 159 (C) | 169 (A) | 179 (D) | 189 (D) | 199 (B) |
| 110 (A) | 120 (B) | 130 (A) | 140 (A) | 150 (D) | 160 (A) | 170 (B) | 180 (A) | 190 (D) | 200 (A) |

# TEST 2

| | | | | | | | | | |
|---|---|---|---|---|---|---|---|---|---|
| 101 (A) | 111 (B) | 121 (A) | 131 (D) | 141 (D) | 151 (C) | 161 (B) | 171 (C) | 181 (C) | 191 (C) |
| 102 (B) | 112 (A) | 122 (D) | 132 (C) | 142 (C) | 152 (A) | 162 (A) | 172 (A) | 182 (D) | 192 (B) |
| 103 (D) | 113 (D) | 123 (C) | 133 (C) | 143 (D) | 153 (A) | 163 (C) | 173 (B) | 183 (B) | 193 (D) |
| 104 (C) | 114 (B) | 124 (D) | 134 (A) | 144 (A) | 154 (D) | 164 (C) | 174 (B) | 184 (D) | 194 (A) |
| 105 (B) | 115 (D) | 125 (D) | 135 (C) | 145 (D) | 155 (A) | 165 (D) | 175 (A) | 185 (A) | 195 (D) |
| 106 (C) | 116 (B) | 126 (A) | 136 (B) | 146 (C) | 156 (A) | 166 (B) | 176 (C) | 186 (A) | 196 (D) |
| 107 (C) | 117 (C) | 127 (A) | 137 (D) | 147 (A) | 157 (B) | 167 (A) | 177 (B) | 187 (A) | 197 (D) |
| 108 (A) | 118 (B) | 128 (A) | 138 (C) | 148 (A) | 158 (C) | 168 (D) | 178 (B) | 188 (B) | 198 (D) |
| 109 (C) | 119 (D) | 129 (B) | 139 (B) | 149 (C) | 159 (A) | 169 (D) | 179 (B) | 189 (A) | 199 (A) |
| 110 (D) | 120 (C) | 130 (A) | 140 (A) | 150 (C) | 160 (A) | 170 (A) | 180 (A) | 190 (C) | 200 (C) |

# TEST 3

| | | | | | | | | | |
|---|---|---|---|---|---|---|---|---|---|
| 101 (C) | 111 (B) | 121 (D) | 131 (A) | 141 (D) | 151 (A) | 161 (B) | 171 (A) | 181 (A) | 191 (D) |
| 102 (D) | 112 (C) | 122 (D) | 132 (B) | 142 (A) | 152 (C) | 162 (C) | 172 (A) | 182 (D) | 192 (C) |
| 103 (B) | 113 (B) | 123 (D) | 133 (D) | 143 (C) | 153 (D) | 163 (A) | 173 (A) | 183 (D) | 193 (B) |
| 104 (D) | 114 (A) | 124 (B) | 134 (A) | 144 (A) | 154 (A) | 164 (B) | 174 (C) | 184 (A) | 194 (A) |
| 105 (A) | 115 (D) | 125 (C) | 135 (A) | 145 (D) | 155 (B) | 165 (A) | 175 (A) | 185 (A) | 195 (D) |
| 106 (B) | 116 (D) | 126 (D) | 136 (D) | 146 (C) | 156 (A) | 166 (A) | 176 (D) | 186 (A) | 196 (C) |
| 107 (C) | 117 (B) | 127 (B) | 137 (B) | 147 (B) | 157 (B) | 167 (B) | 177 (A) | 187 (C) | 197 (C) |
| 108 (D) | 118 (D) | 128 (B) | 138 (B) | 148 (D) | 158 (D) | 168 (B) | 178 (C) | 188 (B) | 198 (D) |
| 109 (A) | 119 (B) | 129 (A) | 139 (A) | 149 (D) | 159 (A) | 169 (B) | 179 (B) | 189 (D) | 199 (B) |
| 110 (A) | 120 (C) | 130 (A) | 140 (B) | 150 (A) | 160 (C) | 170 (C) | 180 (D) | 190 (A) | 200 (C) |

# TEST 4

| | | | | | | | | | |
|---|---|---|---|---|---|---|---|---|---|
| 101 (A) | 111 (A) | 121 (D) | 131 (B) | 141 (C) | 151 (B) | 161 (B) | 171 (A) | 181 (B) | 191 (D) |
| 102 (A) | 112 (C) | 122 (B) | 132 (D) | 142 (C) | 152 (D) | 162 (B) | 172 (B) | 182 (A) | 192 (B) |
| 103 (C) | 113 (D) | 123 (D) | 133 (C) | 143 (D) | 153 (A) | 163 (A) | 173 (C) | 183 (D) | 193 (D) |
| 104 (B) | 114 (B) | 124 (C) | 134 (A) | 144 (D) | 154 (D) | 164 (D) | 174 (D) | 184 (C) | 194 (C) |
| 105 (B) | 115 (D) | 125 (C) | 135 (D) | 145 (B) | 155 (B) | 165 (B) | 175 (A) | 185 (B) | 195 (D) |
| 106 (D) | 116 (C) | 126 (C) | 136 (A) | 146 (C) | 156 (D) | 166 (C) | 176 (D) | 186 (A) | 196 (C) |
| 107 (A) | 117 (A) | 127 (D) | 137 (C) | 147 (C) | 157 (D) | 167 (B) | 177 (D) | 187 (B) | 197 (D) |
| 108 (C) | 118 (B) | 128 (C) | 138 (A) | 148 (B) | 158 (B) | 168 (B) | 178 (B) | 188 (D) | 198 (B) |
| 109 (C) | 119 (A) | 129 (A) | 139 (C) | 149 (D) | 159 (B) | 169 (A) | 179 (C) | 189 (D) | 199 (C) |
| 110 (B) | 120 (B) | 130 (B) | 140 (A) | 150 (D) | 160 (A) | 170 (D) | 180 (A) | 190 (C) | 200 (D) |

# TEST 5

| | | | | | | | | | |
|---|---|---|---|---|---|---|---|---|---|
| 101 (A) | 111 (C) | 121 (B) | 131 (C) | 141 (A) | 151 (D) | 161 (A) | 171 (A) | 181 (A) | 191 (D) |
| 102 (A) | 112 (C) | 122 (C) | 132 (A) | 142 (B) | 152 (D) | 162 (A) | 172 (C) | 182 (A) | 192 (B) |
| 103 (C) | 113 (C) | 123 (B) | 133 (A) | 143 (B) | 153 (D) | 163 (B) | 173 (B) | 183 (C) | 193 (C) |
| 104 (B) | 114 (B) | 124 (D) | 134 (D) | 144 (C) | 154 (D) | 164 (B) | 174 (C) | 184 (B) | 194 (B) |
| 105 (D) | 115 (A) | 125 (B) | 135 (D) | 145 (B) | 155 (A) | 165 (A) | 175 (C) | 185 (D) | 195 (B) |
| 106 (B) | 116 (D) | 126 (D) | 136 (D) | 146 (D) | 156 (C) | 166 (A) | 176 (B) | 186 (C) | 196 (D) |
| 107 (C) | 117 (B) | 127 (B) | 137 (A) | 147 (A) | 157 (C) | 167 (D) | 177 (D) | 187 (A) | 197 (B) |
| 108 (C) | 118 (A) | 128 (A) | 138 (B) | 148 (B) | 158 (D) | 168 (B) | 178 (C) | 188 (C) | 198 (C) |
| 109 (D) | 119 (B) | 129 (A) | 139 (D) | 149 (D) | 159 (B) | 169 (B) | 179 (D) | 189 (D) | 199 (C) |
| 110 (B) | 120 (B) | 130 (A) | 140 (B) | 150 (C) | 160 (B) | 170 (D) | 180 (B) | 190 (B) | 200 (B) |

# TEST 6

| | | | | | | | | | |
|---|---|---|---|---|---|---|---|---|---|
| 101 (C) | 111 (A) | 121 (C) | 131 (C) | 141 (B) | 151 (B) | 161 (A) | 171 (D) | 181 (D) | 191 (C) |
| 102 (C) | 112 (B) | 122 (A) | 132 (D) | 142 (A) | 152 (A) | 162 (D) | 172 (B) | 182 (B) | 192 (A) |
| 103 (B) | 113 (D) | 123 (C) | 133 (C) | 143 (C) | 153 (D) | 163 (B) | 173 (B) | 183 (A) | 193 (B) |
| 104 (A) | 114 (D) | 124 (B) | 134 (C) | 144 (B) | 154 (B) | 164 (C) | 174 (A) | 184 (C) | 194 (D) |
| 105 (D) | 115 (B) | 125 (B) | 135 (C) | 145 (B) | 155 (A) | 165 (D) | 175 (C) | 185 (B) | 195 (D) |
| 106 (A) | 116 (B) | 126 (B) | 136 (A) | 146 (C) | 156 (D) | 166 (D) | 176 (B) | 186 (B) | 196 (C) |
| 107 (C) | 117 (D) | 127 (A) | 137 (D) | 147 (A) | 157 (B) | 167 (D) | 177 (D) | 187 (D) | 197 (A) |
| 108 (D) | 118 (D) | 128 (B) | 138 (A) | 148 (D) | 158 (B) | 168 (B) | 178 (A) | 188 (C) | 198 (B) |
| 109 (B) | 119 (B) | 129 (D) | 139 (B) | 149 (B) | 159 (D) | 169 (A) | 179 (C) | 189 (C) | 199 (A) |
| 110 (D) | 120 (B) | 130 (A) | 140 (A) | 150 (B) | 160 (D) | 170 (B) | 180 (B) | 190 (C) | 200 (A) |

## TEST 7

| | | | | | | | | | |
|---|---|---|---|---|---|---|---|---|---|
| 101 (C) | 111 (B) | 121 (B) | 131 (D) | 141 (C) | 151 (B) | 161 (C) | 171 (D) | 181 (A) | 191 (A) |
| 102 (A) | 112 (C) | 122 (D) | 132 (B) | 142 (B) | 152 (D) | 162 (B) | 172 (A) | 182 (D) | 192 (D) |
| 103 (B) | 113 (D) | 123 (D) | 133 (C) | 143 (B) | 153 (D) | 163 (D) | 173 (C) | 183 (C) | 193 (C) |
| 104 (D) | 114 (B) | 124 (C) | 134 (A) | 144 (A) | 154 (A) | 164 (A) | 174 (D) | 184 (A) | 194 (B) |
| 105 (A) | 115 (C) | 125 (A) | 135 (C) | 145 (A) | 155 (D) | 165 (B) | 175 (D) | 185 (A) | 195 (B) |
| 106 (B) | 116 (D) | 126 (A) | 136 (A) | 146 (D) | 156 (A) | 166 (C) | 176 (B) | 186 (B) | 196 (B) |
| 107 (B) | 117 (B) | 127 (B) | 137 (C) | 147 (D) | 157 (B) | 167 (A) | 177 (A) | 187 (D) | 197 (D) |
| 108 (C) | 118 (C) | 128 (D) | 138 (B) | 148 (A) | 158 (D) | 168 (C) | 178 (A) | 188 (A) | 198 (A) |
| 109 (A) | 119 (B) | 129 (D) | 139 (B) | 149 (C) | 159 (B) | 169 (C) | 179 (C) | 189 (D) | 199 (D) |
| 110 (C) | 120 (C) | 130 (B) | 140 (A) | 150 (D) | 160 (B) | 170 (B) | 180 (A) | 190 (B) | 200 (A) |

## TEST 8

| | | | | | | | | | |
|---|---|---|---|---|---|---|---|---|---|
| 101 (D) | 111 (B) | 121 (B) | 131 (D) | 141 (A) | 151 (B) | 161 (A) | 171 (D) | 181 (B) | 191 (B) |
| 102 (D) | 112 (C) | 122 (D) | 132 (A) | 142 (B) | 152 (A) | 162 (D) | 172 (B) | 182 (C) | 192 (A) |
| 103 (B) | 113 (D) | 123 (A) | 133 (D) | 143 (C) | 153 (B) | 163 (C) | 173 (B) | 183 (A) | 193 (C) |
| 104 (B) | 114 (B) | 124 (C) | 134 (B) | 144 (A) | 154 (D) | 164 (A) | 174 (C) | 184 (C) | 194 (D) |
| 105 (A) | 115 (B) | 125 (B) | 135 (C) | 145 (D) | 155 (C) | 165 (B) | 175 (B) | 185 (B) | 195 (D) |
| 106 (D) | 116 (D) | 126 (D) | 136 (A) | 146 (B) | 156 (D) | 166 (D) | 176 (D) | 186 (D) | 196 (B) |
| 107 (A) | 117 (B) | 127 (A) | 137 (A) | 147 (A) | 157 (C) | 167 (D) | 177 (A) | 187 (D) | 197 (D) |
| 108 (C) | 118 (C) | 128 (C) | 138 (D) | 148 (A) | 158 (B) | 168 (A) | 178 (B) | 188 (A) | 198 (C) |
| 109 (A) | 119 (A) | 129 (D) | 139 (D) | 149 (A) | 159 (B) | 169 (C) | 179 (C) | 189 (A) | 199 (A) |
| 110 (A) | 120 (C) | 130 (D) | 140 (D) | 150 (A) | 160 (A) | 170 (C) | 180 (A) | 190 (C) | 200 (A) |

# TEST 9

| | | | | | | | | | |
|---|---|---|---|---|---|---|---|---|---|
| 101 (A) | 111 (D) | 121 (C) | 131 (C) | 141 (C) | 151 (D) | 161 (C) | 171 (C) | 181 (D) | 191 (A) |
| 102 (C) | 112 (B) | 122 (D) | 132 (D) | 142 (B) | 152 (B) | 162 (B) | 172 (A) | 182 (C) | 192 (D) |
| 103 (A) | 113 (A) | 123 (C) | 133 (A) | 143 (C) | 153 (A) | 163 (C) | 173 (A) | 183 (B) | 193 (A) |
| 104 (C) | 114 (D) | 124 (D) | 134 (A) | 144 (A) | 154 (D) | 164 (B) | 174 (D) | 184 (C) | 194 (D) |
| 105 (A) | 115 (D) | 125 (D) | 135 (C) | 145 (D) | 155 (D) | 165 (A) | 175 (B) | 185 (B) | 195 (C) |
| 106 (D) | 116 (D) | 126 (C) | 136 (B) | 146 (B) | 156 (C) | 166 (D) | 176 (D) | 186 (A) | 196 (C) |
| 107 (C) | 117 (A) | 127 (B) | 137 (A) | 147 (B) | 157 (C) | 167 (C) | 177 (A) | 187 (D) | 197 (B) |
| 108 (D) | 118 (B) | 128 (A) | 138 (C) | 148 (B) | 158 (D) | 168 (A) | 178 (B) | 188 (A) | 198 (B) |
| 109 (B) | 119 (B) | 129 (A) | 139 (D) | 149 (A) | 159 (A) | 169 (D) | 179 (D) | 189 (C) | 199 (B) |
| 110 (A) | 120 (A) | 130 (B) | 140 (A) | 150 (A) | 160 (B) | 170 (D) | 180 (D) | 190 (D) | 200 (C) |

# TEST 10

| | | | | | | | | | |
|---|---|---|---|---|---|---|---|---|---|
| 101 (B) | 111 (D) | 121 (A) | 131 (D) | 141 (B) | 151 (B) | 161 (B) | 171 (B) | 181 (C) | 191 (C) |
| 102 (D) | 112 (A) | 122 (C) | 132 (A) | 142 (D) | 152 (C) | 162 (C) | 172 (D) | 182 (A) | 192 (B) |
| 103 (C) | 113 (C) | 123 (C) | 133 (B) | 143 (C) | 153 (A) | 163 (C) | 173 (D) | 183 (D) | 193 (C) |
| 104 (C) | 114 (D) | 124 (B) | 134 (B) | 144 (C) | 154 (B) | 164 (A) | 174 (B) | 184 (B) | 194 (A) |
| 105 (C) | 115 (B) | 125 (B) | 135 (B) | 145 (A) | 155 (C) | 165 (A) | 175 (A) | 185 (D) | 195 (A) |
| 106 (D) | 116 (A) | 126 (D) | 136 (B) | 146 (A) | 156 (C) | 166 (D) | 176 (A) | 186 (A) | 196 (B) |
| 107 (C) | 117 (A) | 127 (C) | 137 (D) | 147 (B) | 157 (A) | 167 (D) | 177 (A) | 187 (C) | 197 (B) |
| 108 (A) | 118 (D) | 128 (C) | 138 (A) | 148 (D) | 158 (C) | 168 (A) | 178 (D) | 188 (A) | 198 (D) |
| 109 (D) | 119 (C) | 129 (B) | 139 (B) | 149 (C) | 159 (B) | 169 (C) | 179 (D) | 189 (D) | 199 (A) |
| 110 (B) | 120 (B) | 130 (A) | 140 (D) | 150 (A) | 160 (B) | 170 (C) | 180 (C) | 190 (B) | 200 (D) |

# 토익 점수 환산표

## Section I  Listening Comprehension

| 정답 수 | 환산 점수대 |
|---|---|
| 96 ~ 100 | 480 ~ 495 |
| 91 ~ 95 | 470 ~ 495 |
| 86 ~ 90 | 440 ~ 490 |
| 81 ~ 85 | 410 ~ 460 |
| 76 ~ 80 | 390 ~ 430 |
| 71 ~ 75 | 360 ~ 400 |
| 66 ~ 70 | 330 ~ 370 |
| 61 ~ 65 | 300 ~ 345 |
| 56 ~ 60 | 270 ~ 315 |
| 51 ~ 55 | 240 ~ 285 |
| 46 ~ 50 | 210 ~ 255 |
| 41 ~ 45 | 180 ~ 225 |
| 36 ~ 40 | 150 ~ 195 |
| 31 ~ 35 | 120 ~ 165 |
| 26 ~ 30 | 90 ~ 135 |
| 21 ~ 25 | 60 ~ 105 |
| 16 ~ 20 | 40 ~ 75 |
| 11 ~ 15 | 10 ~ 45 |
| 6 ~ 10 | 5 ~ 20 |
| 1 ~ 5 | 5 |
| 0 | 0 |

## Section II  Reading Comprehension

| 정답 수 | 환산 점수대 |
|---|---|
| 96 ~ 100 | 450 ~ 495 |
| 91 ~ 95 | 420 ~ 465 |
| 86 ~ 90 | 400 ~ 435 |
| 81 ~ 85 | 370 ~ 410 |
| 76 ~ 80 | 340 ~ 380 |
| 71 ~ 75 | 310 ~ 355 |
| 66 ~ 70 | 280 ~ 325 |
| 61 ~ 65 | 260 ~ 300 |
| 56 ~ 60 | 230 ~ 270 |
| 51 ~ 55 | 200 ~ 245 |
| 46 ~ 50 | 170 ~ 215 |
| 41 ~ 45 | 140 ~ 185 |
| 36 ~ 40 | 120 ~ 160 |
| 31 ~ 35 | 90 ~ 130 |
| 26 ~ 30 | 60 ~ 105 |
| 21 ~ 25 | 30 ~ 75 |
| 16 ~ 20 | 10 ~ 50 |
| 11 ~ 15 | 5 ~ 20 |
| 6 ~ 10 | 5 |
| 1 ~ 5 | 5 |
| 0 | 0 |

# ANSWER SHEET

## 파고다 토익 적중 실전 RC - TEST 1

### READING (Part V - VII)

| NO. | ANSWER<br>A B C D | NO. | ANSWER<br>A B C D | NO. | ANSWER<br>A B C D | NO. | ANSWER<br>A B C D | NO. | ANSWER<br>A B C D |
|---|---|---|---|---|---|---|---|---|---|
| 101 | Ⓐ Ⓑ Ⓒ Ⓓ | 121 | Ⓐ Ⓑ Ⓒ Ⓓ | 141 | Ⓐ Ⓑ Ⓒ Ⓓ | 161 | Ⓐ Ⓑ Ⓒ Ⓓ | 181 | Ⓐ Ⓑ Ⓒ Ⓓ |
| 102 | Ⓐ Ⓑ Ⓒ Ⓓ | 122 | Ⓐ Ⓑ Ⓒ Ⓓ | 142 | Ⓐ Ⓑ Ⓒ Ⓓ | 162 | Ⓐ Ⓑ Ⓒ Ⓓ | 182 | Ⓐ Ⓑ Ⓒ Ⓓ |
| 103 | Ⓐ Ⓑ Ⓒ Ⓓ | 123 | Ⓐ Ⓑ Ⓒ Ⓓ | 143 | Ⓐ Ⓑ Ⓒ Ⓓ | 163 | Ⓐ Ⓑ Ⓒ Ⓓ | 183 | Ⓐ Ⓑ Ⓒ Ⓓ |
| 104 | Ⓐ Ⓑ Ⓒ Ⓓ | 124 | Ⓐ Ⓑ Ⓒ Ⓓ | 144 | Ⓐ Ⓑ Ⓒ Ⓓ | 164 | Ⓐ Ⓑ Ⓒ Ⓓ | 184 | Ⓐ Ⓑ Ⓒ Ⓓ |
| 105 | Ⓐ Ⓑ Ⓒ Ⓓ | 125 | Ⓐ Ⓑ Ⓒ Ⓓ | 145 | Ⓐ Ⓑ Ⓒ Ⓓ | 165 | Ⓐ Ⓑ Ⓒ Ⓓ | 185 | Ⓐ Ⓑ Ⓒ Ⓓ |
| 106 | Ⓐ Ⓑ Ⓒ Ⓓ | 126 | Ⓐ Ⓑ Ⓒ Ⓓ | 146 | Ⓐ Ⓑ Ⓒ Ⓓ | 166 | Ⓐ Ⓑ Ⓒ Ⓓ | 186 | Ⓐ Ⓑ Ⓒ Ⓓ |
| 107 | Ⓐ Ⓑ Ⓒ Ⓓ | 127 | Ⓐ Ⓑ Ⓒ Ⓓ | 147 | Ⓐ Ⓑ Ⓒ Ⓓ | 167 | Ⓐ Ⓑ Ⓒ Ⓓ | 187 | Ⓐ Ⓑ Ⓒ Ⓓ |
| 108 | Ⓐ Ⓑ Ⓒ Ⓓ | 128 | Ⓐ Ⓑ Ⓒ Ⓓ | 148 | Ⓐ Ⓑ Ⓒ Ⓓ | 168 | Ⓐ Ⓑ Ⓒ Ⓓ | 188 | Ⓐ Ⓑ Ⓒ Ⓓ |
| 109 | Ⓐ Ⓑ Ⓒ Ⓓ | 129 | Ⓐ Ⓑ Ⓒ Ⓓ | 149 | Ⓐ Ⓑ Ⓒ Ⓓ | 169 | Ⓐ Ⓑ Ⓒ Ⓓ | 189 | Ⓐ Ⓑ Ⓒ Ⓓ |
| 110 | Ⓐ Ⓑ Ⓒ Ⓓ | 130 | Ⓐ Ⓑ Ⓒ Ⓓ | 150 | Ⓐ Ⓑ Ⓒ Ⓓ | 170 | Ⓐ Ⓑ Ⓒ Ⓓ | 190 | Ⓐ Ⓑ Ⓒ Ⓓ |
| 111 | Ⓐ Ⓑ Ⓒ Ⓓ | 131 | Ⓐ Ⓑ Ⓒ Ⓓ | 151 | Ⓐ Ⓑ Ⓒ Ⓓ | 171 | Ⓐ Ⓑ Ⓒ Ⓓ | 191 | Ⓐ Ⓑ Ⓒ Ⓓ |
| 112 | Ⓐ Ⓑ Ⓒ Ⓓ | 132 | Ⓐ Ⓑ Ⓒ Ⓓ | 152 | Ⓐ Ⓑ Ⓒ Ⓓ | 172 | Ⓐ Ⓑ Ⓒ Ⓓ | 192 | Ⓐ Ⓑ Ⓒ Ⓓ |
| 113 | Ⓐ Ⓑ Ⓒ Ⓓ | 133 | Ⓐ Ⓑ Ⓒ Ⓓ | 153 | Ⓐ Ⓑ Ⓒ Ⓓ | 173 | Ⓐ Ⓑ Ⓒ Ⓓ | 193 | Ⓐ Ⓑ Ⓒ Ⓓ |
| 114 | Ⓐ Ⓑ Ⓒ Ⓓ | 134 | Ⓐ Ⓑ Ⓒ Ⓓ | 154 | Ⓐ Ⓑ Ⓒ Ⓓ | 174 | Ⓐ Ⓑ Ⓒ Ⓓ | 194 | Ⓐ Ⓑ Ⓒ Ⓓ |
| 115 | Ⓐ Ⓑ Ⓒ Ⓓ | 135 | Ⓐ Ⓑ Ⓒ Ⓓ | 155 | Ⓐ Ⓑ Ⓒ Ⓓ | 175 | Ⓐ Ⓑ Ⓒ Ⓓ | 195 | Ⓐ Ⓑ Ⓒ Ⓓ |
| 116 | Ⓐ Ⓑ Ⓒ Ⓓ | 136 | Ⓐ Ⓑ Ⓒ Ⓓ | 156 | Ⓐ Ⓑ Ⓒ Ⓓ | 176 | Ⓐ Ⓑ Ⓒ Ⓓ | 196 | Ⓐ Ⓑ Ⓒ Ⓓ |
| 117 | Ⓐ Ⓑ Ⓒ Ⓓ | 137 | Ⓐ Ⓑ Ⓒ Ⓓ | 157 | Ⓐ Ⓑ Ⓒ Ⓓ | 177 | Ⓐ Ⓑ Ⓒ Ⓓ | 197 | Ⓐ Ⓑ Ⓒ Ⓓ |
| 118 | Ⓐ Ⓑ Ⓒ Ⓓ | 138 | Ⓐ Ⓑ Ⓒ Ⓓ | 158 | Ⓐ Ⓑ Ⓒ Ⓓ | 178 | Ⓐ Ⓑ Ⓒ Ⓓ | 198 | Ⓐ Ⓑ Ⓒ Ⓓ |
| 119 | Ⓐ Ⓑ Ⓒ Ⓓ | 139 | Ⓐ Ⓑ Ⓒ Ⓓ | 159 | Ⓐ Ⓑ Ⓒ Ⓓ | 179 | Ⓐ Ⓑ Ⓒ Ⓓ | 199 | Ⓐ Ⓑ Ⓒ Ⓓ |
| 120 | Ⓐ Ⓑ Ⓒ Ⓓ | 140 | Ⓐ Ⓑ Ⓒ Ⓓ | 160 | Ⓐ Ⓑ Ⓒ Ⓓ | 180 | Ⓐ Ⓑ Ⓒ Ⓓ | 200 | Ⓐ Ⓑ Ⓒ Ⓓ |

ANSWER SHEET

# ANSWER SHEET

**파고다 토익 적중 실전 RC - TEST 2**

## READING (Part V - VII)

| NO. | ANSWER A B C D | NO. | ANSWER A B C D | NO. | ANSWER A B C D | NO. | ANSWER A B C D | NO. | ANSWER A B C D |
|-----|------|-----|------|-----|------|-----|------|-----|------|
| 101 | Ⓐ Ⓑ Ⓒ Ⓓ | 121 | Ⓐ Ⓑ Ⓒ Ⓓ | 141 | Ⓐ Ⓑ Ⓒ Ⓓ | 161 | Ⓐ Ⓑ Ⓒ Ⓓ | 181 | Ⓐ Ⓑ Ⓒ Ⓓ |
| 102 | Ⓐ Ⓑ Ⓒ Ⓓ | 122 | Ⓐ Ⓑ Ⓒ Ⓓ | 142 | Ⓐ Ⓑ Ⓒ Ⓓ | 162 | Ⓐ Ⓑ Ⓒ Ⓓ | 182 | Ⓐ Ⓑ Ⓒ Ⓓ |
| 103 | Ⓐ Ⓑ Ⓒ Ⓓ | 123 | Ⓐ Ⓑ Ⓒ Ⓓ | 143 | Ⓐ Ⓑ Ⓒ Ⓓ | 163 | Ⓐ Ⓑ Ⓒ Ⓓ | 183 | Ⓐ Ⓑ Ⓒ Ⓓ |
| 104 | Ⓐ Ⓑ Ⓒ Ⓓ | 124 | Ⓐ Ⓑ Ⓒ Ⓓ | 144 | Ⓐ Ⓑ Ⓒ Ⓓ | 164 | Ⓐ Ⓑ Ⓒ Ⓓ | 184 | Ⓐ Ⓑ Ⓒ Ⓓ |
| 105 | Ⓐ Ⓑ Ⓒ Ⓓ | 125 | Ⓐ Ⓑ Ⓒ Ⓓ | 145 | Ⓐ Ⓑ Ⓒ Ⓓ | 165 | Ⓐ Ⓑ Ⓒ Ⓓ | 185 | Ⓐ Ⓑ Ⓒ Ⓓ |
| 106 | Ⓐ Ⓑ Ⓒ Ⓓ | 126 | Ⓐ Ⓑ Ⓒ Ⓓ | 146 | Ⓐ Ⓑ Ⓒ Ⓓ | 166 | Ⓐ Ⓑ Ⓒ Ⓓ | 186 | Ⓐ Ⓑ Ⓒ Ⓓ |
| 107 | Ⓐ Ⓑ Ⓒ Ⓓ | 127 | Ⓐ Ⓑ Ⓒ Ⓓ | 147 | Ⓐ Ⓑ Ⓒ Ⓓ | 167 | Ⓐ Ⓑ Ⓒ Ⓓ | 187 | Ⓐ Ⓑ Ⓒ Ⓓ |
| 108 | Ⓐ Ⓑ Ⓒ Ⓓ | 128 | Ⓐ Ⓑ Ⓒ Ⓓ | 148 | Ⓐ Ⓑ Ⓒ Ⓓ | 168 | Ⓐ Ⓑ Ⓒ Ⓓ | 188 | Ⓐ Ⓑ Ⓒ Ⓓ |
| 109 | Ⓐ Ⓑ Ⓒ Ⓓ | 129 | Ⓐ Ⓑ Ⓒ Ⓓ | 149 | Ⓐ Ⓑ Ⓒ Ⓓ | 169 | Ⓐ Ⓑ Ⓒ Ⓓ | 189 | Ⓐ Ⓑ Ⓒ Ⓓ |
| 110 | Ⓐ Ⓑ Ⓒ Ⓓ | 130 | Ⓐ Ⓑ Ⓒ Ⓓ | 150 | Ⓐ Ⓑ Ⓒ Ⓓ | 170 | Ⓐ Ⓑ Ⓒ Ⓓ | 190 | Ⓐ Ⓑ Ⓒ Ⓓ |
| 111 | Ⓐ Ⓑ Ⓒ Ⓓ | 131 | Ⓐ Ⓑ Ⓒ Ⓓ | 151 | Ⓐ Ⓑ Ⓒ Ⓓ | 171 | Ⓐ Ⓑ Ⓒ Ⓓ | 191 | Ⓐ Ⓑ Ⓒ Ⓓ |
| 112 | Ⓐ Ⓑ Ⓒ Ⓓ | 132 | Ⓐ Ⓑ Ⓒ Ⓓ | 152 | Ⓐ Ⓑ Ⓒ Ⓓ | 172 | Ⓐ Ⓑ Ⓒ Ⓓ | 192 | Ⓐ Ⓑ Ⓒ Ⓓ |
| 113 | Ⓐ Ⓑ Ⓒ Ⓓ | 133 | Ⓐ Ⓑ Ⓒ Ⓓ | 153 | Ⓐ Ⓑ Ⓒ Ⓓ | 173 | Ⓐ Ⓑ Ⓒ Ⓓ | 193 | Ⓐ Ⓑ Ⓒ Ⓓ |
| 114 | Ⓐ Ⓑ Ⓒ Ⓓ | 134 | Ⓐ Ⓑ Ⓒ Ⓓ | 154 | Ⓐ Ⓑ Ⓒ Ⓓ | 174 | Ⓐ Ⓑ Ⓒ Ⓓ | 194 | Ⓐ Ⓑ Ⓒ Ⓓ |
| 115 | Ⓐ Ⓑ Ⓒ Ⓓ | 135 | Ⓐ Ⓑ Ⓒ Ⓓ | 155 | Ⓐ Ⓑ Ⓒ Ⓓ | 175 | Ⓐ Ⓑ Ⓒ Ⓓ | 195 | Ⓐ Ⓑ Ⓒ Ⓓ |
| 116 | Ⓐ Ⓑ Ⓒ Ⓓ | 136 | Ⓐ Ⓑ Ⓒ Ⓓ | 156 | Ⓐ Ⓑ Ⓒ Ⓓ | 176 | Ⓐ Ⓑ Ⓒ Ⓓ | 196 | Ⓐ Ⓑ Ⓒ Ⓓ |
| 117 | Ⓐ Ⓑ Ⓒ Ⓓ | 137 | Ⓐ Ⓑ Ⓒ Ⓓ | 157 | Ⓐ Ⓑ Ⓒ Ⓓ | 177 | Ⓐ Ⓑ Ⓒ Ⓓ | 197 | Ⓐ Ⓑ Ⓒ Ⓓ |
| 118 | Ⓐ Ⓑ Ⓒ Ⓓ | 138 | Ⓐ Ⓑ Ⓒ Ⓓ | 158 | Ⓐ Ⓑ Ⓒ Ⓓ | 178 | Ⓐ Ⓑ Ⓒ Ⓓ | 198 | Ⓐ Ⓑ Ⓒ Ⓓ |
| 119 | Ⓐ Ⓑ Ⓒ Ⓓ | 139 | Ⓐ Ⓑ Ⓒ Ⓓ | 159 | Ⓐ Ⓑ Ⓒ Ⓓ | 179 | Ⓐ Ⓑ Ⓒ Ⓓ | 199 | Ⓐ Ⓑ Ⓒ Ⓓ |
| 120 | Ⓐ Ⓑ Ⓒ Ⓓ | 140 | Ⓐ Ⓑ Ⓒ Ⓓ | 160 | Ⓐ Ⓑ Ⓒ Ⓓ | 180 | Ⓐ Ⓑ Ⓒ Ⓓ | 200 | Ⓐ Ⓑ Ⓒ Ⓓ |

ANSWER SHEET

# ANSWER SHEET

## 파고다 토익 적중 실전 RC - TEST 3

### READING (Part V - VII)

| NO. | ANSWER A B C D | NO. | ANSWER A B C D | NO. | ANSWER A B C D | NO. | ANSWER A B C D | NO. | ANSWER A B C D |
|---|---|---|---|---|---|---|---|---|---|
| 101 | Ⓐ Ⓑ Ⓒ Ⓓ | 121 | Ⓐ Ⓑ Ⓒ Ⓓ | 141 | Ⓐ Ⓑ Ⓒ Ⓓ | 161 | Ⓐ Ⓑ Ⓒ Ⓓ | 181 | Ⓐ Ⓑ Ⓒ Ⓓ |
| 102 | Ⓐ Ⓑ Ⓒ Ⓓ | 122 | Ⓐ Ⓑ Ⓒ Ⓓ | 142 | Ⓐ Ⓑ Ⓒ Ⓓ | 162 | Ⓐ Ⓑ Ⓒ Ⓓ | 182 | Ⓐ Ⓑ Ⓒ Ⓓ |
| 103 | Ⓐ Ⓑ Ⓒ Ⓓ | 123 | Ⓐ Ⓑ Ⓒ Ⓓ | 143 | Ⓐ Ⓑ Ⓒ Ⓓ | 163 | Ⓐ Ⓑ Ⓒ Ⓓ | 183 | Ⓐ Ⓑ Ⓒ Ⓓ |
| 104 | Ⓐ Ⓑ Ⓒ Ⓓ | 124 | Ⓐ Ⓑ Ⓒ Ⓓ | 144 | Ⓐ Ⓑ Ⓒ Ⓓ | 164 | Ⓐ Ⓑ Ⓒ Ⓓ | 184 | Ⓐ Ⓑ Ⓒ Ⓓ |
| 105 | Ⓐ Ⓑ Ⓒ Ⓓ | 125 | Ⓐ Ⓑ Ⓒ Ⓓ | 145 | Ⓐ Ⓑ Ⓒ Ⓓ | 165 | Ⓐ Ⓑ Ⓒ Ⓓ | 185 | Ⓐ Ⓑ Ⓒ Ⓓ |
| 106 | Ⓐ Ⓑ Ⓒ Ⓓ | 126 | Ⓐ Ⓑ Ⓒ Ⓓ | 146 | Ⓐ Ⓑ Ⓒ Ⓓ | 166 | Ⓐ Ⓑ Ⓒ Ⓓ | 186 | Ⓐ Ⓑ Ⓒ Ⓓ |
| 107 | Ⓐ Ⓑ Ⓒ Ⓓ | 127 | Ⓐ Ⓑ Ⓒ Ⓓ | 147 | Ⓐ Ⓑ Ⓒ Ⓓ | 167 | Ⓐ Ⓑ Ⓒ Ⓓ | 187 | Ⓐ Ⓑ Ⓒ Ⓓ |
| 108 | Ⓐ Ⓑ Ⓒ Ⓓ | 128 | Ⓐ Ⓑ Ⓒ Ⓓ | 148 | Ⓐ Ⓑ Ⓒ Ⓓ | 168 | Ⓐ Ⓑ Ⓒ Ⓓ | 188 | Ⓐ Ⓑ Ⓒ Ⓓ |
| 109 | Ⓐ Ⓑ Ⓒ Ⓓ | 129 | Ⓐ Ⓑ Ⓒ Ⓓ | 149 | Ⓐ Ⓑ Ⓒ Ⓓ | 169 | Ⓐ Ⓑ Ⓒ Ⓓ | 189 | Ⓐ Ⓑ Ⓒ Ⓓ |
| 110 | Ⓐ Ⓑ Ⓒ Ⓓ | 130 | Ⓐ Ⓑ Ⓒ Ⓓ | 150 | Ⓐ Ⓑ Ⓒ Ⓓ | 170 | Ⓐ Ⓑ Ⓒ Ⓓ | 190 | Ⓐ Ⓑ Ⓒ Ⓓ |
| 111 | Ⓐ Ⓑ Ⓒ Ⓓ | 131 | Ⓐ Ⓑ Ⓒ Ⓓ | 151 | Ⓐ Ⓑ Ⓒ Ⓓ | 171 | Ⓐ Ⓑ Ⓒ Ⓓ | 191 | Ⓐ Ⓑ Ⓒ Ⓓ |
| 112 | Ⓐ Ⓑ Ⓒ Ⓓ | 132 | Ⓐ Ⓑ Ⓒ Ⓓ | 152 | Ⓐ Ⓑ Ⓒ Ⓓ | 172 | Ⓐ Ⓑ Ⓒ Ⓓ | 192 | Ⓐ Ⓑ Ⓒ Ⓓ |
| 113 | Ⓐ Ⓑ Ⓒ Ⓓ | 133 | Ⓐ Ⓑ Ⓒ Ⓓ | 153 | Ⓐ Ⓑ Ⓒ Ⓓ | 173 | Ⓐ Ⓑ Ⓒ Ⓓ | 193 | Ⓐ Ⓑ Ⓒ Ⓓ |
| 114 | Ⓐ Ⓑ Ⓒ Ⓓ | 134 | Ⓐ Ⓑ Ⓒ Ⓓ | 154 | Ⓐ Ⓑ Ⓒ Ⓓ | 174 | Ⓐ Ⓑ Ⓒ Ⓓ | 194 | Ⓐ Ⓑ Ⓒ Ⓓ |
| 115 | Ⓐ Ⓑ Ⓒ Ⓓ | 135 | Ⓐ Ⓑ Ⓒ Ⓓ | 155 | Ⓐ Ⓑ Ⓒ Ⓓ | 175 | Ⓐ Ⓑ Ⓒ Ⓓ | 195 | Ⓐ Ⓑ Ⓒ Ⓓ |
| 116 | Ⓐ Ⓑ Ⓒ Ⓓ | 136 | Ⓐ Ⓑ Ⓒ Ⓓ | 156 | Ⓐ Ⓑ Ⓒ Ⓓ | 176 | Ⓐ Ⓑ Ⓒ Ⓓ | 196 | Ⓐ Ⓑ Ⓒ Ⓓ |
| 117 | Ⓐ Ⓑ Ⓒ Ⓓ | 137 | Ⓐ Ⓑ Ⓒ Ⓓ | 157 | Ⓐ Ⓑ Ⓒ Ⓓ | 177 | Ⓐ Ⓑ Ⓒ Ⓓ | 197 | Ⓐ Ⓑ Ⓒ Ⓓ |
| 118 | Ⓐ Ⓑ Ⓒ Ⓓ | 138 | Ⓐ Ⓑ Ⓒ Ⓓ | 158 | Ⓐ Ⓑ Ⓒ Ⓓ | 178 | Ⓐ Ⓑ Ⓒ Ⓓ | 198 | Ⓐ Ⓑ Ⓒ Ⓓ |
| 119 | Ⓐ Ⓑ Ⓒ Ⓓ | 139 | Ⓐ Ⓑ Ⓒ Ⓓ | 159 | Ⓐ Ⓑ Ⓒ Ⓓ | 179 | Ⓐ Ⓑ Ⓒ Ⓓ | 199 | Ⓐ Ⓑ Ⓒ Ⓓ |
| 120 | Ⓐ Ⓑ Ⓒ Ⓓ | 140 | Ⓐ Ⓑ Ⓒ Ⓓ | 160 | Ⓐ Ⓑ Ⓒ Ⓓ | 180 | Ⓐ Ⓑ Ⓒ Ⓓ | 200 | Ⓐ Ⓑ Ⓒ Ⓓ |

ANSWER SHEET

# ANSWER SHEET

## 파고다 토익 적중 실전 RC – TEST 4

### READING (Part V-VII)

| NO. | ANSWER A B C D | NO. | ANSWER A B C D | NO. | ANSWER A B C D | NO. | ANSWER A B C D | NO. | ANSWER A B C D |
|-----|-----|-----|-----|-----|-----|-----|-----|-----|-----|-----|
| 101 | Ⓐ Ⓑ Ⓒ Ⓓ | 121 | Ⓐ Ⓑ Ⓒ Ⓓ | 141 | Ⓐ Ⓑ Ⓒ Ⓓ | 161 | Ⓐ Ⓑ Ⓒ Ⓓ | 181 | Ⓐ Ⓑ Ⓒ Ⓓ |
| 102 | Ⓐ Ⓑ Ⓒ Ⓓ | 122 | Ⓐ Ⓑ Ⓒ Ⓓ | 142 | Ⓐ Ⓑ Ⓒ Ⓓ | 162 | Ⓐ Ⓑ Ⓒ Ⓓ | 182 | Ⓐ Ⓑ Ⓒ Ⓓ |
| 103 | Ⓐ Ⓑ Ⓒ Ⓓ | 123 | Ⓐ Ⓑ Ⓒ Ⓓ | 143 | Ⓐ Ⓑ Ⓒ Ⓓ | 163 | Ⓐ Ⓑ Ⓒ Ⓓ | 183 | Ⓐ Ⓑ Ⓒ Ⓓ |
| 104 | Ⓐ Ⓑ Ⓒ Ⓓ | 124 | Ⓐ Ⓑ Ⓒ Ⓓ | 144 | Ⓐ Ⓑ Ⓒ Ⓓ | 164 | Ⓐ Ⓑ Ⓒ Ⓓ | 184 | Ⓐ Ⓑ Ⓒ Ⓓ |
| 105 | Ⓐ Ⓑ Ⓒ Ⓓ | 125 | Ⓐ Ⓑ Ⓒ Ⓓ | 145 | Ⓐ Ⓑ Ⓒ Ⓓ | 165 | Ⓐ Ⓑ Ⓒ Ⓓ | 185 | Ⓐ Ⓑ Ⓒ Ⓓ |
| 106 | Ⓐ Ⓑ Ⓒ Ⓓ | 126 | Ⓐ Ⓑ Ⓒ Ⓓ | 146 | Ⓐ Ⓑ Ⓒ Ⓓ | 166 | Ⓐ Ⓑ Ⓒ Ⓓ | 186 | Ⓐ Ⓑ Ⓒ Ⓓ |
| 107 | Ⓐ Ⓑ Ⓒ Ⓓ | 127 | Ⓐ Ⓑ Ⓒ Ⓓ | 147 | Ⓐ Ⓑ Ⓒ Ⓓ | 167 | Ⓐ Ⓑ Ⓒ Ⓓ | 187 | Ⓐ Ⓑ Ⓒ Ⓓ |
| 108 | Ⓐ Ⓑ Ⓒ Ⓓ | 128 | Ⓐ Ⓑ Ⓒ Ⓓ | 148 | Ⓐ Ⓑ Ⓒ Ⓓ | 168 | Ⓐ Ⓑ Ⓒ Ⓓ | 188 | Ⓐ Ⓑ Ⓒ Ⓓ |
| 109 | Ⓐ Ⓑ Ⓒ Ⓓ | 129 | Ⓐ Ⓑ Ⓒ Ⓓ | 149 | Ⓐ Ⓑ Ⓒ Ⓓ | 169 | Ⓐ Ⓑ Ⓒ Ⓓ | 189 | Ⓐ Ⓑ Ⓒ Ⓓ |
| 110 | Ⓐ Ⓑ Ⓒ Ⓓ | 130 | Ⓐ Ⓑ Ⓒ Ⓓ | 150 | Ⓐ Ⓑ Ⓒ Ⓓ | 170 | Ⓐ Ⓑ Ⓒ Ⓓ | 190 | Ⓐ Ⓑ Ⓒ Ⓓ |
| 111 | Ⓐ Ⓑ Ⓒ Ⓓ | 131 | Ⓐ Ⓑ Ⓒ Ⓓ | 151 | Ⓐ Ⓑ Ⓒ Ⓓ | 171 | Ⓐ Ⓑ Ⓒ Ⓓ | 191 | Ⓐ Ⓑ Ⓒ Ⓓ |
| 112 | Ⓐ Ⓑ Ⓒ Ⓓ | 132 | Ⓐ Ⓑ Ⓒ Ⓓ | 152 | Ⓐ Ⓑ Ⓒ Ⓓ | 172 | Ⓐ Ⓑ Ⓒ Ⓓ | 192 | Ⓐ Ⓑ Ⓒ Ⓓ |
| 113 | Ⓐ Ⓑ Ⓒ Ⓓ | 133 | Ⓐ Ⓑ Ⓒ Ⓓ | 153 | Ⓐ Ⓑ Ⓒ Ⓓ | 173 | Ⓐ Ⓑ Ⓒ Ⓓ | 193 | Ⓐ Ⓑ Ⓒ Ⓓ |
| 114 | Ⓐ Ⓑ Ⓒ Ⓓ | 134 | Ⓐ Ⓑ Ⓒ Ⓓ | 154 | Ⓐ Ⓑ Ⓒ Ⓓ | 174 | Ⓐ Ⓑ Ⓒ Ⓓ | 194 | Ⓐ Ⓑ Ⓒ Ⓓ |
| 115 | Ⓐ Ⓑ Ⓒ Ⓓ | 135 | Ⓐ Ⓑ Ⓒ Ⓓ | 155 | Ⓐ Ⓑ Ⓒ Ⓓ | 175 | Ⓐ Ⓑ Ⓒ Ⓓ | 195 | Ⓐ Ⓑ Ⓒ Ⓓ |
| 116 | Ⓐ Ⓑ Ⓒ Ⓓ | 136 | Ⓐ Ⓑ Ⓒ Ⓓ | 156 | Ⓐ Ⓑ Ⓒ Ⓓ | 176 | Ⓐ Ⓑ Ⓒ Ⓓ | 196 | Ⓐ Ⓑ Ⓒ Ⓓ |
| 117 | Ⓐ Ⓑ Ⓒ Ⓓ | 137 | Ⓐ Ⓑ Ⓒ Ⓓ | 157 | Ⓐ Ⓑ Ⓒ Ⓓ | 177 | Ⓐ Ⓑ Ⓒ Ⓓ | 197 | Ⓐ Ⓑ Ⓒ Ⓓ |
| 118 | Ⓐ Ⓑ Ⓒ Ⓓ | 138 | Ⓐ Ⓑ Ⓒ Ⓓ | 158 | Ⓐ Ⓑ Ⓒ Ⓓ | 178 | Ⓐ Ⓑ Ⓒ Ⓓ | 198 | Ⓐ Ⓑ Ⓒ Ⓓ |
| 119 | Ⓐ Ⓑ Ⓒ Ⓓ | 139 | Ⓐ Ⓑ Ⓒ Ⓓ | 159 | Ⓐ Ⓑ Ⓒ Ⓓ | 179 | Ⓐ Ⓑ Ⓒ Ⓓ | 199 | Ⓐ Ⓑ Ⓒ Ⓓ |
| 120 | Ⓐ Ⓑ Ⓒ Ⓓ | 140 | Ⓐ Ⓑ Ⓒ Ⓓ | 160 | Ⓐ Ⓑ Ⓒ Ⓓ | 180 | Ⓐ Ⓑ Ⓒ Ⓓ | 200 | Ⓐ Ⓑ Ⓒ Ⓓ |

ANSWER SHEET

# ANSWER SHEET

## 파고다 토익 적중 실전 RC – TEST 5

### READING (Part Ⅴ-Ⅶ)

| NO. | ANSWER A B C D | NO. | ANSWER A B C D | NO. | ANSWER A B C D | NO. | ANSWER A B C D | NO. | ANSWER A B C D |
|---|---|---|---|---|---|---|---|---|---|
| 101 | Ⓐ Ⓑ Ⓒ Ⓓ | 121 | Ⓐ Ⓑ Ⓒ Ⓓ | 141 | Ⓐ Ⓑ Ⓒ Ⓓ | 161 | Ⓐ Ⓑ Ⓒ Ⓓ | 181 | Ⓐ Ⓑ Ⓒ Ⓓ |
| 102 | Ⓐ Ⓑ Ⓒ Ⓓ | 122 | Ⓐ Ⓑ Ⓒ Ⓓ | 142 | Ⓐ Ⓑ Ⓒ Ⓓ | 162 | Ⓐ Ⓑ Ⓒ Ⓓ | 182 | Ⓐ Ⓑ Ⓒ Ⓓ |
| 103 | Ⓐ Ⓑ Ⓒ Ⓓ | 123 | Ⓐ Ⓑ Ⓒ Ⓓ | 143 | Ⓐ Ⓑ Ⓒ Ⓓ | 163 | Ⓐ Ⓑ Ⓒ Ⓓ | 183 | Ⓐ Ⓑ Ⓒ Ⓓ |
| 104 | Ⓐ Ⓑ Ⓒ Ⓓ | 124 | Ⓐ Ⓑ Ⓒ Ⓓ | 144 | Ⓐ Ⓑ Ⓒ Ⓓ | 164 | Ⓐ Ⓑ Ⓒ Ⓓ | 184 | Ⓐ Ⓑ Ⓒ Ⓓ |
| 105 | Ⓐ Ⓑ Ⓒ Ⓓ | 125 | Ⓐ Ⓑ Ⓒ Ⓓ | 145 | Ⓐ Ⓑ Ⓒ Ⓓ | 165 | Ⓐ Ⓑ Ⓒ Ⓓ | 185 | Ⓐ Ⓑ Ⓒ Ⓓ |
| 106 | Ⓐ Ⓑ Ⓒ Ⓓ | 126 | Ⓐ Ⓑ Ⓒ Ⓓ | 146 | Ⓐ Ⓑ Ⓒ Ⓓ | 166 | Ⓐ Ⓑ Ⓒ Ⓓ | 186 | Ⓐ Ⓑ Ⓒ Ⓓ |
| 107 | Ⓐ Ⓑ Ⓒ Ⓓ | 127 | Ⓐ Ⓑ Ⓒ Ⓓ | 147 | Ⓐ Ⓑ Ⓒ Ⓓ | 167 | Ⓐ Ⓑ Ⓒ Ⓓ | 187 | Ⓐ Ⓑ Ⓒ Ⓓ |
| 108 | Ⓐ Ⓑ Ⓒ Ⓓ | 128 | Ⓐ Ⓑ Ⓒ Ⓓ | 148 | Ⓐ Ⓑ Ⓒ Ⓓ | 168 | Ⓐ Ⓑ Ⓒ Ⓓ | 188 | Ⓐ Ⓑ Ⓒ Ⓓ |
| 109 | Ⓐ Ⓑ Ⓒ Ⓓ | 129 | Ⓐ Ⓑ Ⓒ Ⓓ | 149 | Ⓐ Ⓑ Ⓒ Ⓓ | 169 | Ⓐ Ⓑ Ⓒ Ⓓ | 189 | Ⓐ Ⓑ Ⓒ Ⓓ |
| 110 | Ⓐ Ⓑ Ⓒ Ⓓ | 130 | Ⓐ Ⓑ Ⓒ Ⓓ | 150 | Ⓐ Ⓑ Ⓒ Ⓓ | 170 | Ⓐ Ⓑ Ⓒ Ⓓ | 190 | Ⓐ Ⓑ Ⓒ Ⓓ |
| 111 | Ⓐ Ⓑ Ⓒ Ⓓ | 131 | Ⓐ Ⓑ Ⓒ Ⓓ | 151 | Ⓐ Ⓑ Ⓒ Ⓓ | 171 | Ⓐ Ⓑ Ⓒ Ⓓ | 191 | Ⓐ Ⓑ Ⓒ Ⓓ |
| 112 | Ⓐ Ⓑ Ⓒ Ⓓ | 132 | Ⓐ Ⓑ Ⓒ Ⓓ | 152 | Ⓐ Ⓑ Ⓒ Ⓓ | 172 | Ⓐ Ⓑ Ⓒ Ⓓ | 192 | Ⓐ Ⓑ Ⓒ Ⓓ |
| 113 | Ⓐ Ⓑ Ⓒ Ⓓ | 133 | Ⓐ Ⓑ Ⓒ Ⓓ | 153 | Ⓐ Ⓑ Ⓒ Ⓓ | 173 | Ⓐ Ⓑ Ⓒ Ⓓ | 193 | Ⓐ Ⓑ Ⓒ Ⓓ |
| 114 | Ⓐ Ⓑ Ⓒ Ⓓ | 134 | Ⓐ Ⓑ Ⓒ Ⓓ | 154 | Ⓐ Ⓑ Ⓒ Ⓓ | 174 | Ⓐ Ⓑ Ⓒ Ⓓ | 194 | Ⓐ Ⓑ Ⓒ Ⓓ |
| 115 | Ⓐ Ⓑ Ⓒ Ⓓ | 135 | Ⓐ Ⓑ Ⓒ Ⓓ | 155 | Ⓐ Ⓑ Ⓒ Ⓓ | 175 | Ⓐ Ⓑ Ⓒ Ⓓ | 195 | Ⓐ Ⓑ Ⓒ Ⓓ |
| 116 | Ⓐ Ⓑ Ⓒ Ⓓ | 136 | Ⓐ Ⓑ Ⓒ Ⓓ | 156 | Ⓐ Ⓑ Ⓒ Ⓓ | 176 | Ⓐ Ⓑ Ⓒ Ⓓ | 196 | Ⓐ Ⓑ Ⓒ Ⓓ |
| 117 | Ⓐ Ⓑ Ⓒ Ⓓ | 137 | Ⓐ Ⓑ Ⓒ Ⓓ | 157 | Ⓐ Ⓑ Ⓒ Ⓓ | 177 | Ⓐ Ⓑ Ⓒ Ⓓ | 197 | Ⓐ Ⓑ Ⓒ Ⓓ |
| 118 | Ⓐ Ⓑ Ⓒ Ⓓ | 138 | Ⓐ Ⓑ Ⓒ Ⓓ | 158 | Ⓐ Ⓑ Ⓒ Ⓓ | 178 | Ⓐ Ⓑ Ⓒ Ⓓ | 198 | Ⓐ Ⓑ Ⓒ Ⓓ |
| 119 | Ⓐ Ⓑ Ⓒ Ⓓ | 139 | Ⓐ Ⓑ Ⓒ Ⓓ | 159 | Ⓐ Ⓑ Ⓒ Ⓓ | 179 | Ⓐ Ⓑ Ⓒ Ⓓ | 199 | Ⓐ Ⓑ Ⓒ Ⓓ |
| 120 | Ⓐ Ⓑ Ⓒ Ⓓ | 140 | Ⓐ Ⓑ Ⓒ Ⓓ | 160 | Ⓐ Ⓑ Ⓒ Ⓓ | 180 | Ⓐ Ⓑ Ⓒ Ⓓ | 200 | Ⓐ Ⓑ Ⓒ Ⓓ |

ANSWER SHEET

# ANSWER SHEET

## READING (Part Ⅴ-Ⅶ)

| NO. | ANSWER A B C D | NO. | ANSWER A B C D | NO. | ANSWER A B C D | NO. | ANSWER A B C D | NO. | ANSWER A B C D |
|-----|------|-----|------|-----|------|-----|------|-----|------|
| 101 | Ⓐ Ⓑ Ⓒ Ⓓ | 121 | Ⓐ Ⓑ Ⓒ Ⓓ | 141 | Ⓐ Ⓑ Ⓒ Ⓓ | 161 | Ⓐ Ⓑ Ⓒ Ⓓ | 181 | Ⓐ Ⓑ Ⓒ Ⓓ |
| 102 | Ⓐ Ⓑ Ⓒ Ⓓ | 122 | Ⓐ Ⓑ Ⓒ Ⓓ | 142 | Ⓐ Ⓑ Ⓒ Ⓓ | 162 | Ⓐ Ⓑ Ⓒ Ⓓ | 182 | Ⓐ Ⓑ Ⓒ Ⓓ |
| 103 | Ⓐ Ⓑ Ⓒ Ⓓ | 123 | Ⓐ Ⓑ Ⓒ Ⓓ | 143 | Ⓐ Ⓑ Ⓒ Ⓓ | 163 | Ⓐ Ⓑ Ⓒ Ⓓ | 183 | Ⓐ Ⓑ Ⓒ Ⓓ |
| 104 | Ⓐ Ⓑ Ⓒ Ⓓ | 124 | Ⓐ Ⓑ Ⓒ Ⓓ | 144 | Ⓐ Ⓑ Ⓒ Ⓓ | 164 | Ⓐ Ⓑ Ⓒ Ⓓ | 184 | Ⓐ Ⓑ Ⓒ Ⓓ |
| 105 | Ⓐ Ⓑ Ⓒ Ⓓ | 125 | Ⓐ Ⓑ Ⓒ Ⓓ | 145 | Ⓐ Ⓑ Ⓒ Ⓓ | 165 | Ⓐ Ⓑ Ⓒ Ⓓ | 185 | Ⓐ Ⓑ Ⓒ Ⓓ |
| 106 | Ⓐ Ⓑ Ⓒ Ⓓ | 126 | Ⓐ Ⓑ Ⓒ Ⓓ | 146 | Ⓐ Ⓑ Ⓒ Ⓓ | 166 | Ⓐ Ⓑ Ⓒ Ⓓ | 186 | Ⓐ Ⓑ Ⓒ Ⓓ |
| 107 | Ⓐ Ⓑ Ⓒ Ⓓ | 127 | Ⓐ Ⓑ Ⓒ Ⓓ | 147 | Ⓐ Ⓑ Ⓒ Ⓓ | 167 | Ⓐ Ⓑ Ⓒ Ⓓ | 187 | Ⓐ Ⓑ Ⓒ Ⓓ |
| 108 | Ⓐ Ⓑ Ⓒ Ⓓ | 128 | Ⓐ Ⓑ Ⓒ Ⓓ | 148 | Ⓐ Ⓑ Ⓒ Ⓓ | 168 | Ⓐ Ⓑ Ⓒ Ⓓ | 188 | Ⓐ Ⓑ Ⓒ Ⓓ |
| 109 | Ⓐ Ⓑ Ⓒ Ⓓ | 129 | Ⓐ Ⓑ Ⓒ Ⓓ | 149 | Ⓐ Ⓑ Ⓒ Ⓓ | 169 | Ⓐ Ⓑ Ⓒ Ⓓ | 189 | Ⓐ Ⓑ Ⓒ Ⓓ |
| 110 | Ⓐ Ⓑ Ⓒ Ⓓ | 130 | Ⓐ Ⓑ Ⓒ Ⓓ | 150 | Ⓐ Ⓑ Ⓒ Ⓓ | 170 | Ⓐ Ⓑ Ⓒ Ⓓ | 190 | Ⓐ Ⓑ Ⓒ Ⓓ |
| 111 | Ⓐ Ⓑ Ⓒ Ⓓ | 131 | Ⓐ Ⓑ Ⓒ Ⓓ | 151 | Ⓐ Ⓑ Ⓒ Ⓓ | 171 | Ⓐ Ⓑ Ⓒ Ⓓ | 191 | Ⓐ Ⓑ Ⓒ Ⓓ |
| 112 | Ⓐ Ⓑ Ⓒ Ⓓ | 132 | Ⓐ Ⓑ Ⓒ Ⓓ | 152 | Ⓐ Ⓑ Ⓒ Ⓓ | 172 | Ⓐ Ⓑ Ⓒ Ⓓ | 192 | Ⓐ Ⓑ Ⓒ Ⓓ |
| 113 | Ⓐ Ⓑ Ⓒ Ⓓ | 133 | Ⓐ Ⓑ Ⓒ Ⓓ | 153 | Ⓐ Ⓑ Ⓒ Ⓓ | 173 | Ⓐ Ⓑ Ⓒ Ⓓ | 193 | Ⓐ Ⓑ Ⓒ Ⓓ |
| 114 | Ⓐ Ⓑ Ⓒ Ⓓ | 134 | Ⓐ Ⓑ Ⓒ Ⓓ | 154 | Ⓐ Ⓑ Ⓒ Ⓓ | 174 | Ⓐ Ⓑ Ⓒ Ⓓ | 194 | Ⓐ Ⓑ Ⓒ Ⓓ |
| 115 | Ⓐ Ⓑ Ⓒ Ⓓ | 135 | Ⓐ Ⓑ Ⓒ Ⓓ | 155 | Ⓐ Ⓑ Ⓒ Ⓓ | 175 | Ⓐ Ⓑ Ⓒ Ⓓ | 195 | Ⓐ Ⓑ Ⓒ Ⓓ |
| 116 | Ⓐ Ⓑ Ⓒ Ⓓ | 136 | Ⓐ Ⓑ Ⓒ Ⓓ | 156 | Ⓐ Ⓑ Ⓒ Ⓓ | 176 | Ⓐ Ⓑ Ⓒ Ⓓ | 196 | Ⓐ Ⓑ Ⓒ Ⓓ |
| 117 | Ⓐ Ⓑ Ⓒ Ⓓ | 137 | Ⓐ Ⓑ Ⓒ Ⓓ | 157 | Ⓐ Ⓑ Ⓒ Ⓓ | 177 | Ⓐ Ⓑ Ⓒ Ⓓ | 197 | Ⓐ Ⓑ Ⓒ Ⓓ |
| 118 | Ⓐ Ⓑ Ⓒ Ⓓ | 138 | Ⓐ Ⓑ Ⓒ Ⓓ | 158 | Ⓐ Ⓑ Ⓒ Ⓓ | 178 | Ⓐ Ⓑ Ⓒ Ⓓ | 198 | Ⓐ Ⓑ Ⓒ Ⓓ |
| 119 | Ⓐ Ⓑ Ⓒ Ⓓ | 139 | Ⓐ Ⓑ Ⓒ Ⓓ | 159 | Ⓐ Ⓑ Ⓒ Ⓓ | 179 | Ⓐ Ⓑ Ⓒ Ⓓ | 199 | Ⓐ Ⓑ Ⓒ Ⓓ |
| 120 | Ⓐ Ⓑ Ⓒ Ⓓ | 140 | Ⓐ Ⓑ Ⓒ Ⓓ | 160 | Ⓐ Ⓑ Ⓒ Ⓓ | 180 | Ⓐ Ⓑ Ⓒ Ⓓ | 200 | Ⓐ Ⓑ Ⓒ Ⓓ |

ANSWER SHEET

# ANSWER SHEET

## 파고다 토익 적중 실전 RC - TEST 7

### READING (Part Ⅴ-Ⅶ)

| NO. | ANSWER<br>A B C D | NO. | ANSWER<br>A B C D | NO. | ANSWER<br>A B C D | NO. | ANSWER<br>A B C D | NO. | ANSWER<br>A B C D |
|---|---|---|---|---|---|---|---|---|---|
| 101 | Ⓐ Ⓑ Ⓒ Ⓓ | 121 | Ⓐ Ⓑ Ⓒ Ⓓ | 141 | Ⓐ Ⓑ Ⓒ Ⓓ | 161 | Ⓐ Ⓑ Ⓒ Ⓓ | 181 | Ⓐ Ⓑ Ⓒ Ⓓ |
| 102 | Ⓐ Ⓑ Ⓒ Ⓓ | 122 | Ⓐ Ⓑ Ⓒ Ⓓ | 142 | Ⓐ Ⓑ Ⓒ Ⓓ | 162 | Ⓐ Ⓑ Ⓒ Ⓓ | 182 | Ⓐ Ⓑ Ⓒ Ⓓ |
| 103 | Ⓐ Ⓑ Ⓒ Ⓓ | 123 | Ⓐ Ⓑ Ⓒ Ⓓ | 143 | Ⓐ Ⓑ Ⓒ Ⓓ | 163 | Ⓐ Ⓑ Ⓒ Ⓓ | 183 | Ⓐ Ⓑ Ⓒ Ⓓ |
| 104 | Ⓐ Ⓑ Ⓒ Ⓓ | 124 | Ⓐ Ⓑ Ⓒ Ⓓ | 144 | Ⓐ Ⓑ Ⓒ Ⓓ | 164 | Ⓐ Ⓑ Ⓒ Ⓓ | 184 | Ⓐ Ⓑ Ⓒ Ⓓ |
| 105 | Ⓐ Ⓑ Ⓒ Ⓓ | 125 | Ⓐ Ⓑ Ⓒ Ⓓ | 145 | Ⓐ Ⓑ Ⓒ Ⓓ | 165 | Ⓐ Ⓑ Ⓒ Ⓓ | 185 | Ⓐ Ⓑ Ⓒ Ⓓ |
| 106 | Ⓐ Ⓑ Ⓒ Ⓓ | 126 | Ⓐ Ⓑ Ⓒ Ⓓ | 146 | Ⓐ Ⓑ Ⓒ Ⓓ | 166 | Ⓐ Ⓑ Ⓒ Ⓓ | 186 | Ⓐ Ⓑ Ⓒ Ⓓ |
| 107 | Ⓐ Ⓑ Ⓒ Ⓓ | 127 | Ⓐ Ⓑ Ⓒ Ⓓ | 147 | Ⓐ Ⓑ Ⓒ Ⓓ | 167 | Ⓐ Ⓑ Ⓒ Ⓓ | 187 | Ⓐ Ⓑ Ⓒ Ⓓ |
| 108 | Ⓐ Ⓑ Ⓒ Ⓓ | 128 | Ⓐ Ⓑ Ⓒ Ⓓ | 148 | Ⓐ Ⓑ Ⓒ Ⓓ | 168 | Ⓐ Ⓑ Ⓒ Ⓓ | 188 | Ⓐ Ⓑ Ⓒ Ⓓ |
| 109 | Ⓐ Ⓑ Ⓒ Ⓓ | 129 | Ⓐ Ⓑ Ⓒ Ⓓ | 149 | Ⓐ Ⓑ Ⓒ Ⓓ | 169 | Ⓐ Ⓑ Ⓒ Ⓓ | 189 | Ⓐ Ⓑ Ⓒ Ⓓ |
| 110 | Ⓐ Ⓑ Ⓒ Ⓓ | 130 | Ⓐ Ⓑ Ⓒ Ⓓ | 150 | Ⓐ Ⓑ Ⓒ Ⓓ | 170 | Ⓐ Ⓑ Ⓒ Ⓓ | 190 | Ⓐ Ⓑ Ⓒ Ⓓ |
| 111 | Ⓐ Ⓑ Ⓒ Ⓓ | 131 | Ⓐ Ⓑ Ⓒ Ⓓ | 151 | Ⓐ Ⓑ Ⓒ Ⓓ | 171 | Ⓐ Ⓑ Ⓒ Ⓓ | 191 | Ⓐ Ⓑ Ⓒ Ⓓ |
| 112 | Ⓐ Ⓑ Ⓒ Ⓓ | 132 | Ⓐ Ⓑ Ⓒ Ⓓ | 152 | Ⓐ Ⓑ Ⓒ Ⓓ | 172 | Ⓐ Ⓑ Ⓒ Ⓓ | 192 | Ⓐ Ⓑ Ⓒ Ⓓ |
| 113 | Ⓐ Ⓑ Ⓒ Ⓓ | 133 | Ⓐ Ⓑ Ⓒ Ⓓ | 153 | Ⓐ Ⓑ Ⓒ Ⓓ | 173 | Ⓐ Ⓑ Ⓒ Ⓓ | 193 | Ⓐ Ⓑ Ⓒ Ⓓ |
| 114 | Ⓐ Ⓑ Ⓒ Ⓓ | 134 | Ⓐ Ⓑ Ⓒ Ⓓ | 154 | Ⓐ Ⓑ Ⓒ Ⓓ | 174 | Ⓐ Ⓑ Ⓒ Ⓓ | 194 | Ⓐ Ⓑ Ⓒ Ⓓ |
| 115 | Ⓐ Ⓑ Ⓒ Ⓓ | 135 | Ⓐ Ⓑ Ⓒ Ⓓ | 155 | Ⓐ Ⓑ Ⓒ Ⓓ | 175 | Ⓐ Ⓑ Ⓒ Ⓓ | 195 | Ⓐ Ⓑ Ⓒ Ⓓ |
| 116 | Ⓐ Ⓑ Ⓒ Ⓓ | 136 | Ⓐ Ⓑ Ⓒ Ⓓ | 156 | Ⓐ Ⓑ Ⓒ Ⓓ | 176 | Ⓐ Ⓑ Ⓒ Ⓓ | 196 | Ⓐ Ⓑ Ⓒ Ⓓ |
| 117 | Ⓐ Ⓑ Ⓒ Ⓓ | 137 | Ⓐ Ⓑ Ⓒ Ⓓ | 157 | Ⓐ Ⓑ Ⓒ Ⓓ | 177 | Ⓐ Ⓑ Ⓒ Ⓓ | 197 | Ⓐ Ⓑ Ⓒ Ⓓ |
| 118 | Ⓐ Ⓑ Ⓒ Ⓓ | 138 | Ⓐ Ⓑ Ⓒ Ⓓ | 158 | Ⓐ Ⓑ Ⓒ Ⓓ | 178 | Ⓐ Ⓑ Ⓒ Ⓓ | 198 | Ⓐ Ⓑ Ⓒ Ⓓ |
| 119 | Ⓐ Ⓑ Ⓒ Ⓓ | 139 | Ⓐ Ⓑ Ⓒ Ⓓ | 159 | Ⓐ Ⓑ Ⓒ Ⓓ | 179 | Ⓐ Ⓑ Ⓒ Ⓓ | 199 | Ⓐ Ⓑ Ⓒ Ⓓ |
| 120 | Ⓐ Ⓑ Ⓒ Ⓓ | 140 | Ⓐ Ⓑ Ⓒ Ⓓ | 160 | Ⓐ Ⓑ Ⓒ Ⓓ | 180 | Ⓐ Ⓑ Ⓒ Ⓓ | 200 | Ⓐ Ⓑ Ⓒ Ⓓ |

ANSWER SHEET

# ANSWER SHEET

## 파고다 토익 적중 실전 RC - TEST 8

### READING (Part V-VII)

| NO. | ANSWER A B C D | NO. | ANSWER A B C D | NO. | ANSWER A B C D | NO. | ANSWER A B C D | NO. | ANSWER A B C D |
|-----|------|-----|------|-----|------|-----|------|-----|------|
| 101 | Ⓐ Ⓑ Ⓒ Ⓓ | 121 | Ⓐ Ⓑ Ⓒ Ⓓ | 141 | Ⓐ Ⓑ Ⓒ Ⓓ | 161 | Ⓐ Ⓑ Ⓒ Ⓓ | 181 | Ⓐ Ⓑ Ⓒ Ⓓ |
| 102 | Ⓐ Ⓑ Ⓒ Ⓓ | 122 | Ⓐ Ⓑ Ⓒ Ⓓ | 142 | Ⓐ Ⓑ Ⓒ Ⓓ | 162 | Ⓐ Ⓑ Ⓒ Ⓓ | 182 | Ⓐ Ⓑ Ⓒ Ⓓ |
| 103 | Ⓐ Ⓑ Ⓒ Ⓓ | 123 | Ⓐ Ⓑ Ⓒ Ⓓ | 143 | Ⓐ Ⓑ Ⓒ Ⓓ | 163 | Ⓐ Ⓑ Ⓒ Ⓓ | 183 | Ⓐ Ⓑ Ⓒ Ⓓ |
| 104 | Ⓐ Ⓑ Ⓒ Ⓓ | 124 | Ⓐ Ⓑ Ⓒ Ⓓ | 144 | Ⓐ Ⓑ Ⓒ Ⓓ | 164 | Ⓐ Ⓑ Ⓒ Ⓓ | 184 | Ⓐ Ⓑ Ⓒ Ⓓ |
| 105 | Ⓐ Ⓑ Ⓒ Ⓓ | 125 | Ⓐ Ⓑ Ⓒ Ⓓ | 145 | Ⓐ Ⓑ Ⓒ Ⓓ | 165 | Ⓐ Ⓑ Ⓒ Ⓓ | 185 | Ⓐ Ⓑ Ⓒ Ⓓ |
| 106 | Ⓐ Ⓑ Ⓒ Ⓓ | 126 | Ⓐ Ⓑ Ⓒ Ⓓ | 146 | Ⓐ Ⓑ Ⓒ Ⓓ | 166 | Ⓐ Ⓑ Ⓒ Ⓓ | 186 | Ⓐ Ⓑ Ⓒ Ⓓ |
| 107 | Ⓐ Ⓑ Ⓒ Ⓓ | 127 | Ⓐ Ⓑ Ⓒ Ⓓ | 147 | Ⓐ Ⓑ Ⓒ Ⓓ | 167 | Ⓐ Ⓑ Ⓒ Ⓓ | 187 | Ⓐ Ⓑ Ⓒ Ⓓ |
| 108 | Ⓐ Ⓑ Ⓒ Ⓓ | 128 | Ⓐ Ⓑ Ⓒ Ⓓ | 148 | Ⓐ Ⓑ Ⓒ Ⓓ | 168 | Ⓐ Ⓑ Ⓒ Ⓓ | 188 | Ⓐ Ⓑ Ⓒ Ⓓ |
| 109 | Ⓐ Ⓑ Ⓒ Ⓓ | 129 | Ⓐ Ⓑ Ⓒ Ⓓ | 149 | Ⓐ Ⓑ Ⓒ Ⓓ | 169 | Ⓐ Ⓑ Ⓒ Ⓓ | 189 | Ⓐ Ⓑ Ⓒ Ⓓ |
| 110 | Ⓐ Ⓑ Ⓒ Ⓓ | 130 | Ⓐ Ⓑ Ⓒ Ⓓ | 150 | Ⓐ Ⓑ Ⓒ Ⓓ | 170 | Ⓐ Ⓑ Ⓒ Ⓓ | 190 | Ⓐ Ⓑ Ⓒ Ⓓ |
| 111 | Ⓐ Ⓑ Ⓒ Ⓓ | 131 | Ⓐ Ⓑ Ⓒ Ⓓ | 151 | Ⓐ Ⓑ Ⓒ Ⓓ | 171 | Ⓐ Ⓑ Ⓒ Ⓓ | 191 | Ⓐ Ⓑ Ⓒ Ⓓ |
| 112 | Ⓐ Ⓑ Ⓒ Ⓓ | 132 | Ⓐ Ⓑ Ⓒ Ⓓ | 152 | Ⓐ Ⓑ Ⓒ Ⓓ | 172 | Ⓐ Ⓑ Ⓒ Ⓓ | 192 | Ⓐ Ⓑ Ⓒ Ⓓ |
| 113 | Ⓐ Ⓑ Ⓒ Ⓓ | 133 | Ⓐ Ⓑ Ⓒ Ⓓ | 153 | Ⓐ Ⓑ Ⓒ Ⓓ | 173 | Ⓐ Ⓑ Ⓒ Ⓓ | 193 | Ⓐ Ⓑ Ⓒ Ⓓ |
| 114 | Ⓐ Ⓑ Ⓒ Ⓓ | 134 | Ⓐ Ⓑ Ⓒ Ⓓ | 154 | Ⓐ Ⓑ Ⓒ Ⓓ | 174 | Ⓐ Ⓑ Ⓒ Ⓓ | 194 | Ⓐ Ⓑ Ⓒ Ⓓ |
| 115 | Ⓐ Ⓑ Ⓒ Ⓓ | 135 | Ⓐ Ⓑ Ⓒ Ⓓ | 155 | Ⓐ Ⓑ Ⓒ Ⓓ | 175 | Ⓐ Ⓑ Ⓒ Ⓓ | 195 | Ⓐ Ⓑ Ⓒ Ⓓ |
| 116 | Ⓐ Ⓑ Ⓒ Ⓓ | 136 | Ⓐ Ⓑ Ⓒ Ⓓ | 156 | Ⓐ Ⓑ Ⓒ Ⓓ | 176 | Ⓐ Ⓑ Ⓒ Ⓓ | 196 | Ⓐ Ⓑ Ⓒ Ⓓ |
| 117 | Ⓐ Ⓑ Ⓒ Ⓓ | 137 | Ⓐ Ⓑ Ⓒ Ⓓ | 157 | Ⓐ Ⓑ Ⓒ Ⓓ | 177 | Ⓐ Ⓑ Ⓒ Ⓓ | 197 | Ⓐ Ⓑ Ⓒ Ⓓ |
| 118 | Ⓐ Ⓑ Ⓒ Ⓓ | 138 | Ⓐ Ⓑ Ⓒ Ⓓ | 158 | Ⓐ Ⓑ Ⓒ Ⓓ | 178 | Ⓐ Ⓑ Ⓒ Ⓓ | 198 | Ⓐ Ⓑ Ⓒ Ⓓ |
| 119 | Ⓐ Ⓑ Ⓒ Ⓓ | 139 | Ⓐ Ⓑ Ⓒ Ⓓ | 159 | Ⓐ Ⓑ Ⓒ Ⓓ | 179 | Ⓐ Ⓑ Ⓒ Ⓓ | 199 | Ⓐ Ⓑ Ⓒ Ⓓ |
| 120 | Ⓐ Ⓑ Ⓒ Ⓓ | 140 | Ⓐ Ⓑ Ⓒ Ⓓ | 160 | Ⓐ Ⓑ Ⓒ Ⓓ | 180 | Ⓐ Ⓑ Ⓒ Ⓓ | 200 | Ⓐ Ⓑ Ⓒ Ⓓ |

ANSWER SHEET

# ANSWER SHEET

## 파고다 토익 적중 실전 RC - TEST 9

### READING (Part Ⅴ-Ⅶ)

| NO. | ANSWER | NO. | ANSWER | NO. | ANSWER | NO. | ANSWER | NO. | ANSWER |
|---|---|---|---|---|---|---|---|---|---|
| | A B C D | | A B C D | | A B C D | | A B C D | | A B C D |
| 101 | Ⓐ Ⓑ Ⓒ Ⓓ | 121 | Ⓐ Ⓑ Ⓒ Ⓓ | 141 | Ⓐ Ⓑ Ⓒ Ⓓ | 161 | Ⓐ Ⓑ Ⓒ Ⓓ | 181 | Ⓐ Ⓑ Ⓒ Ⓓ |
| 102 | Ⓐ Ⓑ Ⓒ Ⓓ | 122 | Ⓐ Ⓑ Ⓒ Ⓓ | 142 | Ⓐ Ⓑ Ⓒ Ⓓ | 162 | Ⓐ Ⓑ Ⓒ Ⓓ | 182 | Ⓐ Ⓑ Ⓒ Ⓓ |
| 103 | Ⓐ Ⓑ Ⓒ Ⓓ | 123 | Ⓐ Ⓑ Ⓒ Ⓓ | 143 | Ⓐ Ⓑ Ⓒ Ⓓ | 163 | Ⓐ Ⓑ Ⓒ Ⓓ | 183 | Ⓐ Ⓑ Ⓒ Ⓓ |
| 104 | Ⓐ Ⓑ Ⓒ Ⓓ | 124 | Ⓐ Ⓑ Ⓒ Ⓓ | 144 | Ⓐ Ⓑ Ⓒ Ⓓ | 164 | Ⓐ Ⓑ Ⓒ Ⓓ | 184 | Ⓐ Ⓑ Ⓒ Ⓓ |
| 105 | Ⓐ Ⓑ Ⓒ Ⓓ | 125 | Ⓐ Ⓑ Ⓒ Ⓓ | 145 | Ⓐ Ⓑ Ⓒ Ⓓ | 165 | Ⓐ Ⓑ Ⓒ Ⓓ | 185 | Ⓐ Ⓑ Ⓒ Ⓓ |
| 106 | Ⓐ Ⓑ Ⓒ Ⓓ | 126 | Ⓐ Ⓑ Ⓒ Ⓓ | 146 | Ⓐ Ⓑ Ⓒ Ⓓ | 166 | Ⓐ Ⓑ Ⓒ Ⓓ | 186 | Ⓐ Ⓑ Ⓒ Ⓓ |
| 107 | Ⓐ Ⓑ Ⓒ Ⓓ | 127 | Ⓐ Ⓑ Ⓒ Ⓓ | 147 | Ⓐ Ⓑ Ⓒ Ⓓ | 167 | Ⓐ Ⓑ Ⓒ Ⓓ | 187 | Ⓐ Ⓑ Ⓒ Ⓓ |
| 108 | Ⓐ Ⓑ Ⓒ Ⓓ | 128 | Ⓐ Ⓑ Ⓒ Ⓓ | 148 | Ⓐ Ⓑ Ⓒ Ⓓ | 168 | Ⓐ Ⓑ Ⓒ Ⓓ | 188 | Ⓐ Ⓑ Ⓒ Ⓓ |
| 109 | Ⓐ Ⓑ Ⓒ Ⓓ | 129 | Ⓐ Ⓑ Ⓒ Ⓓ | 149 | Ⓐ Ⓑ Ⓒ Ⓓ | 169 | Ⓐ Ⓑ Ⓒ Ⓓ | 189 | Ⓐ Ⓑ Ⓒ Ⓓ |
| 110 | Ⓐ Ⓑ Ⓒ Ⓓ | 130 | Ⓐ Ⓑ Ⓒ Ⓓ | 150 | Ⓐ Ⓑ Ⓒ Ⓓ | 170 | Ⓐ Ⓑ Ⓒ Ⓓ | 190 | Ⓐ Ⓑ Ⓒ Ⓓ |
| 111 | Ⓐ Ⓑ Ⓒ Ⓓ | 131 | Ⓐ Ⓑ Ⓒ Ⓓ | 151 | Ⓐ Ⓑ Ⓒ Ⓓ | 171 | Ⓐ Ⓑ Ⓒ Ⓓ | 191 | Ⓐ Ⓑ Ⓒ Ⓓ |
| 112 | Ⓐ Ⓑ Ⓒ Ⓓ | 132 | Ⓐ Ⓑ Ⓒ Ⓓ | 152 | Ⓐ Ⓑ Ⓒ Ⓓ | 172 | Ⓐ Ⓑ Ⓒ Ⓓ | 192 | Ⓐ Ⓑ Ⓒ Ⓓ |
| 113 | Ⓐ Ⓑ Ⓒ Ⓓ | 133 | Ⓐ Ⓑ Ⓒ Ⓓ | 153 | Ⓐ Ⓑ Ⓒ Ⓓ | 173 | Ⓐ Ⓑ Ⓒ Ⓓ | 193 | Ⓐ Ⓑ Ⓒ Ⓓ |
| 114 | Ⓐ Ⓑ Ⓒ Ⓓ | 134 | Ⓐ Ⓑ Ⓒ Ⓓ | 154 | Ⓐ Ⓑ Ⓒ Ⓓ | 174 | Ⓐ Ⓑ Ⓒ Ⓓ | 194 | Ⓐ Ⓑ Ⓒ Ⓓ |
| 115 | Ⓐ Ⓑ Ⓒ Ⓓ | 135 | Ⓐ Ⓑ Ⓒ Ⓓ | 155 | Ⓐ Ⓑ Ⓒ Ⓓ | 175 | Ⓐ Ⓑ Ⓒ Ⓓ | 195 | Ⓐ Ⓑ Ⓒ Ⓓ |
| 116 | Ⓐ Ⓑ Ⓒ Ⓓ | 136 | Ⓐ Ⓑ Ⓒ Ⓓ | 156 | Ⓐ Ⓑ Ⓒ Ⓓ | 176 | Ⓐ Ⓑ Ⓒ Ⓓ | 196 | Ⓐ Ⓑ Ⓒ Ⓓ |
| 117 | Ⓐ Ⓑ Ⓒ Ⓓ | 137 | Ⓐ Ⓑ Ⓒ Ⓓ | 157 | Ⓐ Ⓑ Ⓒ Ⓓ | 177 | Ⓐ Ⓑ Ⓒ Ⓓ | 197 | Ⓐ Ⓑ Ⓒ Ⓓ |
| 118 | Ⓐ Ⓑ Ⓒ Ⓓ | 138 | Ⓐ Ⓑ Ⓒ Ⓓ | 158 | Ⓐ Ⓑ Ⓒ Ⓓ | 178 | Ⓐ Ⓑ Ⓒ Ⓓ | 198 | Ⓐ Ⓑ Ⓒ Ⓓ |
| 119 | Ⓐ Ⓑ Ⓒ Ⓓ | 139 | Ⓐ Ⓑ Ⓒ Ⓓ | 159 | Ⓐ Ⓑ Ⓒ Ⓓ | 179 | Ⓐ Ⓑ Ⓒ Ⓓ | 199 | Ⓐ Ⓑ Ⓒ Ⓓ |
| 120 | Ⓐ Ⓑ Ⓒ Ⓓ | 140 | Ⓐ Ⓑ Ⓒ Ⓓ | 160 | Ⓐ Ⓑ Ⓒ Ⓓ | 180 | Ⓐ Ⓑ Ⓒ Ⓓ | 200 | Ⓐ Ⓑ Ⓒ Ⓓ |

ANSWER SHEET

# ANSWER SHEET

## 파고다 토익 적중 실전 RC - TEST 10

### READING (Part V - VII)

| NO. | ANSWER (A B C D) | NO. | ANSWER (A B C D) | NO. | ANSWER (A B C D) | NO. | ANSWER (A B C D) | NO. | ANSWER (A B C D) |
|-----|------|-----|------|-----|------|-----|------|-----|------|
| 101 | Ⓐ Ⓑ Ⓒ Ⓓ | 121 | Ⓐ Ⓑ Ⓒ Ⓓ | 141 | Ⓐ Ⓑ Ⓒ Ⓓ | 161 | Ⓐ Ⓑ Ⓒ Ⓓ | 181 | Ⓐ Ⓑ Ⓒ Ⓓ |
| 102 | Ⓐ Ⓑ Ⓒ Ⓓ | 122 | Ⓐ Ⓑ Ⓒ Ⓓ | 142 | Ⓐ Ⓑ Ⓒ Ⓓ | 162 | Ⓐ Ⓑ Ⓒ Ⓓ | 182 | Ⓐ Ⓑ Ⓒ Ⓓ |
| 103 | Ⓐ Ⓑ Ⓒ Ⓓ | 123 | Ⓐ Ⓑ Ⓒ Ⓓ | 143 | Ⓐ Ⓑ Ⓒ Ⓓ | 163 | Ⓐ Ⓑ Ⓒ Ⓓ | 183 | Ⓐ Ⓑ Ⓒ Ⓓ |
| 104 | Ⓐ Ⓑ Ⓒ Ⓓ | 124 | Ⓐ Ⓑ Ⓒ Ⓓ | 144 | Ⓐ Ⓑ Ⓒ Ⓓ | 164 | Ⓐ Ⓑ Ⓒ Ⓓ | 184 | Ⓐ Ⓑ Ⓒ Ⓓ |
| 105 | Ⓐ Ⓑ Ⓒ Ⓓ | 125 | Ⓐ Ⓑ Ⓒ Ⓓ | 145 | Ⓐ Ⓑ Ⓒ Ⓓ | 165 | Ⓐ Ⓑ Ⓒ Ⓓ | 185 | Ⓐ Ⓑ Ⓒ Ⓓ |
| 106 | Ⓐ Ⓑ Ⓒ Ⓓ | 126 | Ⓐ Ⓑ Ⓒ Ⓓ | 146 | Ⓐ Ⓑ Ⓒ Ⓓ | 166 | Ⓐ Ⓑ Ⓒ Ⓓ | 186 | Ⓐ Ⓑ Ⓒ Ⓓ |
| 107 | Ⓐ Ⓑ Ⓒ Ⓓ | 127 | Ⓐ Ⓑ Ⓒ Ⓓ | 147 | Ⓐ Ⓑ Ⓒ Ⓓ | 167 | Ⓐ Ⓑ Ⓒ Ⓓ | 187 | Ⓐ Ⓑ Ⓒ Ⓓ |
| 108 | Ⓐ Ⓑ Ⓒ Ⓓ | 128 | Ⓐ Ⓑ Ⓒ Ⓓ | 148 | Ⓐ Ⓑ Ⓒ Ⓓ | 168 | Ⓐ Ⓑ Ⓒ Ⓓ | 188 | Ⓐ Ⓑ Ⓒ Ⓓ |
| 109 | Ⓐ Ⓑ Ⓒ Ⓓ | 129 | Ⓐ Ⓑ Ⓒ Ⓓ | 149 | Ⓐ Ⓑ Ⓒ Ⓓ | 169 | Ⓐ Ⓑ Ⓒ Ⓓ | 189 | Ⓐ Ⓑ Ⓒ Ⓓ |
| 110 | Ⓐ Ⓑ Ⓒ Ⓓ | 130 | Ⓐ Ⓑ Ⓒ Ⓓ | 150 | Ⓐ Ⓑ Ⓒ Ⓓ | 170 | Ⓐ Ⓑ Ⓒ Ⓓ | 190 | Ⓐ Ⓑ Ⓒ Ⓓ |
| 111 | Ⓐ Ⓑ Ⓒ Ⓓ | 131 | Ⓐ Ⓑ Ⓒ Ⓓ | 151 | Ⓐ Ⓑ Ⓒ Ⓓ | 171 | Ⓐ Ⓑ Ⓒ Ⓓ | 191 | Ⓐ Ⓑ Ⓒ Ⓓ |
| 112 | Ⓐ Ⓑ Ⓒ Ⓓ | 132 | Ⓐ Ⓑ Ⓒ Ⓓ | 152 | Ⓐ Ⓑ Ⓒ Ⓓ | 172 | Ⓐ Ⓑ Ⓒ Ⓓ | 192 | Ⓐ Ⓑ Ⓒ Ⓓ |
| 113 | Ⓐ Ⓑ Ⓒ Ⓓ | 133 | Ⓐ Ⓑ Ⓒ Ⓓ | 153 | Ⓐ Ⓑ Ⓒ Ⓓ | 173 | Ⓐ Ⓑ Ⓒ Ⓓ | 193 | Ⓐ Ⓑ Ⓒ Ⓓ |
| 114 | Ⓐ Ⓑ Ⓒ Ⓓ | 134 | Ⓐ Ⓑ Ⓒ Ⓓ | 154 | Ⓐ Ⓑ Ⓒ Ⓓ | 174 | Ⓐ Ⓑ Ⓒ Ⓓ | 194 | Ⓐ Ⓑ Ⓒ Ⓓ |
| 115 | Ⓐ Ⓑ Ⓒ Ⓓ | 135 | Ⓐ Ⓑ Ⓒ Ⓓ | 155 | Ⓐ Ⓑ Ⓒ Ⓓ | 175 | Ⓐ Ⓑ Ⓒ Ⓓ | 195 | Ⓐ Ⓑ Ⓒ Ⓓ |
| 116 | Ⓐ Ⓑ Ⓒ Ⓓ | 136 | Ⓐ Ⓑ Ⓒ Ⓓ | 156 | Ⓐ Ⓑ Ⓒ Ⓓ | 176 | Ⓐ Ⓑ Ⓒ Ⓓ | 196 | Ⓐ Ⓑ Ⓒ Ⓓ |
| 117 | Ⓐ Ⓑ Ⓒ Ⓓ | 137 | Ⓐ Ⓑ Ⓒ Ⓓ | 157 | Ⓐ Ⓑ Ⓒ Ⓓ | 177 | Ⓐ Ⓑ Ⓒ Ⓓ | 197 | Ⓐ Ⓑ Ⓒ Ⓓ |
| 118 | Ⓐ Ⓑ Ⓒ Ⓓ | 138 | Ⓐ Ⓑ Ⓒ Ⓓ | 158 | Ⓐ Ⓑ Ⓒ Ⓓ | 178 | Ⓐ Ⓑ Ⓒ Ⓓ | 198 | Ⓐ Ⓑ Ⓒ Ⓓ |
| 119 | Ⓐ Ⓑ Ⓒ Ⓓ | 139 | Ⓐ Ⓑ Ⓒ Ⓓ | 159 | Ⓐ Ⓑ Ⓒ Ⓓ | 179 | Ⓐ Ⓑ Ⓒ Ⓓ | 199 | Ⓐ Ⓑ Ⓒ Ⓓ |
| 120 | Ⓐ Ⓑ Ⓒ Ⓓ | 140 | Ⓐ Ⓑ Ⓒ Ⓓ | 160 | Ⓐ Ⓑ Ⓒ Ⓓ | 180 | Ⓐ Ⓑ Ⓒ Ⓓ | 200 | Ⓐ Ⓑ Ⓒ Ⓓ |

ANSWER SHEET